296

CONTEMPORARY JEWRY
Volume 7 (First Annual)

CONTEMPORARY JEWRY
Volume 7 (First Annual)

Edited by
Arnold Dashefsky

Transaction Books
New Brunswick (U.S.A.) and Oxford (U.K.)

ISSN: 0147-1694
ISBN: 0-87855-979-5 (cloth)
Printed in the United States of America

Published for the Association for the Sociological Study of Jewry

---

The editors gratefully acknowledge that the publication of this annual was made possible in part by grants from the following organizations:
• Jewish Communal Affairs Department of the American Jewish Committee.
• Endowment Fund of the Greater Hartford Jewish Federation.
We extend a sincere thanks and our deep appreciation to these organizations and the people who represent them.

"Israeli Emigres and the New York Federation: A Case Study in Ambivalent Policymaking for Jewish Communal Deviants," first appeared in the *Jerusalem Letter*.

"The Impact of National Characteristics on Local Citizen Participation: A Developmental Research Framework Applied to Israel," was originally published in Hebrew under the title "National Structural Characteristics in Historical Context and Their Impact on Citizen Participation in Local Planning in Israel," in *Society and Welfare*, vol. 5, no. 3, October 1983, pp. 241-58. Some modifications were made for the English version.

Contents

List of Tables and Figures

PREFACE

Contemporary Jewry: Past, Present, and Future
Arnold Dashefsky

From the Past

Some time ago, in 1969, an idealistic graduate student in sociology wrote to the editor of a national periodical that served the Jewish community, saying:

> The absence of mechanisms of change and the inability to deal effectively and on a large scale with the pressing problems confronting American Jewry highlight . . . the role sociological research can play in this context.
>
> It is my guess that the majority of sociologists of Jewish background (and some of non-Jewish background) at one point in their academic training and research careers have done some work dealing with the Jews. The nature of contemporary sociological research, however, is such that the prestigious and developing subfields are often the ones in which the most funds are made available. . . . With adequate funding . . . [it might be possible] . . . to attract scholars and researchers to study aspects of Jewish life . . . [which study] might be strengthened by the cooperation of scholars and researchers in the formation of one broadly based association for the scientific study of Jewish life.

That student was I. Little did I know at that time that I would have an opportunity to make a modest contribution to achieving these objectives. About two years after the letter was written the Association for the Sociological Study of Jewry was formed, and about five years later the journal *Contemporary Jewry* (*CJ*) was launched. Eight years after the writing of the letter the association entered into an agreement with Transaction Publishers to publish and market the journal. Now a decade and a half later we witness another constructive development in the history of the association: the expansion of *Contemporary Jewry* to book-length size and its appearance as an annual. For me, it has been a privilege and a pleasure to be personally associated with these positive changes and developments, first, as officer of the association and, later, as editor of its journal.

To the Present

It is the shared belief of the officers of the association and the editors that our new format will increase the visibility and credibility of our publication. To make *Contemporary Jewry* a more useful resource for its readers, we have added several new sections. Some explanation is in order.

All articles included in the first two sections, "Feature Articles" and "Research Note," were selected according to the established practice of most scholarly journals, i.e. blind peer review. Articles received were sent out anonymously by one of the editors to at least two reviewers for evaluation. Two reviews, and sometimes three, were used before a final evaluation of the article was forwarded to the author(s). In a small number of cases an in-house editorial decision was made to reject the article when it was clearly not a social scientific piece of research.

During the fifteen months from the fall of 1982 until the end of 1983, the period when manuscripts were first received at the new editorial office of the journal at the University of Connecticut, we received thirteen articles and accepted two: 15 percent acceptance rate. The median turnaround time to authors was forty-eight days. In the first seven months of 1984 we also received fifteen articles. Five were accepted: a 33 percent acceptance rate. The median turnaround time was forty-seven days. In other words, in the more recent period the pace of submissions and the proportion of acceptances doubled. In most cases where papers were not accepted, authors were encouraged to revise and resubmit their articles based on suggestions offered by our reviewers.

A perusal of the current articles reveals the varying approaches to the social scientific analysis of Jewry assumed by the authors, Ronald Tadao Tsukashima, Efraim Ben-Zadok, Arnold Dashefsky, Bernard Lazerwitz, Eva Etzioni-Halevy, and Ann Illy. They reveal general theoretical and methodological concerns that may be applied to the study of Jewry, which in turn may be expanded and enriched by their application.

Ideally *Contemporary Jewry* should become a standard reference work reflecting the diversity of research of scholars in the field. That is the purpose of the two new sections included in this issue. The "Dialogue and Debate" section seeks to bring an issue of methodological or theoretical concern to the fore. In this case we have chosen an assessment of the utility of Distinctive Jewish Names (DJN) in sampling Jewish populations for research purposes. This technique, as can be seen from the discussion in these pages by Bernard Lazerwitz, Mark Abrahamson, Harold Himmelfarb, and Bruce Phillips, has received a good deal of attention.

The next section, entitled "Special Supplemental Section," presents the highlights of a conference on "Israelis in New York" with appropriate research and policy concerns. From time to time, *CJ* will draw attention to special topical interests by publishing research reports on a particular subject. In this case, it is the subject of *yordim* (Israeli emigrants), sometimes talked about in popular forums and sometimes disparaged in political circles and surely not to be ignored by academic researchers. The tendency toward exaggeration in popular and political discussions is tempered by the empirical facts and policy analysis presented by Paul Ritterband, Yael Zerubavel, and their colleagues Marcia Freedman, Josef Korazim, Stephen M. Cohen, and Linda G. Levi.

Of the remaining two sections in this issue, one represents a standard feature of *CJ* and one of a new departure. The "Book Reviews" section presents reviews by Celia S. Heller, George Gershon Kranzler, and Abraham D. Lavender. These reviews were delayed in publication through no fault of the authors. Future issues of *CJ* will present reviews of more recent books of major interest to our readers.

As a further effort to make readers aware of the variety of current research in the social scientific study of Jewry the Appendix "Recent Research" was added. Thanks to the assistance of *Sociological Abstracts* and members of ASSJ, we have included a compendium of abstracts, by Rena Cheskis and your editor, that brings together, for the first time, a systematic review of research on Jews published in social scientific journals for the beginning of the decade (1981 and 1982). It is hoped that subsequent issues of *CJ* will bring the reader the succeeding years. In this way, by 1990 the reader will have a continuing summary of research on Jewry for an entire decade in one source: *Contemporary Jewry*.

Into the Future

We hope that with the interest and support of you, the reader, our common enterprise will flourish. There are several things that you can do: (1) Submit appropriate current articles to *CJ*. (2) Write us a note indicating that you would be available to review articles or books. (3) Join ASSJ if you are not yet a member. (4) Send us your comments about the current volume of *CJ*. (5) Send suggestions about topics you would like considered in future volumes of *CJ*, and any suggestions or comments that would help improve *CJ*.

Acknowledgments

All of our efforts would be impossible without the excellent cooperation of our authors and reviewers. Special thanks are due Associate Editor J. Alan Winter; Assistant Editor Rena Cheskis; Overseas Editor Bernard Lazerwitz; and all of the other editors and reviewers for their devoted service to the journal. (A complete list of all the editors and reviewers appears in this volume.) Hearty thanks are extended to the staff members of the Center for Judaic Studies and Contemporary Jewish Life at the University of Connecticut, Linda Snyder, Celeste Machado, Robert Sweeney, and Anna Albright, who provided invaluable services for *CJ*. In addition, we want to thank the president of Transaction, Irving Louis Horowitz, for his encouragement, and Book Division Editor Dalia Buzin for her dedication. Finally, thanks are owed to all the members and officers of ASSJ and the readers of *Contemporary Jewry* for their sticking by us. All seemed to subscribe to the Hebrew adage *yihyeh tov*! It will be good! We hope you agree.

ARTICLES

1

A Test of Competing Contact Hypotheses in the Study of Black Anti-Semitic Beliefs

Ronald Tadao Tsukashima

The scope of this article concentrates on three specific structural conditions. These structural conditions are represented in the egalitarian social contact and middleman hypotheses. Supporting evidence is reported for both explanations, with the latter being the stronger predictor. Unlike previous studies, the present inquiry does not restrict its focus to a separate analysis of each hypothesis; instead, both are treated as interrelated explanations. Under the reasoning that the first two hypotheses are but different dimensions of a more general formulation called "differential association," they are combined to test their concurrent effect (i.e. specific combination). This last proposition suggests that when Blacks exhibit anti-Semitic beliefs they may do so because of an excess of contacts with Jews that spawn intolerant beliefs (economic mistreatment by middlemen) over contacts that do not (egalitarian social contact). Supporting data and implications are drawn.

This paper argues that the prejudice some Blacks have toward Jews grows out of social and economic exchanges that are in reality unfair or are perceived to be. A first hypothesis states that anti-Semitism is nourished by the fact that most social contacts between Blacks and Jews are unequal, with Jews more powerful. The second states that when Blacks deal with Jews as landlords or merchants they tend to perceive, rightly or wrongly, that they are treated unfairly. Others have tested

1

these two propositions independently. This paper considers them in combination, and proposes a third explanation that I have called differential association.

Competing Hypotheses

Equal-Status Contact

The social contact hypothesis points up the paucity of egalitarian social relations between Blacks and Jews. The findings of studies conducted in many settings indicate that equal-status contacts across racial lines tend to reduce the incidence of intolerant beliefs (Amir 1969; Allport 1954; Brophy 1946; Deutsch and Collins 1951; Jahoda and West 1951; Meer and Freedman 1966; Reed 1980; Simpson and Yinger 1972; Williams 1964; Wilner et al. 1955). Data reported suggest that egalitarian associations reveal the common humanity of others and thus promote communication and shatter prejudicial beliefs (Preston and Robinson 1974; Tsukashima 1973). And the greater the intimacy, the greater the erosion of such beliefs.

Although most of the research on interracial contact and its consequences has been based on white Gentiles, a few studies of Blacks have yielded similar results (Ford 1973; Tsukashima 1973); Tsukashima and Montero 1976; Works 1961). But, as Robinson and Preston (1976) report, the reduction of prejudice is less evident among Blacks than it is among Whites. Nevertheless, Black subordination (relative absence of egalitarian social contact) is proposed as one possible explanation for Blacks' prejudice against Jews.

Middleman Contact

A second perspective concentrates on middleman minorities. Unlike most approaches that focus on minorities who occupy the bottom strata of society, this perspective directs attention to "middle-class" ethnic groups.[1] These groups are unique not only for the intermediate position they hold in the stratification system but, more importantly, because of their concentration in middle-rank entrepreneurial economic roles such as trading, small business, and independent professions. Such groups as Jews in Europe, Japanese in the United States, Chinese in Southeast Asia, Indians in East Africa, Arabs in West Africa, and Scots in Canada provide examples of these roles (Bonacich 1973; Eitzen 1971; Jiang 1968; Rinder 1958–59; Stryker 1959; van der Laan 1975; Zenner and Jarvenpa 1980). Moreover, Bonacich (1980) contends that the middleman phenomenon, "petit bourgeois" in orientation, is not restricted to feudal, slave, or colonial societies. It persists within advanced capitalism too. It has also been noted that middleman minorities sometimes operate beyond the petit bourgeois sector in the realm of the large corporate economy as well (see Zenner and Jarvenpa's work on the Scots in the northern fur trade of Canada's Hudson's Bay Company, 1980).

In a recent attempt to develop a general theory of middleman minorities, Turner and Bonacich (1980) have integrated a body of propositions into a system of interrelated explanations. The basic intent of their theory is to explain the emergence and persistence of this social form. One important proposition relevant to the present study indicates that economic concentration by an ethnic group in middleman roles can often become a force escalating hostility of the majority toward the minority, for hostility grows out of competing interests of buyer and seller, of renter and landlord. Although middlemen provide needed services, the subordinates may believe that the merchant or landlord is gaining an unfair profit. As a result, the concentration of some minorities in middleman occupations makes them especially vulnerable to attack or duress in times of unrest.

Because this theory is framed in sufficiently broad terms to encompass a wide variety of minority-majority relations in different historical and social systems, one can reason that its coverage extends to specific middleman encounters among *minorities* as well. In fact, some (Bonacich 1973; Baldwin 1948; Clark 1946; Marx 1969; Silberman 1979; Tsukashima 1973; Tsukashima and Montero 1976) have already remarked upon the Jewish commercial presence in Black ghettos.[2] Thus the present study of Black hostility toward Jews is conceptualized as a specific case of a more general theoretical framework. Hence, this model would propose that Black anti-Semitism stems from Blacks' disadvantageous economic treatment by Jews in entrepreneurial roles.

Differential Association

The two hypotheses forwarded have been treated independently. As a result, any potential concurrent effects of both have gone unexplored. That is, anti-Semitic beliefs may not result from inegalitarian social contact or economic mistreatment alone but from certain combinations of the two that cannot be inferred from each type of interaction considered individually. The special combination suggested resembles (but is not the same as) Sutherland and Cressey's (1974) concept of differential association.

The logic of this argument contends that the White middleman with whom Blacks have many of their economic dealings are Jews. Correspondingly, when Blacks are exposed primarily to economic (rather than egalitarian) encounters with this group, their perception of the Jewish world becomes limited, serving to reinforce pejorative anti-Semitic images of Jews. If this argument is correct, Black anti-Semitism is a consequence of differential association. Thus, those who report more economic misdealings with Jews than egalitarian contacts would tend to be the most anti-Semitic, and those who report their contacts in the reverse direction, to be the least anti-Semitic. In other words, when Blacks evidence anti-Semitic beliefs, they may do so because of an excess of contacts with Jews that spawn intolerant beliefs (economic mistreatment) over contacts that do not (egalitarian associations). The focus of this hypothesis, then, is not on the exposure to either type of contact, but on the imbalance struck between negative and positive exposure. Moreover, because differential association is not based on the statistical characteristics of both contact variables taken separately, standard statistical techniques such as partial and multiple regression fail to tap its effect.

The present study seeks to test the merits of these competing hypotheses and their relative predictive value. In so doing, the following questions are posed: How well do equal-status contact (social contact) and economic mistreatment (economic contact), taken separately, predict anti-Semitism? More important, when the two contact variables are considered in specific combinations, does the emergent variable, differential association, prove to be at least as efficient a correlate of anti-Semitism as its components? In addressing the latter question, seemingly unrelated propositions about intergroup prejudice are conceptualized as interrelated components of a more general proposition (e.g. although the social contact and the middleman hypotheses can be derived from differential association, the latter cannot be deduced from the separate analysis of the former). Hence, the underlying view is that anti-Semitism among Blacks is due to the conjunction of specific structural conditions (social and economic). Taken together, the above hypotheses permit a test of types of participation and their interrelations (Robinson and Preston 1976) in the study of interminority group prejudice.

Data and Measurements

Sample

The data for the present study are derived from personal interviews conducted between July and December 1970 by Black female interviewers. All respondents (N = 319) were Blacks twenty years of age or older who were residents of the communities of Avalon and Crenshaw in Los Angeles. The two areas differ in their ethnic and class composition. A sample was drawn to represent a cross section of Blacks residing in each area.[3]

Within these communities all census blocks were listed. From this listing, blocks were randomly selected and assigned to interviewers. Each interviewer was then instructed to begin her canvassing with a random dwelling unit as the starting point from a random corner, and to proceed clockwise around the block, stopping at every dwelling unit. Interviewers made no callbacks. This procedure was employed until a quota of eight interviews (per assignment), specified by age, sex, and employment status, was completed to approximate the 1960 population of the two communities.[4]

Although this sampling procedure resembles a probability model, it should be classified as "disproportionately stratified" because persons drawn from these two locations do not correspond to the actual distribution of Blacks in Los Angeles. Hence, the findings of this study are not intended to typify the general Black population but to reflect a subset of them in the research sites of Los Angeles. Of the total 319 respondents, 159 were selected to represent Crenshaw and 160 to represent Avalon. Thus we have oversampled the more educated from Crenshaw to provide sufficient cases for testing the contact hypotheses and related propositions.

Dependent Variable

Anti-Semitism is measured by the endorsement of potentially negative beliefs about Jews. In the selection of the appropriate indicators to construct an index of this construct several criteria were considered. First, interviews with informants during the fieldwork stage of this survey study were consulted. They produced a rich array of cognitive items. Although it is not suggested that there is a distinct system of hostile beliefs regarding Jews, there are recognizable elements that appear to be more commonly associated with this minority than with other groups (Selznick and Steinberg 1969); they include views of Jews as "power oriented" and as "intrusive." Second, two items were employed that are not generally associated with Jews per se; they deal with offensive traits that could be applied to any group of people (e.g. "are too pushy" and "have a lot of irritating faults"). It was reasoned that one could be hostile toward Jews without endorsing items containing anti-Semitic rhetoric (Selznick and Steinberg 1969). Last, with the birth of a new nation, the State of Israel, some Americans felt justified in questioning the patriotism of Jews. In tapping the salience of this development and its implications for anti-Semitism, interviewers asked respondents to comment on the "loyalty of American Jews."

After an association among the items was found (gammas that range from a modest .18 to a high of .79, with a mean coefficient of .45), these five indicators were combined into an index of anti-Semitism. Responses intolerant of Jews were given a value of 1; other responses, 0. These values produce a composite measure that ranges from 0 to 5, with a mean score of 2.55 and a standard deviation of 1.47.[5]

Independent Variables

The effect of egalitarian social contact is not restricted to any one context. It can take place in an institutional setting. At work, for example, where formal norms obtain, one's relations with others tend to be structured and limited to a functionally specific set of role relationships. In contrast, the same contacts tend to be more diffuse in a neighborhood milieu. Respondents are expected here to become involved in a wider range of interactions with, and expectations of, others. In each instance, equal-status contact serves to challenge traditionally held intolerant beliefs, especially when intimacy is involved. In regard to the construction of an index of intimate, equal-status contact, subjects were asked to respond to two questions, one of which involved interaction at work and the other in the neighborhood:

Q. 27. "At work, do you come into contact with Jews as often as fellow workers who are doing about the same kind of job as yours?"
Q. 29. "Do you come into contact with Jews who may live in your neighborhood?"

Respondents who acknowledged having contact in each of the above contexts were then queried if they had taken part in any social activity with Jews, thus tapping the intimate aspect (or quality) of equal-status contact:

Q. 27B and 28B. "Have you ever done anything social with them like going to the movies, to a sports event, or visiting each other's home?"

A value of 1 given to those who responded affirmatively and 0 given to those who did not, yield scores that run from 0 (no contact) through 2 (intimate, equal-status contact with Jews at work and in the neighborhood).

Because Los Angeles has large numbers of Blacks and Jews, and the latter are more likely to occupy middle-class occupations (e.g. small property owners, professionals) than the former, it is likely that many Blacks have had economic dealings with Jews. Accordingly, this survey designed several items to evaluate Blacks' relations with this minority as merchants and landlords. More important, however, is the quality of those relations. This point was forcefully illustrated in the urban conflict of the mid-1960s. Many targets of Black violence in ghetto pockets were commercial establishments that local residents had defined as exploiting their community (U.S. National Advisory Commission on Civil Disorders 1968). Considering this aspect of Black-Jewish relations, the following items were framed to devise an instrument of economic mistreatment:[6]

Q. 30G. "Do you feel that Jewish store owners have ever treated you unfairly in any way?"
Q. 38A. "Do you feel that Jewish landlords have ever treated you unfairly in any way?"

Representing the lowest score (0) on this composite measure are those who reported no instance of economic mistreatment by Jews. At the other extreme (2) are those who indicated mistreatment by a Jewish merchant and landlord.

The last independent variable emerges from cross–tabulating the index of intimate, equal-status contact and of economic mistreatment. The results are three categories of differential association: (–1) those who report more contexts of economic mistreatment than intimate, equal-status contact (N = 70); (+ 1) those who report the reverse combination (N = 68); and (0) those who report no association of either type (N = 135).[8] Despite the cited overrepresentation of middleman Jews in Black economic life (Marx 1969), the two opposite combinations are equally split (about 25 percent each).

Findings

For this sample of Los Angeles Blacks, there is evidence for the first two hypotheses (table 1.1) set forth at the beginning of this paper. Whereas intimate, equal-status contact is related to tolerance toward Jews (– .14), economic mistreatment is correlated in the opposite direction (.40).[9] But the two types of contact do not operate independently (data not reported in tables). When controlling for economic contact, the partial correlation coefficient for egalitarian social contact and anti-Semitism is not significant, but is significant (.40, p < .05 for economic mistreatment and anti-Semitism) when social contact is held constant. It is evident, then, that the economic factor, unaffected in this three-way analysis, is the more persuasive determinant of anti-Semitic scores.[10]

TABLE 1.1

Correlating the Index of Anti-Semitism with the Indexes of Intimate, Equal-Status Contact, Economic Mistreatment, and Differential Association*

	Anti-Semitism	Intimate, Equal-Status Contact	Economic Mistreatment	Differential Association
Anti-Semitism	x	-.14	.40	-.34
Intimate, Equal-Status Contact		x	-.12	.70
Economic Mistreatment			x	-.71
Differential Association				x

N = 265

*All correlations significant at the .05 level.

The thrust of both hypotheses remains unchanged, however, when the disproportionate sampling method (place of residence) employed in this survey and the confusion between Black prejudice toward Jewish and non-Jewish Whites (anti-White attitude) are taken into account (table 1.2). If there is any difference, it is that some of the variance due to economic mistreatment reflects prejudice toward Whites in general and not Jews per se (.33). The findings are complicated by still other considerations. In recent years, Black-Jewish relations have been aggravated by conflicts of interests along occupational lines. "This has happened," says Silberman (1979, 13), "because Blacks have tended to choose occupational lines—most notably, teaching and social work—that Jews had chosen a generation earlier as their route to upward mobility. The result has been conflict over the criteria for appointment and promotion to supervisory jobs, and the question of who determines those criteria." When socioeconomic variables (e.g. occupation, income, and education) are partialed out, however, the effects of egalitarian social contact and economic mistreatment remain essentially the same (and statistically significant in each case in table 1.2). Apparently, social and economic contact operate separately from other socioeconomic dimensions of Black anti-Semitism.

TABLE 1.2

Correlating the Index of Anti-Semitism with the Indexes of Intimate, Equal-Status Contact, Economic Mistreatment, Differential Association, Controlling for Residence, Anti-White Attitude, Occupation, Income, and Education

	Zero Order	Partials*					N
		Residence	Anti-White Attitude	Occupation	Income	Education	
Anti-Semitism x Intimate, Equal-Status Contact	-.14	-.14	-.13	-.13	-.17	-.17	242
Anti-Semitism x Economic Mistreatment	.40	.41	.33	.41	.41	.40	242
Anti-Semitism x Differential Association	-.34	-.35	-.29	-.35	-.37	-.37	242

*All significant at the .05 level.

In short, the two structural explanations that characterize the sample generally also characterize a wide range of subgroups in this sample. The consistency with which they hold in the various subgroups further substantiates them. Hence, when tested separately, social and economic interaction with Jews continues to be related to Black anti-Semitism.

Together, both social and economic contact variables explain 17 percent of the total variance (table 1.3), with economic mistreatment the stronger predictor. Compare the beta of .40 (p < .05) with −.09 (not significant). If the task of sociological theory is to discern the significant variables and conditions that bring about the seeming diversity of anti-Semitic responses, then, the middleman argument provides the more productive explanation between the two contact hypotheses.

TABLE 1.3
Regression of Anti-Semitism on Economic Mistreatment and Intimate, Equal-Status Contact

Independent Variable	Beta	F
Index of Economic Mistreatment	.40	56.59*
Index of Intimate, Equal-Status Contact	−.09	2.83**
	N = 286	

R = .41; F = 29.79

R² = .17

* p .05

** Not significant at the .05 level.

Why these variables form this ordering is not clear because of the mutually exclusive manner in which the social contact and middleman hypotheses have been treated. One can surmise that each type of contact exerts its own impact on collective life chances. Accordingly, not all encounters with Jews will have the same consequence. Some will have a more direct and costly impact on group survival and interests than others. For a group that has known subjugation so long, any dealings related to important life chances will undoubtedly have a significant bearing on its beliefs. As a result, this may account for the contexts of economic mistreatment in the neighborhood and the marketplace as stronger determinants of anti-Semitism than the contexts of egalitarian social contact. Although the latter has been found to correlate with tolerant beliefs, it may have little effect on the subordinate status of Blacks as a group. In this sense, equal-status contact may be a "luxury" that only a few can afford.

An examination of intergroup relations should not be restricted, as is so often the case, to either egalitarian social contact or economic mistreatment alone. In reality, a given group will most likely encounter a combination of the two. For some Blacks, for example (N = 68, 24.9 percent), the former type of association with Jews predominates over the latter. For others (N = 70, 25.6 percent), the opposite is true. The third proposition (differential association) is designed to reflect these combinations. These combinations (or any others), however, are not to be confused with any proposed interactive effect.[11]

Consider the mean differences in anti-Semitism scores. Notice that the mean anti-Semitism score for those indicating more contexts of economic mistreatment than egalitarian social contact (coded − 1) is considerably higher than those reporting the reverse combination (coded + 1; compare 3.50, N = 67 with 2.10, N = 64). Falling between the two categories of differential association are those reporting no contact at all coded 0; 2.21, N = 135). The two variables are negatively correlated (− .34 in table 1.1). But this correlation does not stand alone. Like its economic component, the effect of differential association reflects some generalized prejudice toward Whites collectively (− .29 in table 1.2). Nevertheless, the restatement of two different interpretations allows an underlying structural regularity.

Mindful of the general inequality between Blacks and Jews, of the urban folklore about Jewish middlemen as ghetto interlopers, it is unlikely that any shift in the direction of differential association (more egalitarian social contact than economic mistreatment) will produce an immediate and dramatic reduction in the level of Black anti-Semitism. At the same time, the effect of this emergent variable must not be overstated. The normative nature of anti-Semitism in U.S. life is also a contributing factor in Black prejudice toward Jews. These two sources of cognitive prejudice are not necessarily interdependent (Reed 1980; Triandis and Vassiliou 1967), but in the case of U.S. Blacks an argument can be made for the concurrent presence of both. An assessment of the effects of anti-Semitic norms, however, falls beyond the scope of this inquiry.

Summary and Conclusions

Few studies have examined the relationships among minorities. Those that have examined the relationships between Blacks and Jews have generally focused (although not exlusively) on the selective nature of Black hostility toward Jews. This paper concentrated on three specific structural conditions of Black anti-Semitism that were represented in the social contact and the middleman hypotheses. Supporting evidence was observed for both explanations.

Unlike previous inquiries this study did not restrict its focus to a separate test of each hypothesis; instead, both were treated as inter-related propositions and then compared. Two important discoveries were made: (1) a third explanation of anti-Semitism, which integrates the first two through the concept of differential association, and (2) the relative predictive merits of its two structural components.

First, attention was directed toward the interrelation between contact propositions, not toward the propositions themselves as seemingly separate and unrelated interpretations of anti-Semitism. On the basis that the first two hypotheses were but different dimensions of a more general formulation, they were combined to test their concurrent effect (i.e. specific combinations). To examine this alternative, a third variable heretofore untested was contrived, differential association. It suggests that Black antipathy toward Jews results from an excess of the kinds of contacts that stimulate intergroup prejudice (especially those economic exchanges in which there has developed a collective perception on the part of a less powerful, poorer minority that another minority has tended to make undue profit out of it) over the kinds of contacts that stimulate amity (e.g. neighborly associations). The theoretical fruitfulness of this multidimensional concept was evident by its ability to discriminate scores on the index of anti-Semitism, thus providing continuity of present findings with past theoretic formulations (Sutherland and Cressey 1974).

Because this emergent variable possesses a distinct quality, a quality that is different from its two separate component dimensions, it cannot be deduced from the individual examination of each dimension or through adding the dimensions. The converse is not true. By deriving the first two propositions from the third, the differential association argument attempts to explain apparently divergent responses as expressions of underlying structural regularity.

Second, evaluating the first two structural explanations individually and then comparatively afforded a more realistic assessment of the predictive value of each contact hypothesis. For example, intimate, equal-status contact does not provide the basis for as much optimism in the reduction of prejudice as past inquiries suggest when compared with economic mistreatment (Simpson and Yinger 1974). Of the two contact variables, the latter is by far the stronger predictor of anti-Semitism. Thus, the quality of economic dealings between Blacks and Jews may warrant more attention than present research indicates. If so, the question may not be how to encourage greater equal-status contact (e.g. integration) but how to amend conflicting interest along economic lines to combat intergroup prejudice (see Feagin 1978; Jones 1975). Given a society beset by economic uncertainties, the contexts of economic encounters could take on added importance for studies of intergroup relations.

Certainly the full range of Black-Jewish associations is not limited to the types examined here. The "bittersweet" (Weisbord 1970) nature of their political ties is a case in point. On the one hand, Jews have been longtime supporters of and participants in the civil rights movement for Blacks. On the other hand, militant Black criticism during the late 1960s of Israel and Zionism, along with the push for more Black control of civil rights organizations, alienated many Jews. In view of the present findings, how these political encounters affect attitudes of both Blacks and Jews constitutes another critical element in the web of interaction that has been spun between the two groups throughout this century.

Notes

A note of appreciation must go to Jan Allard for her comments of an earlier draft and also to the anonymous reviewers of this journal.
1. By occupying an intermediate position between the elites and the masses, they form a social bridge between the two major groups ("filling the status gap"). But because of their similarity in economic status with the elite and their close contacts with the masses, they come to symbolize the former. In times of stress (conflicting goals in market relations), they temporarily serve as a buffer group, bearing the brunt of mass anger. In this capacity, the intermediate rank of middleman minorities helps to preserve the vested interests of those above them (Blalock 1967; Bonacich 1973).
2. During the first half of the twentieth century, many Blacks moved into lower-income areas being vacated by upwardly mobile Jews, who themselves had replaced earlier migrants. Although once-Jewish communities are now predominantly Black, many of the economic institutions continued in Jewish hands. As a result, in some ghetto pockets, Jews are overrepresented in Black economic life. This scenario has long been a sensitive area of association for Blacks and Jews alike. It is questionable whether a similar process of invasion-succession has occurred in the major "Black belts" of Los Angeles to the extent that it did in Chicago and other cities in the Midwest and Northeast. But because Los Angeles is a metropolitan center inhabited by a goodly number of both Blacks and Jews, and the latter are more likely than the former to occupy middle-class occupations there, it

is likely that many Blacks have encountered Jews in superordinate positions along economic lines.

3. Located in the curfew zone of the Watts riot, the Avalon area is characterized as a working-class neighborhood composed largely of Black residents (94.7 percent). According to the 1960 U.S. census, 14.4 percent of the employed male labor force hold white-collar positions in a district where less than 30 percent (29.2 percent) own their own homes. Educationally, only 7.6 percent have received some college education according to the 1960 census. In contrast, Blacks from Crenshaw come from a more successful socio-economic background. Almost six in ten (57.1 percent) are engaged in white-collar work, and not quite half (45 percent) are home owners. Also in strong contrast to Avalon, 32.1 percent of the Crenshaw district residents have completed some college training. Racially, 60.9 percent are classified as White, 26.8 percent as Black, and the remaining 12.3 percent as other minorities, most of whom are Japanese according to the 1960 census. At the time this study was designed (1970), 1970 census data were not available; now that they are, a comparison of the two communities reveals the same pattern. Avalon residents continue to come from a lower socio-economic stratum and a more segregated setting than Crenshaw residents. For the college-educated, white-collar worker (male), and home owner, the Avalon percentages are 8.6, 18.7, and 24.9, respectively; the corresponding Crenshaw percentages, 34.9, 49.1, and 38.2. Avalon is 95 percent Black; 7 in 10 Crenshaw residents are classified as Black (U.S. Bureau of the Census 1970, pt. 1, 66, 71, 121, 201, 204, 206, 256, 336, 339, 341, 391; U.S. Bureau of the Census 1970, pt. 2, 21, 66, 69, 71).

4. Block sampling techniques like the above, unless modified, tend to over-sample the unemployed. In addition, females and older persons are apt to be more accessible through this procedure, especially when the interviewing is conducted during the day. Consequently, a considerable proportion of the employed male population would be seriously underrepresented, not to mention those in their young and middle years. To overcome these problems, quota sampling was used to approximate the population distribution. Also, interviewers were instructed to canvas daily their assigned areas during morning, afternoon, and evening hours.

5. One method of establishing the validity of this index is to demonstrate its ability to predict intolerant responses about Jews not contained in the index. Two items are used for this purpose. The first item is open-ended: "People have different ideas about other groups. For example, there are different opinions about what Jewish people are like. In your opinion, what are Jewish people like?" The item was introduced very early in the questionnaire to avoid inputing any characterization of Jews that might occur as a result of structuring the items. In this manner, the item allowed one to examine how Blacks view Jews independently of the questionnaire content. If the scores on the index measure prejudice toward Jews, a greater proportion of those with scores of five should elicit "overall unfavorable evaluations" of Jews than those with scores of four; and those with scores of four should endorse such an evaluation in larger proportion than those with three, and so on. The data support this contention (the percentage scores are 56, 45, 36, 24, 11, and 5). When the second item is introduced ("Jews should be prevented from getting into profitable

positions"), a similar pattern is observed (ranging from a high of 48 percent to a low of 4 percent).

6. These items were presented only after respondents indicated having had economic dealings with Jews in the Jews' respective contexts (i.e. as merchants and landlords).

7. For some Blacks, Whites in middleman-related roles in Black areas are often equated with being Jewish. Evidence for this sort of "mistaken identity" was witnessed during the fieldwork preparation for this survey. As a result, the reader must keep in mind that the reported experiences (structural variables, both social and economic) with Jews in some cases may be more "perceived" than "real."

8. Excluded in this cross tabulation are those who report an equal number of contacts of both types (one-one; two-two, N=25). Moreover, when respondents indicated having "more" of one type of association than another, the *number of contexts* in which they report having had specific encounters with Jews is the referent, and not the frequency, intensity, or duration of encounters within each context as employed in the original concept of differential association.

9. That reported economic mistreatment is related to selective Black hostility toward Jews does not warrant the conclusion that Jews in fact treat Blacks more harshly than do other Whites. However, when respondents were asked to compare the economic treatment they thought they might receive in dealing with Jews and white Gentiles as merchants, landlords, and employers, about half (46 percent) did not differentiate between the two groups. But of those who did, Blacks were more likely to evaluate Jews in an unfavorable light (35 percent as against 20 percent.) More than this, when respondents were queried about the ethnicity of merchants whose establishments were burned and looted during the Watts riot, Jewish store owners were perceived as the more likely target over their Gentile counterparts (27 percent, compared with 10 percent.) A fact not to be ignored, however, is that 63 percent reported that they "didn't know" or that "people in general" were the targets of Black anger.

10. It cannot be concluded from these findings that only asymmetrical relations exist between the contact variables and anti-Semitism. For example, one can reason that egalitarian social interaction with outgroups can reduce prejudice. The interpretation employed here conveys in part this perspective, but—as a cautionary note—it should be made clear that the reverse sequence is as plausible. The less-prejudiced person may be more inclined to develop close contacts across ethnic lines than one who is highly intolerant toward Jews. Conversely, the prejudiced respondent might be the likelier candidate to avoid contact with Jews. The possibility of a reciprocal association applies with equal force to the middleman hypothesis. (Whereas one can argue on behalf of this proposition, the reverse is arguable too. An anti-Semite may be more bent on reporting personal economic dealings with Jews as mistreatment than would be someone who is much less intolerant.)

11. Analysis shows that there is no significant interaction ($p. > 05$) between intimate, equal-status contact and economic mistreatment.

References

Allport, G.W. 1954.*The Nature of Prejudice*. Cambridge, Mass.: Addison-Wesley.

Amir, Y. 1969. "The Contact Hypothesis in Ethnic Relations." *Psychological Bulletin* 71:319-42.

Baldwin, J. 1948. "The Harlem Ghetto." *Commentary* 5:165-70.

Blalock, H.M., Jr. 1967. *Toward a Theory of Minority Group Relations*. New York: Wiley & Sons.

Bonacich, E. 1973. "A Theory of Middleman Minorities." *American Sociological Review* 38:583-94.

――――. 1980. "Middleman Minorities and Advanced Capitalism." *Ethnic Groups* 2:211-19.

Brophy, I.N. 1946. "The Luxury of Anti-Negro Prejudice." *Public Opinion Quarterly* 9:456-66.

Clark, K. 1946. "Candor of Negro-Jewish Relations." *Commentary* 1:8-14.

Deutsch, M., and Collins, M.E. 1951. *Interracial Housing: A Psychological Evaluation of a Social Experiment*. Minneapolis: University of Minnesota Press.

Eitzen, D.S. 1971. "Two Minorities: The Jews of Poland and the Chinese of the Philippines." In *Majority and Minority Relations: The Dynamics of Racial and Ethnic Relations*, ed. N.R. Yetman and C. Hoy Steele, 117-38. Boston: Allyn & Bacon.

Feagin, J.R. 1978. *Racial and Ethnic Relations*. Englewood Cliffs, N.J.: Prentice-Hall.

Ford, W.S. 1973. "Interracial Public Housing in a Border City: Another Look at the Contact Hypothesis." *American Journal of Sociology* 78:1426-47.

Jahoda, M. and West, P.S. 1951. "Race Relations in Public Housing." *Journal of Social Issues* 7:132-39.

Jiang, J.P.L. 1968. "Towards a Theory of Pariah Enterpreneurship." In *Leadership and Authority: A Symposium*, ed. G. Wijeyewardene, 147-62. Singapore: University of Malaya Press.

Jones, N.B. 1975. "The Failure of Black-Jewish Relations." *Crisis* 82:24-27.

Marx, G.T. 1969. *Protest and Prejudice: A Study of Beliefs in the Black Community*. New York: Harper & Row.

Meer, B., and Freedman, E. 1966. "The Impact of Negro Neighbors on White House Owners." *Social Forces* 5:11-19.

Preston, J.D., and Robinson, J.W. 1974. "On Modification of Inter-Racial Interaction." *American Sociological Review* 39:282-85.

Reed, J.W. 1980. "Getting to Know You: The Contact Hypothesis Applied to the Sectional Beliefs and Attitudes of White Southerners." *Social Forces* 59:123-35.

Rinder, I.D. 1958-59. "Stranger in the Land: Social Relations in the Status Gap." *Social Problems* 6:253-60.

Robinson, J.W., and Preston, J.D. 1976. "Equal-Status Contact and Modifi-

cation of Racial Prejudice: A Reexamination of the Contact Hypothesis.''
Social Forces 54:911-24.

Silberman, C. 1979. "Jesse and the Jews." *New Republic* 180:12-14.

Selznick, G., and Steinberg, S. 1969. *The Tenacity of Prejudice: Anti-Semitism in Contemporary America*. New York: Harper & Row.

Simpson, G., and Yinger, M. 1972. *Racial and Cultural Minorities*. New York: Harper & Row.

Stryker, S. 1959. "Social Structure and Prejudice." *Social Problems* 6:340-54.

Sutherland, E.H., and Cressey, D.R. 1974. *Crimonology*. Philadelphia: Lippincott.

Triandis, H.C., and Vassiliou, V. 1967. "Frequency of Contact of Stereotyping." *Journal of Personality and Social Psychology* 7:316-28.

Tsukashima, R.T. 1973. "The Social and Psychological Correlates of Anti-Semitism in the Black Community." Ph.D. dissertation, University of California, Los Angeles.

Tsukashima, R.T., and Montero, D. 1976. "The Contact Hypothesis: Social and Economic Contact and Generational Changes in the Study of Black Anti-Semitism." *Social Forces* 55:149-65.

Turner, J., and Bonacich, E. 1980. "Toward a Composite Theory of Middleman Minorities." *Ethnicity* 7:144—58.

U.S. National Advisory Commission on Civil Disorders 1968. *Supplementary Studies for the National Advisory Commission on Civil Disorders*. Washington, D.C.: Government Printing Office.

van der Laan, H.D., ed. 1975. "Asian Minorities in Africa: Indians and Lebanese." *Kroniek van Afrika,* Special Issue, No. 6.

Williams, R.M., Jr. 1964. *Strangers Next Door*. Englewood Cliffs, N.J.: Prentice-Hall.

Wilner, D.M., Walkley, R.P., and Cook, S.W. 1955. *Human Relations in Interracial Housing*. Minneapolis: University of Minnesota Press.

Weisbord, R.G. 1970. *Bittersweet Encounter*. Westport, Conn.: Negro University Press.

Works, E. 1961. "The Negro-Interaction Hypothesis from the Point of View of the Negro Minority Group." *American Journal of Sociology* 67:47-52.

Zenner, W.P., and Jarvenpa, R. 1980. "Scots in the Northern Fur Trade: A Middleman Minority Perspective." *Ethnic groups* 2:189-210.

2

The Impact of National Characteristics on Local Citizen Participation: A Developmental Research Framework Applied to Israel

Efraim Ben-Zadok

This article suggests that physical, social, political, economic, and national or structural characteristics such as social composition or political culture actually determine patterns and fluctuations in the levels of citizen participation in local planning. Assuming a developmental process, the paper reviews the relationships between these characteristics and local participation in Israel throughout the one hundred years from the inception of the Zionist movement until the 1980s. The main purpose is to design a comprehensive framework that could be used in research. This framework for analyzing causal relationships is presumed to be applicable to other countries. Moreover, it proves that social and political characteristics, which are interrelated in Israel, explain participation significantly; physical characteristics explain less. A general local trend in the 1970s and 1980s toward decentralization, which encourages voluntary participation, is also discussed.

Citizen participation in planning in Western democracies accelerated in the 1960s and 1970s. In Israel modern forms of local participation began only in the 1970s and have recently gained strong momentum with implementation of a national urban renewal project. The project established participation as one of its major goals. This article focuses on the impact of national structural characteristics upon such citizen participation in local planning. The emphasis is on Israel.

Interestingly, much of the literature has addressed the topic of the individual's desire to participate in local planning. Indeed, the effects of social variables, primarily class (which includes such components as income, education, and occupation), have been accepted as explanatory of different levels of local participation (Kornhauser 1959; Wilson and Banfield 1964; Gans 1968; Van Til and Van Til 1970).

Thus, little effort has been directed toward analyzing the impact of national characteristics on community participation, and when such research was conducted, it frequently carried the disadvantage of focusing on just one or two factors. For example, Almond and Verba (1965) sought to demonstrate the influence of local government structure and political culture on people's desire to participate. Their research on local participation stands as one of the few comparative studies on the topic, but it constitutes only a single chapter in their classic, which largely deals with political participation on the national level. Their study examines what they refer to as "the participant political culture"—a political culture in which the actor's orientation is geared toward actively serving the society. Israeli studies have also discussed the relationship between structural characteristics and local participation (Kramer 1971; Lapin 1973). A highly centralized government, bureaucratic paternalism, and a strong party system have been cited as relevant factors limiting participation.

Unlike the literature that has concentrated on personal factors motivating participation, this article analyses the extent to which national structural characteristics have affected participation in local planning. It attempts to design a comprehensive approach stressing two levels. First, it deals with general characteristics (e.g. central-local government relations) as well as more specific characteristics derived from them (e.g. distribution of money from the center to the periphery). Second, the discussion touches upon all national characteristics, physical, social, political, and economic, that are expressed in a wide range of phenomena such as ideology, culture, legislation, management, and organization. These characteristics are examined in a historical context because they change dynamically over time.

The focus is on a specific area of participation: I discuss participation in local planning whether in urban or rural settings. The commitment of planners to public participation has been strong and was recognized as an integral part of the profession, but participation in planning is not defined as a monolithic concept, nor does it imply a single approach or method. In fact, there are many alternative approaches (Alterman 1982). Attempting to avoid confusion, I define participation in local planning as starting from basic voluntary involvement, such as residents' input into a building committee that is responsible for the upkeep and maintenance of the immediate environment, and extending up to decentralized local government activity on the community level, such as citizens' contributions to the preparation of zoning plans. I also include quasi-public organizations of local consumers that try to affect private and public service delivery in the definition of participation. I refer not only to the ability to express one's opinion at some forum but also to the possibility of suggesting and designing programs, and even of implementing and evaluating them.

The purpose of this article, which is based largely on recent Israeli studies, is to offer a comprehensive theoretical research framework for a topic that has thus far remained obscure and confused. A further purpose is to lay the foundation for empirical studies of different aspects of citizen participation in Israel or other countries.

The article has three major sections: the first covers the impact of national *physical* characteristics on citizen participation; the second covers *social* attributes; the third is devoted to the influence of *political* characteristics. Each section treats what I assume to be the two most important characteristics of the attributes in question. The first section discusses the country's physical size and its spatial structure of settlement. The second section elaborates on the functioning of a broad social ideology, and the level of homogeneity-heterogeneity of the country's social composition. The third section analyzes central-local government relationships as expressed in the level of centralization-decentralization, and the political culture as elitist or democratic. The characteristics are analyzed within the historical context provided by the period from the ascendance of Zionism in Israel to the present. We summarize by dividing the topic into periods of historical significance. Thereafter, conclusions are drawn regarding the method of analysis used and the current progress of citizen participation in Israel.

The paper's major contribution is twofold. First, it offers a systematic method of testing the impact of the various national structural characteristics on participation in planning. Second, it presents a review of the development of citizen participation in local planning in Israel from the late nineteenth century until the 1980s.

Physical Characteristics and Their Impact on Citizen Participation

Two physical characteristics are central in influencing local planning participation in Israel. The first is *the physical size of the country*. Israel's small physical size is very important because the short distances facilitate rapid communication from the center to the periphery. It also fosters a high level of involvement of people from the periphery in the center. The second characteristic, *the spatial structure of settlement*, needs further explanation. Shachar (1973) characterizes Israel's spatial structure in the prestate period as "primacy": a system with highly populated central cities, a limited number of small rural communities, and the absence of any middle-sized towns. During the 1950s, the young state attempted to bridge the gap by conducting a policy of population dispersion and by building new towns. Indeed, the government sought to alter the existing structure of "primacy" to one of "rank-size" by trying to establish small to middle-sized towns as centers of commerce and services to provide the needs of nearby small agricultural settlements. Shachar contends that the government has succeeded in altering Israel's structure to become more rank-size in nature, and that this trend is likely to be reinforced as the country's economy continues to become more complex and as middle-sized towns continue to grow. Yet, although the structure has become more rank-sized, the dominance of the four central cities—Tel-Aviv, Jerusalem, Haifa, and Beer-Sheva—in relation to smaller settlements has remained a salient feature, leaving little likelihood of any drastic future alterations in this pattern. In other words, the polarity of the structure, large city versus small settlement, will remain a cornerstone in Israel's urban mold.

Together, the two central physical characteristics have facilitated the development of rapid communication as well as strong political and social bonds between small settlements and large urban centers. The ramifications of the trend to rank-size formation, noted by Shachar, are largely limited to the economics and distribution of services. Thus, while economic ties between medium and small-sized settlements will be encouraged, they will not seriously hinder either the transfer of information from large cities to small communities or their mutual social involvement because the distances between them are so short. Furthermore, technological innovations in communication systems and transportation promise stronger ties between central cities and distant settlements. Clearly, members of the rural communities and the new development towns will continue to frequent the large cities for purposes of trade, leisure, and political and social activities.

The aggregate of these physical factors points to a higher level of participation at the national level. Short distances; strong economic, political, and cultural bonds between large cities and small communities; and rapid communication and transportation have together contributed to a national orientation with strong dependency upon the center. Thus, it is understandable that little importance has been attached to participation at the local level. Finally, while the movement toward a more rank-sized settlement pattern is likely to increase local participation, the new pattern will still remain secondary to the primacy structure.[1]

Social Characteristics and Their
Impact on Citizen Participation

Two social characteristics are cardinal factors in determining local participation in Israel. The first raises the issue of *the functioning of a broad social ideology*; the second is concerned with *the composition of the social structure*, whether it be homogeneous or heterogeneous. I start by discussing the former.

The spatial distribution and polarity of the settlement structure was dictated largely by the Zionist ideology of the Second Aliyah (wave of immigration) dominant since the early years of the twentieth century. Zionist ideals hold that self- and nation-fulfillment are achieved through working the land. These ideals became the pillars of the movement. The attempt to normalize Jewish society in Israel was characterized by the preference for an agrarian way of life to the point of neglecting the functions of the city, which were indeed unrecognized ideologically until the early 1960s (Cohen 1970). The partial neglect in developing large and medium-sized cities was apparent in the allocation of economic resources. It was not until the mid-1960s that the importance of urban centers was recognized and such centers were free to assume their natural positions in the country's settlement pattern.

An antiurban bias is not an exclusively Israeli phenomenon. In fact, different societies have bred antiurban movements of their own. For instance, White and White (1962) portray an American view of the city as a corrupter of American values, and as both an ethical and aesthetic failure. In Wirth's (1938) classic article, the city is depicted as a unit devoid of basic social organization and characterized by formal and anonymous relationships accompanied by loneliness, crime, and psychological stress. Yet, the antiurban ideology in the United States had little impact on the political or economic spheres. Unregulated market forces and private enterprise have continued to be the main features, and the big city remained at the heart of the country's economic and cultural life.

In both Israel and the United States, the antiurban bias has encouraged the blossoming of communal rural settlements with full participation. These were the Israeli kibbutz and the utopian communities that sprouted up in the United States from the mid-eighteenth century throughout the first half of the nineteenth century. Socialist-Zionist ideology dictated more than just settlement patterns and a distribution of political and economic power; it also gave birth to the kibbutz, one of the most comprehensive models of community participation in history. The kibbutz's weekly general assembly of all members, each with one vote, discusses and implements in a highly democratic fashion an array of resolutions relating to physical and social aspects of local planning issues. However, it should be noted that the kibbutz's planning constraints are fewer than the city's, for it is a small and homogeneous group whose members view the communal, family-oriented way of life as a source of individual fulfillment. Kibbutzim have not been reluctant to introduce a system of rotation based on equality in which even high-level administrators are interchanged with simple farmers in daily tasks. These agricultural settlements have obviously been active in regional planning frameworks as well as in contributing to national goals.

The growth of such autonomous communities, accentuating participation, egalitarianism, and an extremist code of morals and ethics, was typical of the utopian societies in the United States as well. The goals of such communities evolved around religious reform and from living an idealistic utopian way of life (Hine 1966). Over a hundred communities were established, but they usually failed after ten or thirty years.

From an organizational viewpoint, the kibbutz has remained unique. No similar communal model evolved in urban areas. Although participation on a smaller scale has appeared in the Israeli moshav (village), plans for urban communal forms have all remained in the discussion stage. Furthermore, a major contrast between the U.S. utopian communities and the Israeli kibbutzim is that the settlers of the former sought to isolate themselves by escaping from society while those of the latter, who constitute only 3 percent of Israel's population, have tried to dominate societal values. Indeed, they have done so with great success.

It can be deduced from the Israeli and U.S. experiences that the existence of such models, with high levels of participation, will remain limited. This lesson is stringently applicable to economies where free enterprise prevails. On the other hand, in socialist societies, the survivability of communal structures is much higher. Moreover, their effect on, and support from, the larger society is usually apparent. While the city is taking its natural position in the Israeli society, the existence of a strong communal setting, such as the kibbutz or moshav, is continually nourished by ideological inspirations of the entire society. Additionally, although communal living has remained the domain of small groups in the country, these values have echoed throughout the whole population. The rural sector dictated national values in the areas of settlement, defense, and security. The cities did not adopt the extreme democratic collective forms more appropriate for small ideologically motivated homogeneous elite groups, but they were influenced by the value system of these groups. Thus, participation in planning in the city was reduced to a secondary level of importance, while the attention of urban dwellers was diverted toward pursuing national goals central to the overall cohesive social framework. This climate enabled political parties to become the cities' main channels of participation, whether at the local or national level (Katan 1980, 52-54).

Our discussion of the urban sector turns now to the second social feature that affects citizen participation: the level of homogeneity or heterogeneity of the social composition. From the start, the population diversity in Israel's major cities was relatively low. In comparison to the United States and Europe, large differences in class and racial groups related to different life-styles have been lacking in Israel. This is illustrated by juxtaposing Israel and the United States. Both are highly urbanized societies. Seventy percent of the U.S. population is urban; in Israel, 86 percent (Efrat 1979, 15). Yet, one must recognize an indispensable difference: Israel has only a few cities measured in the hundreds of thousands; such cities would be considered small in the United States, where a significant number of cities exceed the one million mark. Hawley (1971, 135) explains tht there is a direct correlation between city size and ability to specialize in a wider range of areas, i.e. more stores, commerce, and related services, as well as more leisure and cultural opportunities. Most important, large size breeds a wider variety of social groups with dissimilar backgrounds and styles. Because size is an essential element for social diversity, the U.S. urban system must sustain the needs of many different groups. Consequently, a variety of participatory strategies have developed in the central cities and metropolitan areas, from which most of the academic documentation has emerged.

The relatively homogeneous makeup of Israel's Jewish urban population was influenced largely by natural collective values that stressed equality and classlessness, and offered little in terms of different life-styles. It can be inferred that the homogeneity of the population was one of the main barriers to the introduction of plans for local participation until the mid-1960s. Because specialization on a territorial basis was fairly limited, divergence in participatory strategies was not required. Finally, it was not likely that such a need would arise in a society that invested so much energy in solving national problems.

In the late 1960s, however, Israel's social structure underwent important changes that raised the level of participation. The major shifts involved increases in the levels of heterogeneity, pluralism, and specialization. Intraclass boundaries became more defined, facilitating the development and adoption of new life-styles. The attempt to answer different needs meant that local participation became a tool for regulating the demands of specific groups on the general system. The proclivity for pluralism was a function of the growth of urban communities, more specifically, of the four central cities which began their surge in the 1950s. The expansion, which came as a reslt of natural growth and immigration, increased the level of urbanization and supported social specialization. The rise in heterogeneity may also be explained by an improved economy and by the increased adaptation of affluent Western life-style symbols.

The pluralistic trend legitimized both individualistic interests and identification on the basis of class, religion, or life-style. Ethnic awareness was also stressed. The "melting-pot" integration policies of the 1950s were replaced by increasing ethnic identification. A number of mostly anthropological studies are devoted to this topic. Weingrod (1979) focuses on ethnic festivals of Moroccan, Kurdish, and Georgian Jews as expressions of ethnic pride and uniqueness. Similarly, Goldberg (1977) sees the resurgence of the ancient Moroccan Mimouna festival as a clear sign of greater ethnic pride and awareness. Weingrod not only observes that stratification has become a clear feature in Israel's social structure but also explains the evolving phenomenon of class-ethnic intersection. The working class could now be characterized as Oriental Jews with lower income and less formal education. Furthermore, the strengthening of ethno-class identification produced some local protest.[2]

The pluralism discussed above was accompanied by increases in the standard of living, leisure time, and standard level of education. Wilson and Banfield (1964) compared the heightened "public regarding" of the upper-class and well-educated electorate in local planning issues with the "private regarding" ethos of the lower class. Although not central to our discussion, these conditions have, to some extent, contributed to the development of an ethos that elevated the importance of citizen participation in planning.

Heterogeneity and pluralism stimulated an awareness of individualistic needs, which raised different demands and encouraged participation. A parallel feature of the 1960s was the beginning of a steady erosion in the appeal of egalitarianism and collective ideals and with it the strengthening of specific sectorial demands that matched the growing trend toward individualism and materialism. In this manner, the broad social ideology began to lose its ability to function strongly. Thus, changes in these two social characteristics, ideology and social composition, brought about an increase in the level of citizen participation after the late 1960s.

Evidence of the rise of participation at the local level can be seen from the widened scope of activity of voluntary associations as well as the increased participation in environmental associations.[3] Such examples lend support to the increasing citizen participation trend. Finally, this trend is partly the by-product of the social changes discussed above, changes that are likely to continue developing in the current direction.

Political Characteristics and Their
Impact on Citizen Participation

The two most important political characteristics that affect citizen participation at the local level are *the relationships between central and local governments as expressed in the level of centralization or decentralization*, and *the political culture as elitist or democratic*. The two characteristics are closely interrelated. Indeed, they often appear inseparable, and therefore will be discussed together.

The Jewish community in Europe and in the Arab countries developed as an autonomous ethnic framework that provided religious, economic, and social services for hundreds of years. This framework was duplicated in Palestine at the end of the eighteenth century with the establishment of the *Kolel*, a community organized on the basis of country or city of origin in Europe. The *Kolels* were later united under one federation, which in the late nineteenth century became known as the General Committee of Knesset Yisrael (Weiss 1979, 21). From the end of the nineteenth century until World War I, the Zionist settlement movement was composed of local initiatives, which included the first *Moshavot* (agricultural towns), moshavim (cooperative villages), kibbutzim, and cities that started as independent neighborhoods (National Committee for Local Government Affairs 1981, 11-12). Municipal reforms, enacted by the Ottoman Empire of those days, sought to increase the authority of the central government but had little effect on the Jewish communities (Weiss 1979, 22). In fact, it is possible to observe the continuation until the end of World War I of the local political tradition of European and Oriental Jewry: an effective social autonomous framework created on a territorial basis, enjoying voluntary support with a defined organizational structure fostered by various informal processes.

British rule (1918-48) strongly influenced the government structure and the judicial system later adopted by the State of Israel. During the British mandate, local governments enjoyed only limited authority. Government policy was dictated from the center, where decisions were made. Many Jewish communities organized themselves by forming local committees that lacked legal authority, yet were successful in collecting taxes and developing services (Weiss 1979, 23-24).

The Jewish community (Yishuv) in Palestine became officially organized in 1921 under the title of Knesset Yisrael. In 1928, the Knesset Yisrael administrative structure was established. Its national institutions took the tasks of planning and budgeting the settlement of the country. The Zionist movement delegated the responsibility of caring for daily needs and community development to the local level. Although the Yishuv developed a centralized structure that formulated guidelines for national policy, the settlements themselves enjoyed autonomy, provided their own services, and made local and regional development decisions.

With the establishment of the State of Israel in 1948, most tasks were transferred from the Jewish Agency, the national institutions, and local communities directly to government offices. Power was consolidated at the expense of local bodies. Centralization was legislated but also informally established in the negotiation patterns between the center and periphery. An emphasis on strengthening state authority and statism itself as the highest national values eroded the political power of the periphery and contributed to its economic dependency (Weiss 1979). The central government became the focus of power and thus served to maintain the control of the older elites. Municipalities were relegated to a position of dependency for matters of legislation, construction, education, health, welfare, and industrial development. The services that remained distinctly local were sanitation, garbage collecting, gardening, water utilities, and sewage. The rationale for the division of services was based upon differentiating basic technical services from services that were instrumental in fulfilling national values. The centralization trend continued until the end of the 1960s.

The centralized structure was essential to answer the immediate national needs of the young state, which faced many acute problems. Defense, immigrant absorption, population dispersion, and economic self-sufficiency were top priorities; the quality of the individual's life and the needs of the local community were secondary. Most of the country's political power and economic resources were channeled to broad national goals, and the centralized bureaucratic structure was an effective tool toward their realization. Both the process of immigration and the need to safeguard the country's rate of development for such massive absorption contributed to the dependency of localities upon the center, as illustrated by the immigrant settlements and the new development towns. Local development, initiated for the purpose of advancing national goals, was not always contingent on economic rationality. This situation necessitated intense involvement on the part of the central government, the only entity that could offer major planning and budgetary support to construction, industry, agriculture, education, and welfare services. Serving the immigrants, who were needy of individual, professional, and social counseling in adapting to their new surroundings, was yet another important function delegated to central agencies.

The centralized hierarchy in government was naturally accepted because the forebears, themselves from Eastern Europe, were familiar with this form of governing. Additionally, the center's intervention in implementation served as an essential element of socialist policies. The centralized methods were accepted by most immigrants, especially the Oriental ones, out of necessity and because most came from political cultures that lacked any democratic tradition. Thus, the democratic norms that were institutionalized emphasized formal aspects of democracy, such as free elections, proportional representation and the need for a majority in parliamentary decision making; liberal aspects of individual freedom and minority rights were less stressed (Shapiro 1977). Israeli politics, characterized as highly ideological (Eisenstadt 1967), encouraged public interest in ideological cleavage on the national level. In this system, there was little sign of any crystallization of a tradition of participatory democracy or organizational decision making from below. The individual's dependency on the state was almost complete, especially that of the immigrant. Such a situation did little to encourage standing up for citizen's rights—especially if one was a newcomer.

The political structure, created out of necessity and buttressed by the political tradition of the immigrants' countries of origin did not foster resident participation in planning at the local level. In fact, the first two decades of statehood were characterized by citizen apathy. The most significant expressions of the centralized structure can be seen in four arrangements—more specific structural characteristics derived from the central-local government interrelationship—which deprived local governments of much of their power, lowered their level of political autonomy, and consequently weakened participation from below.

The first arrangement was the system of local elections, which were similar to the parliament (Knesset) elections that were usually held on the same day. The elections were proportional and were based on the European parliamentary model: members of the local council elected the mayor by majority vote. In such a system, legislative authority overlapped executive authority; carried out the decisions of the council but had limited power. The electorate did not vote for individual candidates; candidates were selected from lists compiled in the parties' headquarters. The ability of the voters, mostly immigrants, to differentiate the Knesset elections from municipal elections was limited, and so they were often inclined to vote a single party line.

The second arrangement was the structure that positioned the parties as intermediaries between the government and municipalities. The parties tried to secure the votes of the immigrants who were dependent upon them and who did not necessarily distinguish between the party, the state, or the Histadrut (the largest trade union).[4] In addition, there was a tacit coalitional identification between central and local authorities. The Labor party (Mapai) and its religious coalition partners were at the helm of the entire system. With a resurgence of immigration, there was a minimal number of locales that differed from the pattern of power distribution of the center. Israel is described as a country with an intense party system. Parties are numerous, and they oversee many social, political, economic, and educational activities. Dependence on party headquarters impaired the growth of democratic forces from below. Local activists were drafted and eventually assumed jobs in their communities under the auspices of the parties. Thus, the parties, which actually maintained the power of the older elites, continued to dominate and manipulate the electoral potential of the immigrants. Furthermore, many of the traditional leaders of the Oriental Jewry failed to migrate to Israel with their masses. A tendency for strong party loyalty was very much present among the new immigrants. They lacked the tools to integrate into their new society, and thus many of them underwent a painful transition from a traditional society to a modern society with formal welfare services (Katan 1980).

The third arrangement was the method of allocating funds from the center to local authorities. Because the government structure is especially sensitive to political forces, the potential for improvisation is always present. This invites lobbying by local party officials, with personal ties, informal contacts, and party membership influencing economic policy in regard to the municipalities (Weiss 1979, 16-18). The pressures are evident in the budget making for the Ministries of Interior, Education, Housing, Commerce and Industry, Labor, and Welfare. The municipalities are also monitored by the state comptroller. All these factors have contributed to the municipalities' dependency for most of their revenues, upon the government. Often budgetary motives could be measured only in terms of their national social value and not their economic feasibility. Such was especially the case in regard to new settlements and development towns. These were not natural ecological growth processes but projects initiated at the top with the local, sometimes unstable, socioeconomic structure always dependent on capital from the center.[5]

The fourth arrangement that limited the power of municipalities and citizen participation was the administrative structure of local planning in Israel. The 1965 Planning and Building Law had its origins in the British 1936 Town Planning Ordinance. The hierarchical structure—National Council, district commission, and local commission—secured central control at each level. The achievement of public goals and national planning objectives was guaranteed by a parallel hierarchy of legal plans, each incorporating the general directions assigned to the level below. A small clause in the law allowed the public to receive information and to submit objections concerning certain plans, an opportunity to participate that was not extensively utilized. The effectiveness of the system was assured by the public ownership of 92 percent of the land through the Israel Lands Authority. Most planning before the end of the 1960s was done by architects and engineers, with little involvement of technically unskilled citizens in committees or agencies of local planning.

Let us pause here to read a passage about the growth of a political culture in Israel until the end of the 1960s; we can identify three distinct elements that coexist, albeit unblended and in mutual conflict (Elazar 1977, 48-49):

> (1) A statist-bureaucratic political culture which implicitly accepts the concept of a reified state existing independently of its citizens and which views political organization as essentially centralized, hierarchical, and bureaucratic in character (a view shared by the vast majority of those Israelis coming from continental Europe), (2) an Oriental subject political culture, which views government as the private preserve of an elite, functioning to serve the interests of that elite and hence a potentially malevolent force in the lives of ordinary people (a view shared by the great majority of the Israeli population coming from the subject cultures of Eastern Europe and the Arab countries of the Middle East and North Africa), and (3) a Jewish political culture, which is civic and republican in its orientation, viewing the policy as a partnership of its members who are fundamentally equal as citizens and who are entitled to an equal share of the benefits resulting from the pooling of common resources. This culture combines a high level of citizen participation with a clear responsibility on the part of the governing authorities to set the polity's overall direction and is shared to a greater or lesser degree by the 85% of the population that is Jewish.

These three elements have been in constant conflict because of the large gap between the country's formal institutional structure and its actual political behavior. The country can be characterized as having a bureaucratic, centralized, hierarchical structure that allows for informal arrangements executed through individual counseling and negotiation, which, in turn, bring some dispersion of power (Elazar 1977). As explained, the Jewish community structure has always enjoyed autonomy and participation from below. The formal centralization that developed in the new state was foreign to the cultural political orientation of the Jewish public. There is no doubt that the conflict between the Jewish political culture and the Israeli bureaucratic structure was a cause of a great deal of tension and deficiency in governmental functioning.

The 1970s brought a lull in pressures from economic, social, security, and immigrant-absorption problems. The economic situation had improved, and the standard of living rose. The army became stronger, and territorial boundaries were expanded. The absorption process was coming to a close, and the number of new immigrants fell steadily. These improved conditions contributed to a renewal of decentralization trends. Concern for individual needs and local communities increased. More signs of participation from below began to surface. Simultaneously, local municipalities were strengthened. As a result, public participation was legitimated and accelerated.

The decentralizing trend of the 1970s is clearly expressed in the four arrangements discussed above that had weakened local participation until that time. If we return to review these arrangements, it will become evident that each incorporates the new trend of strengthening local authority, increasing its political autonomy, and broadening public participation in planning.

We begin by analyzing the first two closely connected arrangements: the local elections system and the party structure. In the 1969 elections, the number of mayors coming from local lists reached seventeen compared to nine in 1965. The 1973 elections, following the Yom Kippur War, marked a turning point; they clearly demonstrated the dwindling power of the parties and a heightened electoral ability to differentiate between the Knesset and municipal elections. The new peak of split-ticket voting (a trend first recognized in 1969) and the appearance of independent lists indicated citizen desire for a more meaningful expression of local interests and a need to differentiate between national and local policy. This trend is described by Elazar (1975) as a transformation from ideologically based to territorially based politics. It is seen as a sign of voter maturity. The trend was formally recognized in 1975 with passage of a law calling for election of mayors and deputies on an individual rather than list basis. The law also separated mayoral and council elections. The legislative and executive functions continued to overlap, with council members holding executive positions. It was still possible to form large coalitions and distribute the positions accordingly, yet the law originated in natural developments calling for local and unique expression, and was an indication of further changes.

In assessing major changes in Israel's party formation since the Yom Kippur War, Galnoor (1980, 130, 135) argued:

> "Statism," in the sense of a reduction in the degree of party-politicization, gained legitimacy in 1967, and became an even more vigorously presented demand after the Yom Kippur War. . . .Following the Yom Kippur war, the erosion in the power of the parties reached a peak, principally affecting those parties which had formed the cabinet—diminishing their capacity to serve as coordinating centers and channels of communication.

The erosion of party power and the new method of elections encouraged the emergence of a spontaneous local leadership, replacing local officials and other representatives drafted from the parties' headquarters in the central cities. These factors also facilitated the independent functioning of local leaders, who formerly were dominated by the parties. Local leaders successfully gained widespread local support with which to counter external influences, especially those from party headquarters. Thus, they were able to function in accordance with the needs of the community. The leaders, many of them from the development towns, were relatively young and of Oriental origin. They proved themselves in 1973, and even more so in the 1978 elections, by being elected through party or local lists. A number of them reached the national level in the 1977 Knesset elections and again in 1981, when local government served as an avenue to positions at the center (Ben-Zadok and Goldberg 1983, 17-18, 21-24). These developments signified a strengthening of democratic participatory trends and political independence at the local level.

The third arrangement, the method of distribution of funds, also contributed to the decentralizing trend. Local budget dependency upon the center diminished as a result of increased local autonomy. The greater power of mayors and the development of local power bases placed the localities in a better bargaining situation in a process that was characterized by informal mechanisms. The preliminary results of an extensive study analyzing patterns of the government's distribution of funds to fifty municipalities between 1968 and 1978 verify that the relationship became more open, and that local authorities are more independent of the center (Torgovnik 1982).

Signs of change can also be detected in the fourth arrangement, the administrative structure of local planning. The emphasis on social planning has proceeded hand-in-hand with an increase in the public's awareness of planning issues. Recently the courts ruled in favor of submitting supplements to zoning plans. In addition, there is a rise in the number of objections by individuals and public bodies to zoning plans submitted to the commissions. In Israel's first comprehensive evaluation of the statutory planning system, the researchers suggest changing from a rigid and detailed approach to one more flexible and general (Alexander, Alterman, and Law-Yone 1979, 45).

The trend toward decentralization in the 1970s was accompanied by an atmosphere of ambivalence toward the modern welfare state, an atmosphere from the Western world. On the one hand, there were demands, which were fulfilled, for more intensive state intervention in the delivery of services to individuals. On the other hand, the complex bureaucracy, high taxation, alienation from the central government, and feelings of class and ethnic deprivation stimulated a resurgence in the public's desire to participate in decision making and a turn against the accepted value of government centralization. As a result, there was a rise of public protest activities. A comprehensive documentation of these activities, e.g. strikes, demonstrations, and even vandalism and violence between 1960 and 1979, appears in Lehman-Wilzig's (1981) study. It points to a steady rise in acts of protest in Israel, particularly since 1970.

The same ambivalent atmosphere and subsequent protests were already present in the United States in the early 1960s. The liberal Great Society programs introduced by the Johnson administration (1964-68), concerned housing, education, employment, health, and other areas. These programs were concurrent with the blossoming of the civil rights, Black, women's, student, and antiwar movements. The interaction among the social policies, the social movements, and the spirit of protest strengthened the trend toward citizen participation in the United States.

The most intensive expression of welfare state involvement, on the one hand, and citizen participation in local planning, on the other, in both the United States and Israel, is seen in urban renewal projects. In 1977, with the change of power from Labor to Likud government, the Israeli government and the Jewish Agency together adopted a comprehensive plan for the rehabilitation of 160 poor neighborhoods at a cost of $1.2 billion. The project was marked by the democratic orientation of the decision making and by the participation of the residents.[6]

One critique, among many, focused on the plan's fuzziness regarding the composition of resident representation and appointment to the neighborhood steering committees (State Comptroller 1980, 227). Another criticism: "The organizational structure of Project Renewal at the national and local level is complex, and actually the roles, authorities and functional processes of the various bodies participating in the plan are unclear." (State Comptroller 1980, 228). The lack of clarity in organization and delegation of authority provided the opportunity for the government and the Jewish Agency to retreat somewhat by limiting decentralization while the project was still under way. Still, the project was a radical change. It was the most comprehensive social planning venture in a state that since its establishment had struggled with the pressures of physical planning. It raised the level of resident participation and attracted the cooperation of Diaspora Jewry.[7]

A preliminary general evaluation of Project Renewal explains that while the administrative structure originally envisioned was quite simplistic, with a local steering committee designing plans and a national committee authorizing them and granting implementation rights, reality dictated development of a more complex structure. The report indicates some initial findings, such as a rise in the level of resident participation and involvement in local organizations, an increase in the number of building committees and new neighborhood committees, and the positive implications of the project for resident involvement in community affairs and decisions regarding their future (International Committee on Project Renewal Evaluation 1983, 4, 20.)

The decentralizing trend, with social and economic changes in the background, has been strengthened in the 1980s.[8] The Israeli structure has remained largely centralized in contrast to the United States, where the government structure allows for the institutionalization of localism. However, a political culture encompassing elements of citizen participation and citizen cooperation with the central government is common to both countries. Thus, the cultural foundation in Israel can be broadened by instilling an appreciation for democratic values. Additionally, the administrative relationships between the central and local governments will continue to decentralize. In conclusion, the changes in the two political characteristics mentioned, the central-local government relationships and the political culture, will continue to contribute to the developing trend towards greater citizen participation in local planning.

Conclusions

The comprehensive framework presented in this article argues that citizen participation in local planning can be explained by national structural characteristics in a historical developmental context. It is important to systematically include all characteristics. As shown in table 2.1, social and political characteristics are held to be closely intertwined and to account significantly for the level of participation. In our case, the

TABLE 2.1
Summary of Major National Structural Characteristics and Citizen Participation in Local Planning in Israel: One Hundred Years, by Historial Periods

Period	Physical Characteristics	Social Characteristics	Political Characteristics	Citizen Particip in Local Plann
Late ninteeth century until World War I (First and Second Aliyah)	Early independent development of cities, *Moshavot,* and villages.	Setting the foundations for collective way of life in agrarian communities. Local organizations in the cities.	Autonomous community framework (continuation of European and Oriental Jewish tradition).	Intermediate level.
From 1920 until the establishment of the State in 1948	"Primacy" settlement structure—polarity and dependency of periphery upon the center.	Effective functioning of a broad social ideology. Full participation (the kibbutz) and partial (the moshav). Collective values influence the city. Cohesiveness around national goals.	Central organization within the Zionist movement; coexisting with autonomous local communities.	High level in ru communities. I mediate level ir cities.
From 1949 until the late 1960s	Small physical size of state—short distances. Structure becomes more "rank-size" oriented with establishment of middle-sized development towns.	Effective functioning of ideology continues. High level of cohesiveness around national goals. Social homogeneity.	Centralization and hierarchy—strong dependency of the periphery upon the center. Conflict between political cultures—elitism or democracy in state-citizen interrelationship.	Generally at a l level.
From 1970 until the early 1980s	Territorial enlargement of state's boundaries. Basically a "primacy" structure but becoming more "rank-size" oriented.	Functioning of ideology weakens. Increased local group demands. Heterogeneity, pluralism, and specialization. Improved standard of living. Rise in standard level of education.	Centralization remains dominant; however, decentralization and local autonomy are on the upsurge. Ambivalent atmosphere toward the welfare state—government intervention versus participation from below.	A steadily rising trend.
Through the 1980s	Continued "rank-size" trend.	Strengthening of previous trends.	Strengthening of decentralization and participation trends.	Strengthening of previous trends.

period from 1949 through the late 1960s was characterized by a high degree of cohesiveness and homogeneity, which was compatible with centralization and hierarchical governmental structure. These factors were crucial determinants of the low level of local participation. The outcome was a small number of voluntary associations and a lack of citizen involvement in planning committees. The period from 1970 until the earily 1980s witnessed a countertrend. During this period, social and political elements of a decentralized nature—such as the weakening of the functions of ideology, heterogeneity, pluralism, specialization, and local autonomy—have increased participation in a wide range of voluntary and environmental associations as well as local planning committees. In addition, economic characteristics were successfully incorporated with social and political ones. For instance, the improvement of the standard of living and the system of the distribution of funds from the center to the periphery have been discussed. Evidently, the combination has been successful in the Israeli system. However, the separate consideration of economic factors in analyzing other systems should not be excluded.

On the other hand, physical characteristics were not always determinants of the level of participation. Their explanatory importance was less than other factors cited above. For example, the continuation of a more "rank-size" settlement structure since 1970 might be used, to some extent, as reference to a rise in participation. On the contrary, this physical transformation, which began in 1949, does not account for the low level of participation that prevailed until the late 1960s. Nevertheless, the small geographical size partially explains participation at the national level. Furthermore, physical characteristics were influenced by ideological motives, such as placing an emphasis on agrarian settlement or the establishment of new medium-size towns.

Evidence of a constant flux in the content of these characteristics necessitates their evaluation within a dynamic historical context. It is interesting that there is a developmental process in the physical structure, from "primacy" to "rank-size," as well as in the social structure, from collectiveness and homogeneity to specialization and heterogeneity. There is no such continuity in either the political dimension or in citizen participation. However, these findings do not allow one to generalize about other periods or countries.

We conclude that the level of citizen participation in Israel is subject to fluctuations and is affected by the periodical interaction of different characteristics. The closely related social and political characteristics are dominant for our explanation; the physical ones have less effect. It should be noted that although our research framework may be universal, the content of the results must be viewed exclusively in terms of Israel.

In any case, this preliminary analysis suggests further research. At present, I recommend two guidelines for future study:

1. Extensive research into the relationship between national structural characteristics and citizen participation at the local level could benefit from a cross-cultural perspective examining the development of different models of participation in various countries.
2. There is need to document and analyze local participation activities in Israel. An effort is being made by the International Committee of Project Renewal Evaluation. Attention should be focused on building committees, community centers, planning committees, and voluntary and environmental associations.

Finally, one must remember that the tradition of communal participation and autonomy is embedded in the political culture of the Jewish people. Over the past hundred years we have witnessed the development of structural characteristics that answered national aspirations. These characteristics affected participation in local planning. It must also be understood that the Israeli system is dynamic. Stages that covered long periods of time in other countries often lasted only one generation in Israel. Undoubtedly, the modern definition of local participation as established in the United States has not yet been embedded in the Israeli society. However, we may assume that with the growing Western influence on Israel—such as heterogeneity, pluralism, specialization, economic prosperity, improved education, decentralization, and political autonomy—local participation, a concept not foreign to Jewish culture, will rise, and elements from below will receive a stronger impetus.

Notes

The author wishes to thank his colleagues at Tel-Aviv University, Dr. Joseph Katan and Dr. Shimon Spiro, for their helpful comments on earlier drafts in Hebrew. This article is based on a Hebrew version published in the Israeli quarterly *Society and Welfare* 5, no. 3 (October 1983). 241-58. Special acknowledgment is due to Mr. Daniel Sisselman for his editorial assistance on the English draft.
1. Comparing Israel with the United States helps in the understanding of the issues just discussed. The United States is a country of enormous size; hundreds of miles may separate small communities from large urban centers. It could be characterized as a country with a "rank-size" structure lacking the tradition of polarity found in Israel. As a result of the decentralized character of the United States, its local units have asserted their automony and strengthened their local awareness. Consequently,

participation is emphasized. Although technological innovations in communication and transportation have "shortened" distances, they have not dominated the system nor radically changed the orientation toward local participation. As a result, the involvement of the periphery in central cities' politics, culture, and economics has been minimal. In fact, non-affiliation with large urban centers, combined with an intense involvement in local issues, is typical of small towns in the United States.

2. An illustration of how ethno-class promotes local participation is evident in the Israeli Black Panthers movement. The movement came into being in deprived neighborhoods in Jerusalem in the early 1970s attracting mostly Moroccan youth. They demonstrated against ethnic discrimination, demanding attention to their needs for education, employment, and housing. Another movement that began in 1973 was the Ohalim (tents) movement, a militant body of lower-class Oriental Jews who called for the improvement of education, cultural, housing, and welfare services (Hasson 1983).

3. The Association for Housing Culture, which opened its first two branches in 1964, reported six regional and seventy-three local offices in 1982. At that time, it provided legal counseling, responded to approximately 275 monthly complaints, and included the membership of 20,000 building committees. The Israeli Council for Consumption has nine branches, provides legal counseling, and handles about 300 monthly complaints. Tens of public demonstrations have taken place in protest of environmental polluters, such as power stations and gas turbines. Other voluntary organizations dealing with environmental issues are the Society for the Preservation of Nature, the Public Council for the Prevention of Noise and Pollution in Israel, and the Council for Beautiful Israel.

4. The role of the urban political machine, as a party apparatus that recruited the votes of new immigrants under economic and cultural adaptation pressures (covered thoroughly in the U.S. literature; see, for example, Banfield and Wilson 1963) is relevant to the Israeli case.

5. In addressing the issue of national planning in Israel between 1952 and 1965, Akzin and Dror (1966, 7-8) make three points: (1) because the economy is governmentally controlled, Israeli society shows a high level of political activity; (2) politicians play a major role in formulating policy, in contrast to professionals, whose input is limited; (3) when outlining economic policy, a balanced and dynamic division of political power is always carefully weighed. One should also assume that because a large percentage of the national budget comes from abroad, the development of a flexible form of allocation subject to political bargaining and exempt from proclamation would be reinforced.

6. The goal was:
   To develop both the influence and responsibility of neighborhood residents. . . . Participation of the residents, so that the inhabitants be partners in each step of the planning, decision making, and implementation process, by means of a significant and fair representation in the neighborhood steering committee. . . . A local steering community, chaired by the mayor, consisting of neighborhood residents (up to 50%), city officials, Government and Jewish Agency representatives [International Committee on Project Renewal Evaluation 1981, 2-3].

7. Every rehabilitated neighborhood is adopted by a Jewish community in the West, which provides not only financial assistance but also expertise, with professionals coming from abroad to assist the neighborhood.
8. The clearest official illustration of the decentralizing trend and of the legitimation of local participation was delivered by the national committee that designed the most comprehensive reform in Israel's local government structure. The committee grants equal status and responsibility to the municipalities and the central government in areas of common interest at the local level. Yet, it obviously reserves government authority to direct national decisions and indicates that the public lends legitimacy to both government levels (National Committee for Local Government Affairs 1981). An important contribution to local planning awareness was made by the rapid sprouting of local newspapers in the 1970s, serving as evidence of the decentralizing trend (Caspi 1980). Further proof can be seen in Jerusalem, where a plan for neighborhood councils is now being operated. Other attempts for local planning from below are developing but have yet to be documented.

References

Akzin, Benjamin, and Dror, Yehezkel. 1966. *Israel: High Pressure Planning.* Syracuse: Syracuse University Press.

Alexander, Ernest R., Alterman, Rachelle, and Law-Yone, Hubert. 1979. *Urban Plan Implementation: An Evaluation of the Israeli Statutory Planning System.* Haifa: Technion, Center for Urban and Regional Studies.

Almond, Gabriel A., and Verba, Sidney. 1965. *The Civic Culture: Political Attitudes and Democracy in Five Nations.* Boston: Little, Brown.

Alterman, Rachelle. 1982. "Planning for Public Participation: The Design of Implementable Strategies." *Environment and Planning* 9:295-313.

Banfield, Edward C., and Wilson, James Q. 1963. *City Politics.* Cambridge: Harvard University Press.

Ben-Zadok, Efraim, and Goldberg, Giora. 1983. "A Sociopolitical Change in the Israeli Development Towns: An Analysis of Voting Patterns of Oriental Jews." Working Paper No. 71 (March). Tel-Aviv University, Center for Urban and Regional Studies.

Caspi, Dan. 1980. "The Growth of the Local Press in Israel: Trends and Early Assessments." Ramat-Gan: Bar-Ilan University. (Hebrew.)

Cohen, Erik. 1970. *The City of Zionist Ideology.* Jerusalem: Hebrew University, Institute of Urban and Regional Studies.

Efrat, Elisha. 1979. *Elements of Urban Geography.* Tel-Aviv: Achiasaf Publishing House. (Hebrew.)

Eisenstadt, Shmuel N. 1967. *Israel Society.* London: Weidenfeld & Nicolson.

Elazar, Daniel J. 1975. "The Local Elections: Sharpening the Trend toward Territorial Democracy." In *The Elections in Israel—1973*, ed. A. Arian, 219-37. Jerusalem: Jerusalem Academic Press.

———. 1977. "The Compound Structure of Public Service Delivery Systems in Israel." In *Comparing Urban Service Delivery Systems Structure and*

Performance, ed. V. Ostrom and F.P. Blish, 47-82. Urban Affairs Annual Reviews, vol. 12. Beverly Hills, Calif.: Sage.

Galnoor, Itzhak. 1980. "Transformation in the Israeli Political System since the Yom Kippur War." In *The Elections in Israel*—1977, ed. A. Arian, 119-48. Jerusalem: Jerusalem Academic Press.

Gans, Herbert J. 1968. "Social and Physical Planning for the Elimination of Urban Poverty." In *People and Plans: Essays on Urban Problems and Solutions,* ed. H.J. Gans, 231-48. New York: Basic Books.

Goldberg, Harvey. 1977. "Introduction: Culture and Ethnicity in the Study of Israeli Society." *Ethnic Groups* 1, no. 3 (February): 163-86.

Hasson, Shlomo. 1983. "The Emergence of an Urban Social Movement in Israeli Society—An Integrated Approach." *International Journal of Urban and Regional Research* 7, no. 2 (June): 157-74.

Hawley, Amos A. 1971.*Urban Society: An Ecological Approach.* New York: Ronald Press Co.

Hine, Robert V. 1966. *California Utopian Colonies.* New Haven: Yale University Press.

International Committee on Project Renewal Evaluation. 1981. "Guidelines for Evaluation Research." (March). Jerusalem: Government of Israel and Jewish Agency.

———. 1983. "Report for 1982." (March). Jerusalem: Government of Israel and Jewish Agency. (Hebrew.)

Katan, Joseph. 1980. *Clients Participation: Theory and Practice.* Jerusalem: Ministry of Labor and Welfare, Community Work Service. (Hebrew.)

Kornhauser, William, 1959. "Power and Participation in the Local Community." *Health Education Monograph* 6:28-37. Oakland: Society of Public Health Educators.

Kramer, Ralph. 1971. *Urban Community Work in Israel.* Hebrew University. (Hebrew.)

Lapin, Ben. 1973. *Community Workers and Social Work Tradition.* Jerusalem: Massada Press.

Lehman-Wilzig, Sam N. 1981. "Public Protest and Systematic Stability in Israel: 1960-1979." In *Public Life in Israel and the Diaspora,* ed. S.N. Lehman-Wilzig and B. Susser, 171-201. Ramat-Gan: Bar-Ilan University Press.

National Committee for Local Government Affairs. 1981. *Local Government in Israel.* (June). Jerusalem. (Hebrew.)

Shachar, Arie. 1973. "The New Towns and Their Impact on the Population Distribution in Israel." In *Towns in Israel,* ed. A. Shachar, D. Weintraub, E. Cohen, and I. Shelach, 70-87. Jerusalem: Hebrew University. (Hebrew.)

Shapiro, Jonathan. 1977. *Israeli Democracy.* Ramat-Gan: Massada Press. (Hebrew.)

State Comptroller. 1980. Annual Report No. 31 for 1980 and for Fiscal Year 1979. Jerusalem. (Hebrew.)

Torgovnik, Ephraim. 1982. "A Research Report: Government Policy and Local Government." (March.) Seminar in Department of Political Science, Tel-Aviv University.

Van Til, Jon, and Van Til, Sally. 1970. "Citizen Participation in Social Policy: The End of the Cycle?" *Social Problems* 17 (Winter): 313-23.

Weingrod, Alex. 1979. "Recent Trends in Israeli Ethnicity." *Ethnic and Racial Studies* 2, no. 1 (January): 55-65.

Weiss, Shevach. 1979. *City, Region and State: Local Government in Israel— Basic Problems*. Tel-Aviv: General Federation of Labor. (Hebrew.)

White, Morton, and White, Lucia. 1962. *The Intellectual versus the City: From Thomas Jefferson to Frank Lloyd Wright*. Cambridge: Harvard University Press.

Wilson, James Q., and Banfield, Edward C. 1964. "Public Regardingness as a Value Premise in Voting Behavior." *American Political Science Review* 58 (December): 876-87.

Wirth, Louis. 1938. "Urbanism as a Way of Life." *American Journal of Sociology* 44 (July): 1-24.

3

North American Migration to Israel: Stayers and Leavers

Arnold Dashefsky and *Bernard Lazerwitz*

This study compares migrants to Israel (1969-71) who remained (Stayers) and those who returned (Leavers) based on interviews (N=560) from the Immigrant Absorption Survey of the Israel Central Bureau of Statistics. These data are also compared to a representative nationwide sample of U.S. Jews (N=5,790) based on the National Jewish Population Survey with respect to biosocial, socioeconomic, and Jewish identification characteristics. Additional comparisons between Stayers and Leavers are reported with respect to adjustment and other variables, and a path model of U.S. migration to Israel is developed. Finally, a group of returned migrants (Returnees) to Israel (N=46) were interviewed in the United States and aspects of their return and reentry process are discussed.

Just as migration is an issue of political importance in many countries, so, too, is it an issue of intellectual significance in many disciplines. As Jansen has pointed out, the explanations for migration cut across demography, economics, political science, sociology, and social psychology (1969,60).

There have been two basic approaches in seeking to explain migration: one is that of studying the various motives for migration; the other examines the degree to which migration motives are resolved by the act of migration and subsequent adjustment. In the first approach, works of Eisenstadt (1954), Lee (1966), and Bogue (1969) are relevant. For the second approach, the studies of Eisenstadt (1954) as well as Herman (1970), who based his work on the field theory of Lewin (1951), are useful.

What much of this literature has in common is a microfunctionalist (or configurationist) approach (associated with gestalt psychology, field theory, dissonance theory, balance theory, and so on). This "viewpoint argues that the human being is constantly driven to achieve an orderly and *balanced* grasp of the world derived from a 'gestalt'—a sudden insight or configuration of phenomena" that permits the individual "to function in social groups on the basis of the consistency achieved" (Dashefsky 1976,112). Implicit in this model is the functionalist assumption that society and the individual strive for equilibrium. Migrants who enter the new system have their equilibrium upset and they upset the equilibrium of the society. Ultimately in most cases they are absorbed, and their equilibrium as well as that of society is restored.

Such an approach, which is also based on the assumption that society is characterized by a good deal of consensus as to the appropriate norms and values governing people's behaviors, tends to emphasize the need for individuals to change their behavior and assimilate to the new culture and social structure. Eisenstadt (1954), for example, reported on the absorption of low-status Afro-Asian Jews in postindependence Israel at a time when economic, political, and social stability were perceived as essential for survival in an emerging heterogeneous society.

An alternative approach to intergroup relations, focusing on pluralism and the extent to which there is conflict and disagreement over the appropriate norms and values governing people's behavior, emerged in the 1960s (see Dashefsky 1976). Because this perspective has been developed relatively recently, it might explain why Matras finds such scant research conducted on the relative "success" of the migrant in the new society (1973,380). There is a need to go beyond the emphasis on the perspective of the social system and the assumption that migrants of necessity must assimilate and adjust to the new society. We cannot assume migrants have little alternative to such adjustment, but we need to examine the ways they define themselves in their new societies. Applying the pluralism perspective permits one to consider the case of migrants who do not assimilate in the system as the functional model expects them to do.

Such an emphasis would more likely emerge in the case of voluntary international migrants, who have the possibility of returning home. As Beijer (1969, 39) has pointed out, they have received little scolarly attention. Such voluntary international migration is frequently ideologically motivated, but only infrequently do scholars note this. Petersen (1975) defines this group as "free" migrants. They are characterized by a small-scale movement of pioneers who are alienated from their home society. Such voluntary international migration represents an estimated 5 to 7 percent of the total international migration since 1945 (Beijer 1969, 23).

North American Migrants in Israel

Much of the previous research on migrants has focused on the adjustment of new immigrants to their adopted country and the reasons they gave for leaving their native country. Few studies have compared individuals who have migrated and remained to those who have returned to their native lands. At least one instance where the data for such a comparison exist is that of U.S. migrants to Israel.[1]

Eisenstadt (1952) laid the theoretical and empirical foundations for the study of immigrant response to Israeli society soon after it became an independent state with his research on the oppressed Jewish migrants from Afro-Asian countries. After 1960, when U.S. migration to Israel increased, studies began to appear on this new migration of persons from a highly industrialized society to the less developed Israeli society—a reverse of the typical pattern. In 1961 the Israeli census counted 3,550 Americans; by 1972 there were 16,105 (an increase of 454 percent in one decade), and by 1979, approximately 29,000 (Dashefsky and Lazerwitz 1983). In the decade following the Yom Kippur War (1973), U.S. migration to Israel *declined* to between 2,000-3,100 per year (see table 3.1).[2]

The rise of U.S. migration in the late 1960s and early 1970s occasioned several empirical studies during and after this period. Sherrow and Ritterband (1970) carried out a study of the determinants of migration to Israel among 47 American Jewish participants in a "Jewish Peace Corps" program called Sherut Laam. They found that with respect to *migration* to Israel, Jewish identification was an important determinant but Zionist identification was not. Later Antonovsky and Katz (1979) examined the factors in the adjustment and absorption process of the U.S. and Canadian population in Israel. They found the following premigration variables positively associated with subjective *adjustment*: membership in a Zionist organization, knowledge of Israel, and interest in Israel. They found postmigration problems negatively associated with subjective adjustment. Engel (1970) studied native U.S. and Canadian Jews who became permanent residents of Israel between 1962 and 1966, and also found Jewish identification more salient for migration than Zionist identification. Engel's study was one of the few that examined the reasons for staying in Israel as well as the reasons for leaving, but separate samples were not gathered for each aspect of migration and absorption, or return; rather, one sample of persons currently living in Israel was analyzed. Goldscheider (1974) analyzed the demographic and social characteristics of U.S. migrants to Israel and found them more likely to be young, at least third-generation Jews, female, single, and high on Jewish identification measures. Finally, Avruch (1981) found in

TABLE 3.1
North American Migrants to Israel, 1967-1983

Year	
1967	4,048
1968	6,216
1969	5,739
1970	6,424
1971	7,364
1972	5,515
1973	4,393
1974	3,089
1975	2,802
1976	2,700
1977	2,571
1978	2,856
1979	2,893
1980	2,053
1981	2,142
1982	2,522
1983	3,095

Sources:

1968-69 Calvin Goldscheider, "American Aliya: Sociological and Demographic perspectives," in *The Jewish American Society*, ed. Marshall Sklare, 337-84 (New York: Behrman House, 1974).

1970-77 Elazar Leshem and Yehudit Rosenbaum, eds., *Mihkarim Bklitat Aliyah (Studies in immgrant absorption)* (Jerusalem: Government of Israel, 1978).

1978-81 Mark Mehler, personal communication (New York Israel Aliyah Center, August 1982).

1982-83 Doug Chandler, personal communication (New York Israel Aliyah Center, March 1984).

an intensive study of 119 U.S. migrants that their Jewish identity was more salient than their American identity.

While to some it may appear that the causes and consequences of internal and international migration are the same, Goldscheider (1971,65) has disagreed. He argued that the generally greater distances, cultural and linguistic obstacles, and legal and political barriers necessitate separate explanations. The aim of this paper is to use a pluralistic approach to intergroup relations as a framework for a study of ideologically motivated, voluntary international migrants, and to explore the factors that explain why some stay in the host country and others return. Such is the situation of American migrants to Israel.

Data Sources

The findings reported here were part of a larger research project, "Americans in Israel," that probed the motivations for migration to Israel of North American Jews and endeavored to develop a path analysis model to try to explain why some migrants remain (Dashefsky and Lazerwitz 1983). The data sources utilized for describing and analyzing this problem included:

1. *National Jewish Population Survey* (NJPS): These data are derived from interviews with a national probability sample of American Jews (N= 5,790) gathered between 1970 and 1972 and described in Lazerwitz (1978) and Lazerwitz and Harrison (1979).
2. *Israel Immigrant Absorption Survey* (IAS): These data were obtained from the Israel Central Bureau of Statistics and consisted of interviews with North Americans who migrated to Israel between 1969 and 1971 (N= 560) and who were followed for a three-year period, as described in Dashefsky and Lazerwitz (1983).
3. *Postmigration Interviews:* A separate sample of 46 persons who had migrated to Israel after 1967 and returned subsequently to the United States ("Returnees") were interviewed in the Boston-Washington metropolitan corridor in 1976-77.[3] The time period of the interviews corresponds to the period of a slowing down of the rate of migration, which peaked in the period 1968-71. (see table 3.1.)

Biosocial and Socioeconomic Background Characteristics

Table 3.2 presents some major biosocial background characteristics of the NJPS sample of American Jews, of the migrants who stayed in Israel, and of the migrants who left (derived from the first wave IAS sample of North Americans in Israel who were interviewed after two months). In most instances the Stayers and Leavers differ significantly in regard to such characteristics from American Jews as a whole. The migrants are much more likely to be single, young, American-born, and college educated, and to have been professionally employed when living in the United States. Generally these characteristics (with the possible exception of being American-born) make for less integration into U.S. society and more mobility. There are, however, some differences between the Stayers and Leavers that help us understand why some stay and some leave. The Leavers are like the Stayers, only *more so*. They are more likely to be single, young, American-born, college educated, and professionally employed; hence, they are even more mobile. An important difference is that the Stayers are less likely to be male (40

TABLE 3.2
Biosocial and Socioeconomic Characteristics of American
Migrants to Israel (Stayers and Leavers) and American Jewish Adults

Characteristics	Stayers[1]	Leavers[1]	American Jews[2]
Born to U.S. born parents	26%	38%	20%
Married	67	51	80
18-29 years	34	54	15
College degree	39	45	33
Professional job in U.S.	39	49	29
Proportion Male	40	49	45

[1]*Source*: Immigrant Absorption Survey (N = 560, Stayers plus Leavers).
[2]*Source*: National Jewish Population Study (N = 5790).

percent) than American Jews (45 percent male) and even more likely to be male than the Leavers (49 percent male). It is likely that the expectation of lengthy Isreali military service for men is an important factor that can help to explain this difference.[4]

Jewish Identification Pattern

Table 3.3 presents some major characteristics of the pattern of Jewish identification among the Stayers, Leavers, and the NJPS sample of American Jews. Again both the Stayers and Leavers tend to differ when compared to American Jews as a whole. The former two groups tend to be much more attached to traditional Jewish practices than American Jews. They are more likely to have had an intensive Jewish (day school) education (6 to 8 times more likely), to prefer the Orthodox Jewish denomination (2 to 3 times more likely), and to attend religious services weekly (2½ to 4½ times more likely). The only exception to this pattern is fasting on the last Yom Kippur: the Stayers are more likely to have fasted, and the Leavers are a little less likely to have fasted than American Jews.

There is, however, some degree of difference between the Stayers and the Leavers. In all instances the Stayers are more highly integrated into a traditional pattern of Jewish experience and identification than are American Jews as a whole and the Leavers. These findings are consistent with those of Berman (1979).

TABLE 3.3
Jewish Characteristics of American Migrants to Israel
(Stayers and Leavers) and American Jewish Adults

Characteristics	Stayers[1]	Leavers[1]	American Jews
Preferring Orthodox Jewish Denomination	35%	19%	11%
Jewish Day School Education	32	24	4
Attending Synagogue once a week in U.S.	36	20	8
Fasted on last U.S. Yom Kippur	68	47	51

[1]*Source*: Immigrant Absorption Survey.
[2]*Source*: National Jewish Population Study.

It appears that the American migrants who returned have less "staying power" because they are not socially integrated into U.S. society, and neither were they successful in socially integrating themselves into Israeli society. One dimension that appears to increase the tendency toward integration is the greater degree of Jewish identification and traditional experience of the Stayers compared to the Leavers. Whether this tendency is due to the greater *inner* personal resolve and commitment of the more religiously traditional Stayers or the greater *outer* state support given to Orthodox Judaism as the "established synagogue" in Israel cannot be determined by this research.[5]

Adjustment Process

Table 3.4 presents some major behavioral and attitudinal characteristics of the adjustment-absorption process of the Stayers and Leavers at various stages.[6] These characteristics can be sorted into three types: satisfaction, contacts, and perceptions.

After two months Stayers were slightly more likely than Leavers to be "well" or "quite" satisfied with their housing and with their progress in Hebrew. They were also more satisfied economically and socially. By the end of the first year, the levels of satisfaction with their own economic progress declined, grew stronger for Hebrew, and remained relatively stable for the other two factors.

TABLE 3.4
Characteristics of Migrants (Stayers and Leavers) at
Varying Stages of the Adjustment-Absorption Process

Characteristics	Leavers – 2 Mos. in Israel	Stayers (in Israel)			
		2 Mos.	1 Yr.	2 Yrs.	3 Yrs.
A. Satisfactions					
Economically Quite Satisfied	33%	40%	33%	32%	34%
Socially Well Satisfied	31	35	35	32	36
Well Satisfied with Housing	46	48	43	46	47
Quite Satisfied with Hebrew Progress	27	30	39	41	42
B. Contacts					
Frequent Social Contacts with Veteran Americans	19	18	28	23	22
Frequent Social Contacts with New American Migrants	46	45	42	42	38
Frequent Social Contacts with New Non-American Migrants	34	30	20	21	15
C. Perceptions					
Feeling Fully Like an Israeli	7	16	17	16	20
Probability of Staying: Quite Sure	25	52	51	52	50

Source: Immigrant Absorption Survey.

With respect to "contacts," Stayers and Leavers had just about the same frequency of contact with other new migrants and veteran Americans after two months. Contacts with new migrants among the Stayers declined substantially after three years, especially contacts with non-American new migrants. Their contacts with veteran Americans increased slightly after a few more years in Israel.

The major differences between Stayers and Leavers occur at the level of perceptions. Stayers are twice as likely as Leavers to be "quite sure" of staying in Israel, and two to three times as likely to feel "fully" like an Israeli.

These findings suggest that the Stayers and Leavers arrive with different initial attitudes toward their new experiences. Those who are more confident of staying are, in fact, more likely to stay and to feel like Israelis, develop satisfactions with their new lives, and reduce contacts with other migrants who may reinforce nonadaptive orientations.

Who Will Stay and Who Will Leave?

It is possible to gain further insights into how to predict who will stay and who will leave by relying on multivariate nominal scale analysis (MNA), which is described in Andrews and Messenger (1973).[7] One feature of the MNA approach is that it predicts Stayers and Leavers on the basis of a wide range of survey variables. The prediction can then be compared with whether the respondents actually stayed or left Israel. The results of this statistical technique are given in table 3.5 for the respondents of the first and second survey waves. The table shows that the data from the Immigrant Absorption Survey effectively predict who will stay but are less effective in predicting who will leave. At the first survey wave, 31 percent of the Leavers were predicted as staying; at the second wave, 52 percent of the Leavers were predicted as staying. Put another way, at the first wave, 22 percent of the respondents were mis-classified by the prediction method (13 percent were those who eventually left Israel). At the second wave, 19 percent were misclassified (14 percent eventually left Israel). Overall, about 15 percent of the survey's respondents at the panel waves belong to a category of people who when interviewed appear to be among those who will stay but leave.

It is possible to use the MNA appraoch to move toward a model of "staying-leaving." Tables 3.6 and 3.7 provide this by giving the various MNA beta values for nineteen survey variables associated with "staying-leaving," with the various categories of the measurement scales on "confidence of remaining in Israel," "satisfaction with one's social life," and "satisfaction with one's economic situation." In table 3.6 we have the basic outcome variable, stay in Israel, and the variable most associated with that outcome, confidence of remaining in Israel. Table 3.7 gives the two satisfaction questions. In regard to tables 3.6 and 3.7, the conventional standard that beta values from .12 to .19 are moderate ones and that beta values .20 or higher are strong variables will be used; values less than .12 are considered weak variables.

The conventional standard enables the meaningful organization of the beta values. Note that for staying at the first wave there are only two strong variables: the ability to speak Hebrew before migration, and confidence of remaining. At the second wave for the same dependent variable, confidence of remaining is the only strong variable. At both panel waves, age and social contact with veteran American settlers are moderate-impact variables. At the first wave, fasting on one's last Yom Kippur abroad, and social contacts with Israelis and veteran non-American settlers are moderate variables. At the second wave, education, membership in Jewish organizations before migration,

TABLE 3.5
MNA Predictions on Staying or Leaving and Actual Results
(Immigrant Absorption Survey, First and Second Panel Waves)

	First Wave		
Actual Outcome	Predicted Outcome		Base
	Leave	Stay	
Leave	69%	31	100%
Stay	15%	85	100%

	Second Wave		
Actual Outcome	Predicted Outcome		Base
	Leave	Stay	
Leave	48%	52	100%
Stay	7%	93	100%

satisfaction with Hebrew progress, feeling like an Israeli, satisfaction with housing, and social contacts with new migrants from the United States fall into the moderate-impact grouping.

With confidence of remaining in Israel such an effective predictor variable, what seems to be associated with it? Age, marital status by sex, education (first wave only), satisfaction with one's social life (second wave only), feeling like an Israeli, preferred religious denomination (first wave only), satisfaction with housing (second wave only), satisfaction with one's economic situation, and only for second wave, social contacts with veteran settlers, social contacts with non-American new migrants and social contacts with other new American migrants.

Note how few variables are common to both staying-leaving and confidence of remaining. Considering both waves together, just age, marital status by sex, feeling like an Israeli (second wave) are common to both. Social contact with American migrants correlates negatively with staying and correlates positively with confidence of remaining.

As can be seen in the table 3.7 attitude columns on satisfaction (with

TABLE 3.6

Predictor Variable MNA Beta Values Associated with Migration Success and Confidence of Remaining in Israel
(Immigrant Absorption Survey First and Second Panel Waves)

MNA BETA VALUES FOR CONFIDENCE OF REMAINING IN ISRAEL

Predictor Values	Stay in Israel		First Wave				Second Wave			
	First Wave	Second Wave	Certain	Pretty Certain	Likely, but not sure	Not Likely	Certain	Pretty Certain	Likely, but not sure	Not Sure
a. Age	.16	.12	.29	.20	.23	.21	.15	.16	.16	.08
b. Marital status by sex	.11	.17	.19	.15	.15	.12	.18	.08	.14	.14
c. Education	.11	.16	.04	.06	.10	.24	.13	.07	.07	.08
d. Synagogue attendance before migration	.05	.09	.06	.09	.08	.12	.11	.07	.09	.05
e. Fast on last Yom Kippur abroad	.13	.05	.02	.02	.04	.07	.03	.12	.09	0
f. Member Jewish Organization before migration	.09	.12	.08	.06	.02	.08	.10	.06	.07	.04
g. Jewish education	.05	.11	.01	.03	.04	.04	.09	.09	.03	0
h. Ability to speak Hebrew before migration	.21	.12	.08	.06	.08	0	.09	.18	.06	.08
i. Social life satisfaction	.03	.11	.05	.10	.03	.09	.16	.10	.05	.06
j. Hebrew progress satisfaction	.08	.15	.03	.06	.08	.02	.04	.07	.06	.02
k. Confidence remaining in Israel	.29	.47								
l. Feeling Israeli	.06	.14	.20	.08	.16	.19	.19	.17	.17	.11
m. Preferred Jewish denomination	.07	.11	.11	.08	.11	.11	.08	.10	.09	.04
n. Housing satisfaction	0	.12	.08	.06	.04	.06	.12	.14	.10	.04
o. Economic situation satisfaction	.05	.07	.16	.02	.16	.06	.24	.08	.12	.12
p. Social contacts with veteran settlers	.18	.05	.11	.08	.09	.06	.07	.07	.12	.13
q. Social contacts with veteran American settlers	.12	.15	.08	.06	.09	.07	.08	.10	.06	.11
r. Social contacts with new migrants from North America	.05	-.16	.01	.10	.08	.05	.25	.21	.10	.08
s. Social contacts with new migrants from outside North America	.07	.05	.10	.07	.07	.13	.17	.14	.07	.11

TABLE 3.7
Predictor Variable MNA Beta Values
Associated with Social and Economic Satisfactions
(Immigrant Absorption Survey Panel First and Second Panel Waves)

MNA BETA VALUES FOR

Predictor Values	Satisfaction with Social Life						Satisfaction with Economic Situation					
	First Wave			Second Wave			First Wave			Second Wave		
	Quite	Fairly	Not Satis.	Quite	Fairly	Not Satis.	Quite	Fairly	Not Satis.	Quite	Fairly	Not Satis.
a. Age	.09	.12	.13	.20	.20	.12	.10	.11	.11	.13	.14	.11
b. Marital status by sex	.17	.14	.14	.11	.11	.09	.14	.09	.11	.13	.18	.11
c. Education	.04	.02	.06	.02	.14	.15	.10	.07	.09	.21	.15	.06
d. Synagogue attendance before migration	.14	.11	.10	.05	.06	.07	.04	.08	.10	.10	.11	.06
e. Fast on last Yom Kippur abroad	.02	0	.02	.09	.04	.05	0	.01	0	0	.01	.02
f. Member Jewish organization before migration	.07	.06	.09	.08	.04	.05	.08	.12	.08	.04	.11	.08
g. Jewish education	.06	.06	.03	.01	.05	.04	.09	.08	.05	.07	.09	.04
h. Ability to speak Hebrew before migration	.07	.02	.07	.08	.08	.03	.01	.07	.07	.09	.07	.07
i. Social life satisfaction	---	---	---	---	---	---	.21	.16	.10	.18	.17	.01
j. Hebrew progress satisfaction	.10	.04	.08	.04	.09	.16	.14	.03	.01	.19	.04	.07
k. Confidence remaining in Israel	.04	.10	.11	.12	.17	.17	.12	.06	.15	.16	.03	.23
l. Feeling Israeli	.20	.12	.13	.18	.14	.14	.14	.06	.13	.04	.13	.20
m. Preferred Jewish denomination	.18	.18	.03	.13	.17	.03	.14	.16	.12	.24	.09	.07
n. Housing satisfaction	.15	.05	.12	.21	.12	.13	.32	.19	.35	.20	.17	.17
o. Economic situation satisfaction	.22	.10	.18	.19	.15	.07	---	---	---	---	---	---
p. Social contacts with veteran settlers	.10	.07	.16	.20	.06	.29	.07	.13	.10	.10	.11	.08
q. Social contacts with veteran American settlers	.09	.06	.05	.05	.10	.10	.07	.09	.08	.04	.09	.13
r. Social contacts with new North American migrants	.04	.04	.04	.05	.10	.15	.08	.07	.10	.10	.05	.13
s. Social contacts with new migrants from countries outside North America	.05	.14	.13	.07	.10	.16	.07	.06	.04	.15	.13	.17

one's social life and economic situation) at both waves, satisfaction with social life, housing, economic situation, Hebrew progress, and feeling like an Israeli cluster together. Also, satisfaction with one's economic situation is consistently associated with confidence of remaining in Israel. However, apart from confidence of remaining in Israel, none of these attitude variables consistently has meaningful direct links to the staying-leaving variable. There are clearly none at the first wave. At first glance some seem to be related at the second wave, but careful inspection of the percentage tables and deviations that form the basis of the beta values reveals that, apart from feeling like an Israeli, the other attitude items have inconsistent associations with the staying-leaving categories. Their percentages are either inconsistent, not monotonic when they need to be, or are overly influenced by a few extreme values. The only statistically proper conclusion to reach is that these attitude items fail to have a meaningful association with staying-leaving. Only feeling like an Israeli remains a statistically meaningful variable at the second wave.

How much of the variance between Stayers and Leavers can be explained by this secondary analysis approach? Using the University of Michigan's Survey Research Center's AID technique, and employing nineteen independent variables explained just 24 percent of the variance! Of this 24 percent, 12 percent came from one item, confidence of staying; the remaining 12 percent was scattered among nine other variables with no more than 3 percent accounted for by a single factor (Dashefsky and Lazerwitz 1983). On the whole, one set of factors dominates the initial decision to migrate and another set determines staying or leaving.

A Model of North American Migration to Israel

What kind of a story do these various MNA statistics tell? Can they be formed into a model that will enlighten us on the issue of staying in Israel or leaving? Figure 3.1 tries to do this. In the model, the lines with circles are the stronger connections among model variables. First, there is a set of demographic variables that are directly associated with staying in Israel or leaving, such as age, sex, and marital status. Then, there is a group of variables that reflect background factors that existed prior to migration, such as activity in Jewish organizations, ability to speak Hebrew, and Jewish denominational preferences. Then, we have a set of variables that emerge out of experiences in Israel; foremost among these are contacts with veteran settlers and satisfactions with various aspects of life in Israel.

What variables, in their turn, seem to contribute to the important

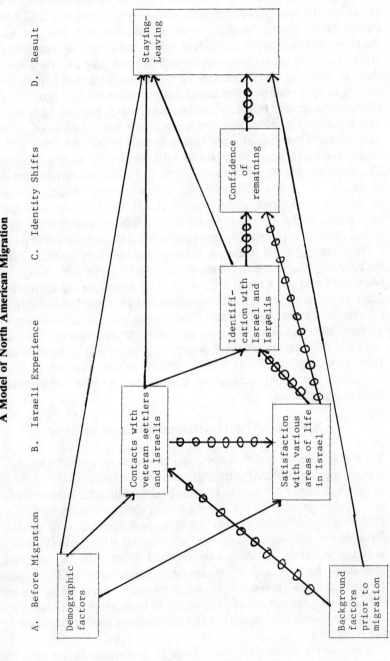

FIGURE 3.1
A Model of North American Migration

A. Before Migration   B. Israeli Experience   C. Identity Shifts   D. Result

factor of confidence of remaining? Here is where the various attitude factors come into play. It is suggested that identification with Israeli life and satisfaction with one's economic situation, social life, housing conditions, and progress with Hebrew appear to contribute to confidence of remaining and, through such confidence, operate indirectly upon staying-leaving. This same suggested model applies to both waves. The only significant model shift between the waves is a tendency for attitudes to move toward a stronger association with staying-leaving. However, here the statistics are far from clear; a solid case can be made only for an emergent stronger association for feeling like an Israeli.

This model indicates that, at the first wave, what really counts is the set of background factors carried to Israel by the migrants. In actuality, the first wave represents not only the beginning of the absorption process but also the end of the process that led to a migration decision. By the time of the second wave, the Israeli experience is the effective determinant of migration success. The main variable stream moves to contacts with veteran settlers and Israelis and then to satisfactions with various areas of Israeli life, which creates an identification with Israel. The identification supports confidence about the ability to remain in Israel, which in turn is the most decisive factor in staying (see Dashefsky and Lazerwitz 1983).

Apparently the initial selective factors are not the ones that keep people in Israel. For remaining in Israel, being somewhat older, marital status by sex, having Hebrew language abilities prior to migration, contacts with the veteran Israeli population, and a set of positive, satisfying experiences in Israel that create confidence all work to separate those who stay from those who leave. Note the sharp decline in the importance of Jewish identification factors with regard to staying. Prior Jewish involvement can move a person to Israel but will not keep the person there.

Reentry of Returnees

Most research in international migration focuses on the motivations and adjustments of migrants but does not report on those who return. Although it was not possible to follow up the Leavers of the Immigrant Absorption Survey, the sample of forty-six returned American migrants, offered some clues to understanding the return and reentry process. Eighteen percent of the sample had lived in Israel for less than one year; 37 percent one year; 34 percent from one to three years; and the rest, more than three years. Two-thirds (68 percent) returned between 1973 and 1976.

In the previous sections we pointed out that confidence of remaining is the most important variable in accounting for those who stay in Israel, and various attitude factors, e.g. satisfaction over one's economic situation, social life, housing condition, and so on, influence that confidence. One satisfaction factor not previously isolated is revealed in the special analysis of the Returnees' file. The most frequently cited factors contributing to their return to the United States dealt with the family. Fully 65 percent of the Returnees stated that relatives in the United States contributed "a lot" or "somewhat" to the decision to return, and 52 percent cited family adjustment difficulties in Israel (see Dashefsky and Lazerwitz 1983). Further analysis of the perceptions of the Returnees revealed that while most saw themselves as pulled to Israel (77 percent) rather than pushed from the United States (44 percent,) most also saw themselves as pushed from Israel (52 percent) rather than pulled to return to the United States (24 percent). These data highlight the need for future systematic research on a probability sample of Returnees to probe the delicate decision-making matrix that explains the motivation for remaining or returning, and to further illuminate what may sustain or undermine confidence of remaining.

Finally, the question arises as to whether any aspects of the experience of living in Israel and the distinctive characteristics of the Leavers as compared to the Stayers influenced their subsequent life in the United States. Seven out of ten returnees (71 percent) indicated that their life in the United States was different after their return from what is was before they left. Although they did not feel any more "Jewish" than "American" after migration than before (72 percent and 74 percent), a majority (53 percent) saw themselves as *more* involved in the American Jewish community. Interestingly, only 38 percent reported attending religious services twice monthly or more, compared to 54 percent who did so before migration. If religious services were not as important a dimension in their Jewish lives, having Israeli friends was. Eighty percent of the Returnees reported having Israeli friends, compared to 60 percent so reporting before migration. Israeli friends and, indeed, Israel seemed to constitute a larger part of their lives. Four-fifths (79 percent) said there was a fifty-fifty chance or better that they would return to live in Israel. Despite the fact that many expressed feelings of anger or embarrassment about their Israel experience, a great majority of Returnees were still thinking about living in Israel.

Because the Leavers were less traditional in their pattern of Jewish identification than the Stayers (as pointed out in a previous section), it is not surprising that the Returnees report a decrease in synagogue attendance. Therefore, the way in which their perceived greater involvement in the American Jewish community manifests itself is likely through Jewish social and cultural experiences, such as speaking Hebrew, or talking about Israel to Israeli friends, or sending their children to a Jewish day school. Because these characteristics are highly atypical for the American Jewish community, they highlight the Returnees' Jewish involvement. Nevertheless, these findings merely probe the surface of the response to the return and reentry process of the Returnees. More comprehensive study of this group is needed.

Summary and Conclusion

This paper compared a sample of North American migrants to Israel who remained (Stayers) to those who returned (Leavers). Stayers and Leavers were also compared to a representative nationwide sample of American Jews with respect to biosocial, socioeconomic, and Jewish identification characteristics. Additional comparisons between Stayers and Leavers were reported with respect to adjustment and other variables, and a path model of American migration to Israel was developed. These data showed that there was a set of demographic variables directly associated with staying or leaving Israel, such as age, sex, and marital status. Following these was a cluster of variables that reflect background factors that existed prior to migration, such as activity in Jewish organizations, ability to speak Hebrew, and Jewish denominational preferences. Then, a set of variables emerged out of experiences in Israel, including contacts with veteran settlers and satisfaction with various aspects of Israeli life. These variables contributed to identification with Israel and Israelis, and ultimately to the most important predictor variable, confidence of remaining. Finally, a group of returned migrants to Israel were interviewed in the United States and aspects of their return and reentry process were reported.

In conclusion, the decisions to migrate to Israel and then to stay or return to the United States should not be seen simply as a zero-sum game or an either-or proposition. Rather, such decisions may be constantly shifting back and forth between the two poles of Israel and the United States as embodied in the perceptions of the alternatives each society provides, the conceptions of self the individual develops, and the patterns of social interaction the individual encounters. Perhaps individuals facing such decisions will never be satisfied with the status quo and will constantly search for new solutions to their marginality and new resolutions to the delicate balance of their aspirations and identities (cf. Katz 1974).

Notes

This article is a revised version of a paper presented at the annual meeting of the Association for the Sociological Study of Jewry and the Society for the Study of Social Problems, San Francisco, September 1982. The authors wish to thank the Israel Central Bureau of Statistics for access to the North American data of the Immigration Absorption Survey. Of particular help in this regard were Dr. Moshe Sicron, Dr. Eitan Sabatello, Mr. Joseph Askenazi, and Mr. Avi Ackerman. The funds to purchase the North American data were provided by the Research Committee of Bar-Ilan University. Valuable research assistance was provided in Israel by Ephraim Tabory and Sarah Cohen. The Computer Center of Bar-Ilan University was most generous in providing free computer time. The funds for the first phase of this project were provided by the National Institute of Mental Health, United States Public Health Service, Grant No. IR03 MH 24072-01A1. In addition, thanks are also due to the University of Connecticut Research Foundation, the Memorial Foundation for Jewish Culture Fellowship and the National Endowment for the Humanities summer stipend, which provided partial funding for this project and to the University of Connecticut for granting a sabbatic leave to work on this project. Additional valuable research assistance in the United States was provided by Arlene Gottshalk, Dan Jansenson, Ann Mardenfield, Jeffrey Schwartz, Millie Spector, Linda Stark, Lynne Stein, Beth Troy, Mark Weinberg, David Wrubel, and Bill Zall. Last but not least thanks are due to the anonymous reviewers of this journal, to Don Waldman who provided valuable assistance and consultation, and to Celeste Machado, Marilyn Horton, and Linda Snyder who typed the drafts for this paper.

1. Such migrants to Israel are called *olim,* and the act of migration is called *aliya,* meaning ascent, both physical and spiritual.
2. The number of reported *olim* in 1983 compared to 1982 is the greatest absolute increase (573 persons) and the greatest percentage increase (23 percent since the boom period of American *aliya* between 1967 and 1973.) Whether this is a mere statistical fluctuation or signals a new trend remains to be seen.
3. The data gathered for the Returnee group relied on a "snowball sample." The initial list was developed in the Greater Hartford area, which produced only twenty persons who had migrated after 1967 and returned; eighteen were interviewed. Two others were interviewed in southern Connecticut, five in the Greater Boston area, and twenty-one in the Washington, D.C. area, which resulted in a total of forty-six interviews. It is possible that some of those interviewed in the IAS study were also interviewed in the Returnees group.
4. The question of statistical significance for the percentage given in tables 3.2, 3.3, and 3.4 can readily be handled by giving a set of generalized percentage levels required for significance. To contrast Stayers and Leavers, differences of 9 percent (or more) have reached the standard "two sigma level." To contrast Stayers or Leavers and those from NJPS, differences of 6 percent (or more) have reached the standard "two sigma level."
5. How do these migrants compare to Israeli adults? The table below shows that the migrants are somewhat younger, slightly more composed of women,

and far better educated than Israeli adults. After one year in Israel, they are more likely than Israeli adults to hold professional jobs. Finally, this migrant group with a high level of Jewish identification falls somewhat short of the percentage of Israelis who fast on Yom Kippur. Obviously, this far from typical migrant group readily moves into the Israeli middle class. Whatever immigrant difficulties they endure, their experiences are far removed from those of the Afro-Asian Jewish immigrants of the 1950s. Nor are their immigrant experiences parallel to those of their immediate forebears who came to the United States from the villages of Eastern Europe. Given their Jewish identification and commitment, the American Jewish migrants in Israel may be placed ideologically between the early twentieth-century Zionist pioneers and the postindependence immigrant groups with their role and value-shift problems.

Characteristics	U.S. Jews in Israel[1]	Israelis[2]
16-29 years	42%	35%
College degree	42%	6%
Professional job	27%	16%
Male, for those 20 years of age or older	43%	46%
Fasted on Yom Kippur	59%	67%

1. *Source*: Immigrant Absorption Survey.
2. *Sources*: Israeli census, 1972, except for Yom Kippur data supplied by Professor Y. Ben-Meir and used with his permission.

6. The Immigrant Absorption Survey gathered data from four repeated surveys conducted over a three-year period upon three annual groups of immigrants and potential immigrants from North America. The three annual groups arrived in 1969, 1970, and 1971. Interviews took place in four stages: two months, one year, two years, and three years.

Number in Original Sample (N = 560)		
Stage	Stayed	Left
Two months	555	5
One year	446	114
Two years	393	167
Three years	331	229

After three years, 331 migrants remained in Israel. Given sample design weighting characteristics, this is 63 percent of the original cohort.

7. This technique is a form of dummy variable multiple regression analysis in which all system variables, both dependent and independent, can be either ordinal or nominal scale variables. MNA does require an additive model. Here, we determine the impact of each independent variable upon the dependent variable categories, over and beyond that of the other independent variables, by a statistic called beta. Beta is just the dummy variable regression equivalent of the familiar standardized multiple regression coefficient also called beta.

References

Andrews, Frank, and Messenger, Robert. 1973. *Multivariate Nominal Scale Analysis*. Ann Arbor: University of Michigan, Institute for Social Research.

Antonovsky, Aaron, and Katz, David. 1979. *From the Golden to the Promised Land*. Darby, Penn.: Norwood Edition.

Avruch, Kevin. 1981. *American Immigrants in Israel: Social Identities and Change*. Chicago: University of Chicago Press.

Beijer, G. 1969. "Modern Patterns of International Migratory Movements." In *Migration*, ed. J.A. Jackson, 11-59. New York: Cambridge University Press.

Berman, Gerald S. 1979. "Why North Americans Migrate to Israel?" *Jewish Journal of Sociology* 21:135-44.

Bogue, Donald. 1969. *Principles of Demography*. New York: Wiley & Sons.

Dashefsky, Arnold, ed. 1976. *Ethnic Identity in Society*. Chicago: Rand McNally.

Dashefsky, Arnold and Lazerwitz, Bernard. 1983. "The Role of Religious Identification in North American Migration to Israel." *Journal for the Scientific Study of Religion* 22, 263-75.

Eisenstadt, S.N. 1952. "The Process of Absorption of New Immigrants in Israel." *Human Relations* 5:223-46.

———. 1954. *The Absorption of Immigrants*. London: Routledge & Kegan Paul.

Engel, Gerald. 1970. "North American Settlers in Israel." In *American Jewish Yearbook* 71:161-87.

Goldscheider, Calvin. 1971. *Population, Modernization, and Social Structure*. Boston: Little, Brown.

———. 1974. "American Aliya: Sociological and Demographic Perspectives." In *The Jew in American Society*, ed. M. Sklare, 335-84. New York: Behrman House.

Herman, Simon N. 1970. *American Students in Israel*. Ithaca: Cornell University Press.

Jansen, Clifford. 1969. "Some sociological aspects of migration." In *Migration*, ed. J.A. Jackson, 60-73. New York: Cambridge University Press.

Katz, Pearl. 1974. "Acculturation and Social Networks of American Immigrants in Israel." Ph.D. dissertation, State University of New York at Buffalo.

Lazerwitz, Bernard. 1978. "An Estimate of a Rare Population Group: The U.S. Jewish Population." *Demography* 15 (August): 389-94.

Lazerwitz, Bernard, and Harrison, Michael. 1979. "American Jewish Denominations: A Social and Religious Profile." *American Sociological Review* 44:656-66.

Lee, Everett S. 1966. "A Theory of Migration." *Demography* 3:47-57.

Leshem, Elazar, and Rosenbaum, Judith, eds. 1978. *Studies in Immigration Absorption in Israel*. Jerusalem: Government of Israel.

Lewin, Kurt. 1951. *Field Theory in Social Science.* Edited by D. Cartwright. New York: Harper.

Matras, Judah. 1973. *Population and Societies.* Englewood Cliffs, N.J.: Prentice-Hall.

Petersen, William. 1975. *Population.* New York: Macmillan.

Sherrow, Fred S., and Ritterband, Paul. 1970. "An analysis of migration to Israel." *Jewish Social Studies* 32 (July): 214-23.

RESEARCH NOTE

4

Women in Legislatures:
Israel in a Comparative Perspective

Eva Etzioni-Halevy and *Ann Illy*

This paper presents a comparison of the proportion of women in the Knesset with the proportion of women in legislatures in other Western-style democracies, and a comparison of this proportion by different parties. It shows that women are underrepresented in the Knesset as in other Western legislatures. It also shows that in the proportion of women parliamentarians Israel is not conspicuously lagging behind other Western countries, but neither is it the expected leader. Although in most countries analyzed the proportion of women in the legislature has been growing in recent years, in Israel it has been slightly decreasing. A comparison of Israel with other systems of proportional representation shows that women have recently been doing much better in some of these societies than in in Israel. This situation is analyzed in terms of a three-tiered structure of impediments. It is argued that (contrary to what might have been expected) in Israel such impediments are exacerbated by the sociopolitical importance of military service.

Introduction

This paper argues (1) that women are generally disadvantaged in the attainment of political power positions in general, and in their representation in legislatures in particular; and (2) that there is a three-tiered structure of impediments to their participation. The first of these tiers of impediments results from women's long-standing patterns of socialization (still prevalent today) toward "feminine" and familial roles that are widely conceived as incompatible with roles of political power holders. Of course, political power is not inherently masculine (and no one has been able to show that it is), nor is the world of politics inherently a man's world—however, it has traditionally been conceived as such. This conception has influenced women's socialization and, hence, their self-images and self-conceptions. As a result women are less likely than men to hold ambitions and aspirations that would lead them toward a career in politics.

The second and third tiers of impediments result from the power struggle that women aspirants must undergo to obtain prominent political positions. This power struggle (once again) is not inherently more appropriate for men than it is for women; however, in the societies under discussion it has been structured in such a way as to put women at a disadvantage. The power struggle may be seen from two angles: that of the potential women aspirants to political positions and that of the more established participants (so far disproportionately male). The second tier of impediments is inherent in women's vantage point on the political power struggle. From this vantage point, it is significant that the power struggle is exceptionally time and energy consuming. In many cases the struggle stretches out over numerous years, requiring much legwork, with an end result that seems distant and uncertain. Persons embarking on this path must be willing and able to work long hours and forgo leisure time that, under normal conditions, could be devoted to the family. Women would be less likely than men to fit this criterion because they would be expected to devote more of their time to their families as well as to household duties. Women might well have to undergo a preliminary power struggle in their own families before they could win the right to devote the time and effort necessary for the political power struggle. Or, at least, women would be less likely than men to have the support of their spouses to embark on such a protracted and time-consuming endeavor. Consequently, the number of women entering the political power struggle would be smaller than that of men.

Furthermore, while the power struggle is uncertain in its outcome in any case, the prospects of a successful outcome are (as indicated below) especially doubtful for women. Moreover, because women cannot fail to be aware of this, even the more ambitious among them would probably think twice before staking their future on a course where the chances of success are so obviously meager. Thus, the underrepresentation of women in politics may set a vicious circle into motion by discouraging prospective women candidates to try for a political career that, in turn, is itself partly responsible for their underrepresentation. Evidence from the United States tends to show that more women compete for political office than is realistic in terms of their chances for success;[1] even so, they do not participate in the political competition in proportion to their numbers.

The third tier of impediments results from the political power struggle as seen from the vantage point of its more established participants. At this level, too, the prospects for women are less than favorable. This is so not necessarily because these participants are intent on disadvantaging women but because they, too, labor under certain constraints, imposed on them by the existent system, and because these constraints work to women's disadvantage. For instance, preselection bodies for parliament (of whatever nature) are under pressure to maximize their parties' chances in elections. They are thus under pressure to select candidates who are relatively well known, popular figures, capable of attracting votes. Therefore, women who have become known to the public through their previous work, have better chances of being preselected. However, in general, preselection bodies apparently are not convinced that there are sufficient numbers of women who are sufficiently well known to the public to be electoral assets to their parties. On the other hand, preselection bodies are under pressure to show that they give "fair" representation to less-advantaged groups, and women are generally regarded as such a group. The result of these cross-pressures may frequently be tokenism as far as women are concerned.

Another constraint preselection bodies (and those who influence them) work under is that of maximizing their own power positions. Thus, they are likely to give preference to persons who have been or may be an asset to them in their own struggles for power. They are people who aided the preselectors' political careers in the past, who, if selected, can reciprocate by further aiding their careers in the future, and who, if not selected, can retaliate by hampering those careers. Hence, to be preselected, candidates must have been previously able to build up power strongholds for themselves within their parties. For that purpose, they must have been politically active in those parties or in other types of politically relevant organizations. Moreover, through their activities they must have been enmeshed in networks of informal relations and patronage. It is through such networks that personal-political support and loyalty (and therefore power) are built up. Potential candidates thus must have been faithful supporters and part of the power bases of politicians who are influential in allocating positions. For their own part, they must have been able to attract supporters, to form their own power bases, and to be able to influence the allocation of positions in favor of their own supporters.

Here, again, women are disadvantaged, either because not many of them have learned how to play the game, or because their male colleagues *think* that not many of them know how to play the game, or because their male colleagues *think* that not many of them are reliable partners in the game. Again, a vicious circle may well be set into motion: If men believe that women cannot be appropriate participants in the network of support and patronage, they are likely to preclude them from such networks, thus fulfilling their own prophecies.

Expectations with Respect to Israel

The existence of a three-tiered structure of impediments would result in women's being underrepresented in all Western legislatures in relation to their proportion in the voting population. Nevertheless, in the case of Israel we expect greater female participation (and even more so in the labor bloc) compared with other Western countries, for three reasons:

1. The egalitarian values—handed down especially from the labor movement and the military underground movement in the *Yishuv* (preindependence) era—including *inter alia* equality between the sexes.
2. The prominence in Israeli life of military service highlights the participation of women as well as men.
3. The kibbutz movement has made a disproportional contribution to Israel's political elite, in particular to the elite of the labor parties, and its ideology propounds equality between sexes. In the kibbutz, women are freed to a greater extend than women in the city from household and child-care duties; hence, it is expected that kibbutz women would have made a contribution similar to kibbutz men in the labor parties' elite participation.

This paper presents a comparison of the proportion of women in the Knesset since independence (1948) with the proportion of women in legislatures in other Western-style democracies over a similar time span. In addition, the proportions of women in left-wing (labor) and center and right-wing parties or blocs in parliament are compared.

The countries were selected for comparison on the basis of a combination of criteria. We intended to make sure that the major democracies (especially the United States and the United Kingdom) would be included, along with some smaller democratic countries more similar in size to Israel. In addition, we wanted countries with both proportional representation and single-member constituencies to be represented. Availability of the information served as another constraint. In all, eleven countries have been included in the analysis.

TABLE 4.1
Percentage of Women in Legislatures in Selected Western-Style Democracies

		1945	1950	1955	1960	1965	1970	1975	1980/81
Australia	House of Representatives	1.3	0.8	0	0	0.8	0	0.8	0/24
Australia	Senate	2.6	6.7	8.3	8.3	8.3	5	6.3	9.4/15.6
Austria	Nationalrat	5.5	5.5	6.1	6.1	6.1	4.8	7.7	9.8
Britain	House of Commons	3.8	3.4	3.8	4.0	4.6	4.1	4.3	3.0
Canada	House of Commons	0.4	0	1.2	1.4	1.5	1.0	3.6	4.1
Finland	Eduskunta	9.3	14.4	15.2	14.0	17.0	22.0	23.4	27.0
France	National Assembly	5.5	6.1	3.5	1.3	1.7	2.1	1.6	4.0
Israel	Knesset	N/A[a]	9.1	8.3	8.3	8.3	6.7	7.5	8.3/67
Norway	Stortinget	—[b]	—	—	6.7	8.0	9.3	15.5	—
Sweden	Riksdag	8.0	10.5	12.25	13.75	13.25	18.5	22.5	—
U.S.A.	House of Representatives	2.5	2.1	3.7	3.7	2.3	2.3	4.4	3.7
U.S.A.	Senate	0	1.0	1.0	2.0	2.0	1.0	0	1.0
West Germany	Bundestag	N/A[c]	6.7	8.2	8.7	6.7	6.5	5.6	8.8

Note: See note 2 for sources.
a Not applicable: First Knesset, 1949
b Not known
c Not applicable: First Bundestag, 1950

Results

The results of the comparison are presented in table 4.1. The proportion of women in legislatures is presented in five-year intervals, beginning from 1950. It must be noted that the elections in each country did not necessarily take place in the years presented in the table. In most cases the data used were for the last previous election year. In the meantime, some women parliamentarians might have left and been replaced by men, and vice versa. Having looked at the data in some detail, we concluded, however, that inaccuracies resulting from such replacements have been only minor and do not change the overall picture. For Israel, the data used were from the *Government Year Book* for the particular year mentioned in the figure.

From table 4.1 it can be seen that in the countries studied, the percentage of women in the legislature ranges from 0 to 27, with most countries' female participation not exceeding 10 percent. In Israel the percentage of women parliamentarians ranges from 9.1 in 1949 to 6.7 in 1969 and 1981. Thus, Israel is not conspicuously lagging behind, but neither is it the expected leader. It is also of interest that while in most countries the proportion of women in parliament has been growing in recent years (the Australian Senate is an impressive example), in Israel there has been a slight trend in the opposite direction.

It is commonly thought that proportional representation is conducive to greater female participation in parliament. This is so because in single-member constituencies preselection bodies (or preselection electorates) are especially likely to worry that women candidates are apt to lose votes.[3] Under the system of proportional representation, on the other hand, preselection bodies would be less hesitant to allocate a certain proportion of "safe" places on the party lists of candidates to women because no single constituency would depend exclusively on their vote-attracting capacity.

Of the countries here compared, Israel, Austria, Finland, Norway, and Sweden have proportional representation; the United Kingdom, the United States, Canada (House of Commons), and France have single-member constituencies; West Germany has a combination of the two systems; and Australia has single-member constituencies for the House of Representatives and proportional representation for the Senate. In table 4.1, it can be seen that where proportional representation prevails—including Israel—women indeed tend to do better than in systems of single-member constituencies. However, when Israel is compared with other systems of proportional representation or with a combined system (West Germany), it does not manifest an especially high rate of female

TABLE 4.2
Proportion of Female Knesset Members in Political Blocks, 1949 Onward

Knesset Political Bloc	1st (1949-51) No. Mem.	1st Prop. female	2nd (1951-55) No. Mem.	2nd Prop. female	3rd (1955-59) No. Mem.	3rd Prop. female	4th (1959-61) No. Mem.	4th Prop. female	5th (1961-65) No. Mem.	5th Prop. female	6th (1965-69) No. Mem.	6th Prop. female	7th (1969-73) No. Mem.	7th Prop. female	8th (1973-77) No. Mem.	8th Prop. female	9th (1977-81) No. Mem.	9th Prop. female	10th (1981-84) No. Mem.	10th Prop. female
Labor[b]	66	12.1	60	10	59	13.5	63	11.1	59	10.1	63	11.3	56	10.7	51	9.8	32	12.5	47	8.5
Center-Right[c]	26	7.6	32	12.5	34	5.8	31	3.3	34	5.8	31	6.4	36	3.1	43	2.2	62	3.2	55	5.5
Communists[d]	4	0	5	20	6	16.6	4	25	5	20	4	0	4	0	4	0	5	0	4	0
Religious[e]	16	0	17	0	18	0	19	0	20	5	18	5.5	18	5.2	17	0	18	5.5	13	0
Other[f]	1	100	0	0	0	0	0	0	0	0	0	0	0	0	4	50	3	33.3	1	100

a The structures of parties taken into account are the ones at the beginning of each Knesset. Splits taking place during sessions are not considered.

b Includes Mapai, Mapam, Ahdut Ha'avodah, Rafi, the Alignment.

c Includes *Herut*, General Zionists, Progressives (Independent Liberals), Liberals, Free-Centre, Democratic Movement for Change, Telem, Tehiya, Flatto-Sharon.

d Includes Maki, Rakah, Moked.

e Includes Ha-Po'el Hamizrahi, Hamizrahi (NRP) Agudat Israel, Tami.

f Includes *Wizo*, Civil Rights Movement, Sheli. Some minor Arab lists, without women parliamentarians, have not been included.

Note: See note 4 for sources.

TABLE 4.3

Percentage of Women in Legislatures from Different Political Blocs, Labor/Communists as Against Center Right (except for the United States)

	Australia - House of Representatives		Australian Senate		Britain House of Commons		France National Assembly		Israel Knesset					United States House of Representatives	
	Australian Labor Party	Liberals, National Country Party	Australian Labor Party	Liberals, National Country Party & Australian Democrats	Labour	Conservatives, Liberals	Socialists, Communists	Rally for the Repub., Union for French Democracy	Labour	Likud Tehiya, Telem	Communist[a]	Religious	Other[b]	Democrats	Republicans
1978							7.6(198)	1.5(265)							
1979					4.1(268)	2.3(350)									
1980														4.5(242)	2.6(192)
1981	5.9(51)[c]	0(74)	14.8(27)	9.5(63)					8.5(47)	5.5(55)	0(4)	0(13)	100(1)		

[a] For Israel, Communists are reported separately because they find their support mainly among the Arab electorate and are concerned with national more than with social issues.

[b] Except for Israel, minute parties have not been reported.

[c] Numbers in parentheses refer to numbers of seats in parliament held by the particular party or bloc.

Note: See note 5 for sources.

participation. Indeed, in some systems of proportional representation, women have recently been doing much better than in Israel.

The next step was to compare women in legislatures according to different parties or political blocs, with special emphasis on the distinction between labor blocs, on the one hand, and center and/or right-wing blocs, on the other. The relevant data for Israel are presented in table 4.2,[4] and the comparison with the other countries is presented in table 4.3.[5] It should be noted that the numbers are very small, and thus differences of one or two members between parties may seem rather large in terms of percentages.

It was argued above that the labor bloc would be more likely to promote equality between the sexes than the center and/or right-wing blocs. The tables show that this has generally been so in Israel throughout its history and in a few other countries in recent years, but only to a limited extent. Moreover, labor's stance represents token rather than real egalitarianism. Even in the labor bloc women are still greatly underrepresented. In the United States, where the division is between a more liberal party (Democratic) and a more conservative party (Republican), women do slightly better in the former, but even there they are greatly underrepresented.

In the Israeli labor bloc, women do rather well in comparison with most other labor and/or liberal blocs shown in the table. This is so, presumably, because the other countries have single-member constituencies (as against Israel's proportional representation). When the Israeli labor bloc is compared with the Labor party in the Australian Senate (which is elected by proportional representation), Israel does considerably worse. In any case, it is clear that even in the Israeli labor bloc women have no more than token representation.

It is worth noting in passing that women in Israel are underrepresented in other power positions as well, and the more powerful the positions, the smaller the representation of women in them. Thus, Weiss and Yishai (1980) report that although women average between 40 and 50 percent of total party membership, their representation in party leadership positions is only around 7.5 percent, and that in the most senior public service posts, there is an almost complete absence of feminine representation. The two most important Knesset committees are foreign affairs and security, and finance. Since the sixth Knesset (1965-69) no woman has served on the former, and apart from the fourth Knesset (1959-61) none has served on the latter.

Interpretation

How can the results of this study be interpreted? Why is it that despite some ostensibly egalitarian tendencies peculiar to Israel, and especially to the labor movement, Israel has not had greater female representation in the legislature than the other comparable countries? Why is it that in comparison with women of other countries featuring proportional representation Israeli women have been marginally less represented in the legislature?

The first interpretation we would like to suggest is in terms of the three-tiered structure of impediments posited above or, in other words, in terms of women's attitudes toward, and in terms of the constraints imposed by, the power struggle in which women must participate to succeed in politics. It seems that in this power struggle Israeli women (no less than their counterparts in other Western democracies) are advertently or inadvertently disadvantaged.

According to this interpretation, Israeli women (like women in other Western countries) are less likely than men to aspire to political or other high-powered careers. This interpretation is supported by a study of Tel-Aviv University students (Shapira, Etzioni-Halevy, and Chopp-Tibbon 1978) that found that female undergraduates and graduate students (ostensibly a most fertile recruitment ground for female politicians) tended to be far less ambitious than their male counterparts and to opt more frequently than not for what were traditionally considered "female" (e.g. child-related) occupations, which usually are relatively low on the ladder of power and prestige. They were also much more likely than their male counterparts to emphasize the need for leisure time to be devoted to family responsibilities. Only a small minority were clearly "career women" in that they opted for high-ranking and demanding occupations and were adamant and self-confident in their choice. The findings were seen as reflecting the cross-pressures likely to be applied to female students. On the one hand, they would have been expected to make use of their academic qualifications and not to opt out of the occupational market altogether. On the other hand, they would have been socialized toward establishing families, and been expected to devote a major part of their time to homemaking and rearing children. Hence the tendency of the majority to compromise on the less-demanding, less-leisure-absorbing type of occupations. Clearly, a political career would not fall into this category.

Interestingly, what has been found for Israeli women students has also been found to be the case for kibbutz women (another ostensibly fertile ground for the recruitment of female politicians). Tiger and Shepher

(1975) show the kibbutz women, too, tend to opt for the traditionally "female" occupations—mainly the services (e.g. cooking, child care). They also show that kibbutz women tend to participate much less than their male counterparts in kibbutz politics, which, in some cases, might serve as a springboard for national politics.

On the basis of these studies, it may be surmised that Israeli women do not tend to enter into, and participate in the political power struggle, and do not tend to seek election in proportion to their numbers. According to this interpretation, the political power struggle as seen from the vantage point of its relatively well-established participants, also works to the disadvantage of Israeli women (no less than it works to the disadvantage of women in other Western countries). And, indeed, in Israel no less than in other countries, preselection bodies[6] for parliament are under pressure to select vote-winning candidates, for even in a system of proportional representation where no single constituency hinges on the popularity of any single candidate, a party still has to put up as strong a list as possible to be attractive to the electorate as a whole. Some Israeli women have, indeed, become known to the public through their previous political activity or through their prominence in women's organizations and the like. In general, however, Israeli preselection bodies are apparently no more convinced than similar bodies in other countries that there are many women who are electoral assets to their parties. To show "fairness" they must select *some* women, and this is usually done through a quota system by which women get a certain, though limited, representation.

It is worth noting that there is, from this viewpoint, a difference among Israeli parties. In some parties (notably the National Religious party, NRP), the number of women who through their previous activities have become well known to the public and/or have established power bases for themselves is smaller than the number of positions allotted to women through the quota system. Hence, paradoxically, even women who are relatively less prominent and successful in the power game than their male counterparts have a chance of being selected. In other parties, notably the Labor Alignment, the number of politically prominent and active women exceeds the number of positions allotted to women through the quota system. Hence, here, women have to struggle especially hard to be preselected.

The second interpretation we would like to suggest is in terms of the factors that might have been expected to work toward greater gender equality in Israel, compared with other democratic countries. It now seems not only that these factors have been outweighed by the above-mentioned constraints but that at least one of the factors, that concerned with military service, has worked to the disadvantage rather than advantage of Israeli women.

In this context, it must be noted that many Israeli politicians have previously made outstanding careers in the army. Because defense and security issues predominate in Israeli politics, a military career is frequently considered useful and legitimate preparation for a political career. Moreover, outstanding army officers are usually well known and popular among the public and thus are considered major electoral assets for the parties they join upon terminating active military service. Here, too, women are disadvantaged.

As noted before, Israel may be considered egalitarian for drafting women as well as men into the army. However, women are not accepted into combat units, and, probably in part for this reason, only few women have made military careers and none has made the kind of outstanding military career that would give her a head start in the political arena. As far as a career in politics is concerned, the prominence of military service, thus, is detrimental to Israeli women.

It is also noteworthy that the feminist movement (which gives women ideological backing in seeking a political career) has never made much headway in Israel. This may well be due, among other things, to the fact that Israeli men are so overburdened with military and reserve service[7] that to make any claim that women are worse off than men seems ludicrous. Thus, the virtual lack of feminist backing for women's political careers also seems to be related to Israel's military service.

Conclusion

The underrepresentation of women in the Israeli parliament (and this holds for other political power positions as well) can be traced to certain attitudes displayed by, and certain cross-pressures applied to, potential women aspirants, on the one hand, and to more established participants in the political power struggle (mostly male), on the other, which seem to work in Israel no less than in other democratic countries. These include relatively weak ambitions among some types of women who could choose to enter politics, probably as a result of their socialization and the pressures brought to bear on them in relation to their roles as home-makers and mothers. They also include lack of confidence on the part of established politicians in women's ability to attract votes and play the political power game. Such lack of confidence would be counterbalanced by pressures to give women "fair" representation but exacerbated by pressures to maximize the parties' chances in elections and the politicians' own power positions within the parties.

The fact that Israeli women are marginally worse off in their prospects of making parliamentary careers than women in comparable countries may be attributed to the prominence of military service in Israel. Rather than promoting greater equality for Israeli women, as might have been expected, military service may well have had the obverse effect. By heightening the burden but also the prospect of prominence for men, it may well have discouraged feminism while at the same time provided some men with a springboard for subsequent political careers.

The resultant state of affairs does not seem to be one that has been consciously designed by anyone in particular; it is, rather, the result of a constellation of factors and forces reflecting women's general position in Israeli society. Awareness of this situation, in addition to being valuable in its own right, may (or may not) spur concerned women and men to work toward change.

Notes

This is a revised version of a paper presented at the International Interdisciplinary Congress on Women, Haifa, December 1981. We are indebted to Ms. Desley Deacon, Dr. Marian Sawer, and Professor Rina Shapira for their most helpful comments. We are also indebted to the Embassy of Israel, Canberra, Australia, for its most valuable aid in gathering the material.

1. We are grateful to Dr. Marian Sawer for making this point.
2. Sources for Table 4.1:

   Annuaire Statistique de la France, 1961, 1965, 1979.

   Annual Abstract of Statistics, 1981. No. 117 (Great Britain: Central Statistical Office).

   M. Charlot, "Women in Politics in France," in *The French National Assembly Elections of 1978,* ed. H.R. Penniman (Washington, D.C.: American Enterprise Institute), 171-91.

   F.W.S. Craig, ed., *British Electoral Facts, 1885-1975* (London: Butler & Tanner, 1976).

   Congressional Quarterly Guide to Congress, 2d ed. (1977).

   Embassy of France, Canberra, Australia.

   Embassy of Irasel, Canberra, Australia.

   Embassy of the Federal Republic of Germany, Australia.

   Cynthia Fuchs Epstein and Rose Laub Coser, eds., *Access to Power* (London: Allen & Unwin, 1981).

   The International Year Book and Statesmen's Who's Who, 1980 (Windsor Court: Kelly's Directories, 1980).

   Israel Government Year Book, 1950, 1956, 1060-61, 1965-66, 1970-71, 1976, 1979).

   Walter S. Kohn, *Women in National Legislatures* (New York: Praeger, 1980).

   Enid Lakeman, *How Democracies Vote* (London: Faber & Faber, 1974).

   Enid Lakeman and James D. Lambert, *Voting in Democracies* (London: Faber & Faber, 1959).

Parliament of the Commonwealth of Australia, List of Senators, Canberra, 10 July 1981.

Parliament of the Commonwealth of Australia, List of Members of Thirty-First and Thirty-Second Parliaments, 1978, 1981.

Robert D. Putnam, *The Comparative Study of Political Elites* (Englewood Cliffs, N.J.: Prentice-Hall, 1976).

Viola A. Smith, *Women in Australian Parliaments and Local Governments* (Sydney: Australian Local Government Women's Association, 1975).

Statesman's Year Book, 1978-79 (London: Macmillan & Co., 1980).

Statistical Abstract of the United States, 1980 (Washington, D.C.: Bureau of the Census, 1980).

Elizabeth Valance, *Women in the House* (London: Athlone Press, 1979).

Yearbook Australia, Nos. 55-60 (Canberra: Australian Bureau of Statistics, 1969-74).

3. Such anxiety is not necessarily justified. In Australia, for instance, it was found that female candidates are not more likely than male candidates to be defeated in single-member constituency elections (Mackerras 1980).

4. Sources for table 4.2:

Shevah Weiss and Yael Yishai, "Women's Representation in Israeli Political Elites," *Jewish Social Studies* 42 (Spring 1980): 165-76.

Embassy of Israel, Canberra, Australia.

5. Sources for table 5.3:

Annuaire Statistique de la France, 1961, 1965-1979.

Annual Abstract of Statistics, 1981, No. 117 (Great Britain: Central Statistical Office).

Embassy of Israel, Canberra, Australia.

Walter S. Kohn, *Women in National Legislatures* (New York: Praeger, 1980).

Parliament of the Commonwealth of Australia, List of Members of Thirty-First and Thirty-Second Parliaments, 1978, 1981.

Parliament of the Commonwealth of Australia, List of Senators, Canberra, 10 July 1981.

Statistical Abstract of the United States, 1980 (Washington, D.C.: Bureau of the Census, 1980).

6. In most Israeli parties, selection committees and/or the parties' central bodies have a major role in preselection of candidates for the Knesset. For instance, in the Labor party (the central partner in the Labor Alignment) candidates who have been members of the Knesset for two terms or more have to be reendorsed by the party's Central Committee. The other candidates are chosen via two separate procedures: part are selected by the Appointments Committee, and part are elected by party members in the party's districts. In Herut (the major partner of the right-wing Likud), the first thirty-five on the list of candidates are chosen by the party's Central Committee. The Liberal party (also a partner in the Likud) has all its candidates selected by the party's Central Committee.

7. Men are drafted for active service for three years, women for eighteen months; men are on reserve duty up to the age of fifty-five, women are released upon the birth of their first child.

References

Mackerras, Malcolm. 1980. "Do Women Candidates Lose Votes?—Further Evidence." *Australian Quarterly* (Summer 1980): 450-55.

Shapira, Rina, Etzioni-Halevy, Eva, and Chopp-Tibbon, Shira. 1978. "Occupational Choice among Female Academicians—The Israeli Case." *Journal of Comparative Family Studies* 9:65-82.

Tiger, L., and Shepher, J. 1975. *Women in the Kibbutz*. New York: Harcourt Brace Jovanovich.

Weiss, Shevah, and Yishai, Yael. 1980. "Women's representation in Israeli political elites." *Jewish Social Studies* 42:165-76.

DIALOGUE AND DEBATE

In this section we present an exchange by several scholars who have carried out research on the use of distinctive Jewish names (DJN) in sample surveys in the Jewish community. We asked Bernard Lazerwitz to write the initial essay in this section, based on his general research contributions to the study of sampling populations and the sociological study of Jewry. Several other scholars who had examined the DJN technique in one of their recent research projects were asked to use the Lazerwitz essay as a starting point for a discussion of their own research; they are Mark Abrahamson, Harold Himmelfarb, and Bruce Phillips. The result is the following series of articles devoted to dialogue and debate on the use of DJN. Additional comments from readers documenting their use of DJN and its appropriateness are welcome and will be considered for publication in future volumes.

5

Some Comments on the Use of Distinctive Jewish Names in Surveys

Bernard Lazerwitz

The usefulness of distinctive Jewish names (DJN) in Jewish research was reintroduced into the published literature by Fred Massarik (1966). In his article, Massarik notes that the technique was originated by Samuel Kohs around 1941.

Kohs devised a list of what he regarded as 35 distinctive Jewish names. These names, it is asserted, are a relatively constant proportion of all Jews. Later the list of distinctive Jewish names was extended to include another 71 names to form a full list of 106.[1] Of course, a quick glance at the list reveals that they are, in reality, distinctive *American* Jewish names. The names are derived from a U.S. Jewish population that is overwhelmingly Ashkenazic in origin and whose forebears went through the "name-modification" procedure that accompanied the process of registering migrants seeking to enter the United States. The list is meant for use in the United States. Given the different origins of the Israeli Jewish population and the differential Israeli name-modification system, with its emphasis on Hebrew names, one would need another list for Israeli distinctive Jewish names.

According to Massarik, the distinctive (American) Jewish names technique is useful for:

1. Situations in which definitive listings of known Jewish households are unavailable.
2. The formation of sampling strata containing different densities of Jewish population.
3. Estimating Jewish population for large areas.

Massarik (1966, 190) also strongly cautions his readers that the technique he presents provides rough Jewish population estimates and must be utilized with "extreme caution and awareness of the need to consider complicating parameters."

Since the 1966 publication by Massarik, our abilities to sample local U.S. Jewish populations have improved with the availability of Jewish Federation lists covering a sizable proportion of Jewish households (outside New York City and its surburan areas) and through the use of the random-digit-dialing sampling technique. This article seeks to update the discussion on the usefulness of distinctive Jewish names in survey work by analyzing the distinctive Jewish names data of the National Jewish Population Survey (NJPS) and commenting on the use of federation lists and random digit dialing.[2]

Statistical Differences between Persons with and without Distinctive Jewish Names

Differences between respondents to the NJPS who had distinctive Jewish names or did not have such names will be considered. First, this is done for the entire sample. Then, the NJPS sample is broken into two major sample-design components. One component consists of Jews "known" to their local federations; being "known" consists of appearing on lists of Jewish households submitted by federations to the NJPS research team that were used for sampling purposes. This component has 2,950 survey respondents. The other component consists of survey respondents not on local federation lists plus all respondents in the New York City and suburbs primary sampling unit. These respondents were obtained by area probability sampling techniques.[3] The yield here was 1,940 interviews in the New York City metropolitan area and 900 interviews with Jews in the rest of the United States who were not known to their local federations.

The very nature of the label, distinctive Jewish names, provides the basis of the necessary research hypothesis. It is expected that those with DJN would, as a group be more traditionally involved with their organized Jewish communities than the group of Jews without DJN. The voluntary retention of a basic label, one's name, which indicates one is Jewish, ought to be a sign of a greater Jewish commitment than that of the group of Jews without DJN. In this latter group would fall those who have done something to their names to reduce the degree to which it labels them as Jewish. Now, to the data.

First, note that the group of Jews having the 106 distinctive names form just 16 percent of the entire NJPS probability sample. This can be further broken down into 11 percent having one of the basic 35 DJN and 5 percent having one of the augmenting 71 DJN. This gives an interview

base of 976 for the 106-DJN group and of 713 for the 35-DJN group.
Immediately, these interview numbers show a major limitation of DJN
work with sample surveys. For many expected survey sample sizes, the
interview base for the 35-DJN group might be too small for stable
statistical work. Hence, one might want to work with the full 106-DJN
group to get a more adequate sample subgroup size.[4]

Table 5.1 displays the differences between the full DJN and non-DJN
subgroups as found in NJPS. The statistical technique used here is rank-
order pattern analysis, which looks into the consistency of the percentage
differences between these two sample subgroups on twenty measures of
Jewish involvement covering items such as lighting candles on shabbat,
saying kiddush, synagogue membership, frequency of attendance at
religious services, activity in Jewish organizations, and so on.[5] Here the
patterns are given for the entire sample, the list-sample substratum, and
the area-sample substratum.

TABLE 5.1
Jewish Involvement Rank-Order Patterns for Distinctive and
Non-distinctive Jewish Names, NJPS Data

Sample Categories	Rank	Patterns
1. All U.S.		
DJN	1	2
Non-DJN	2	1
Pattern Frequencies	12	8
2. List Sample		
DJN	1	2
Non-DJN	2	1
Pattern Frequencies	11	9
3. Area Sample		
DJN	1	2
Non-DJN	2	1
Pattern Frequencies	13	7

There is a 50 percent chance of either the DJN or the non-DJN sub-groups having the larger percentage on any one of the twenty Jewish involvement measures. Hence, ten is the expected number of times our hypothesis that DJN should be more traditionally involved ought to hold on a random basis. In turn, the standard deviation would be 2.24.

Working with this mean-standard deviation combination would require that the DJN subgroup show more Jewish involvement for fourteen to fifteen items out of the twenty to reach the standard 2 sigma level. Lowering standards just a bit to the 90 percent confidence-limit level would require the DJN subgroup to lead on thirteen to fourteen involvement items.

Neither level of significance is achieved for the entire sample nor the list-sample substratum. There is a fingertip grasp on the 90 percent significance level for the area-sample substratum. In the area sample, then, our expectation that the DJN subgroup would be consistently more Jewishly involved than the non-DJN subgroup is fairly well upheld.

The above findings call for a more intensive look at the differences between the DJN and non-DNJ sample categories. This has been done via the MNA multiple regression technique of the Survey Research Center of the University of Michigan (see table 5.2). MNA, or multivariate nominal scale analysis, is a dummy variable, multiple regression technique that handles data from complex sample designs, such as NJPS. Further, MNA is designed to work with any combination of interval, ordinal, or nominal independent variables together with either an ordinal or nominal dependent variable. It also handles multicollinearity among the

TABLE 5.2

Sizable MNA Beta Values for Area Sample Distinctive and Non-distinctive Jewish Names, NJPS Data

Items	Area Sample Beta Values for	
	DJN	Non-DJN
U.S. Generations	.14	.16
Education	.11	.10
Denomination	.09	.11
Synagogue Member	.09	.03
Activity in Jewish Organizations	.13	.17

independent variables. When applied, it indicates the amount of impact each independent variable has on the dependent variable above and beyond the impacts of the other independent variables. Such impact is measured by the MNA equivalent of the standardized multiple regression coefficient, better known as beta. These betas are given for each category of the dependent variable. Here, an independent variable will be considered to have a meaningful impact on the DJN, non-DJN dependent variable if its beta is .09 or larger for either the DJN or non-DJN category.[6]

The beta values of table 5.2 introduce the five factors that best differentiate between the DJN and non-DJN sample subgroups. The two subgroups differ on number of generations in the United States, with the DJN subgroups having fewer foriegn-born and more second-generation Jews than the non-DJN subgroups. The DJN also have more education than the non-DJN.

On demoninational preference, DJN are more concentrated in the Conservative denomination, and are especially less likely to be among those with no preferences than are the non-DJN. Then, DJN are more likely to be synagogue members than non-DJN. Finally, area-sample DJN are definitely less likely to be active in Jewish community voluntary associations than are area-sample non-DJN.

Among the basic claims for the DJN technique is that this subgroup represents a relatively constant proportion of the total Jewish population. Hence, after counting DJN, for example, in a local telephone directory, one can estimate the locality's Jewish population. In a personal communication, Massarik wrote that he has used the ratio of 6.67 non-DJN to each DJN. This gives the DJN proportion as 15 percent of the Los Angeles Jewish population. How well does this figure hold for other Jewish communities?

Clearly, the 15 percent holds for the entire NJPS sample, which has 16 percent DJN. Previously published work with NJPS (Lazerwitz 1977) has given an eleven-category geographic classification that can be formed from the NJPS sample within the limitations of its sample size and design. Table 5.3 gives the DJN percentages for the eleven geographic categories. Note that the New York City metropolitan area yields 14 percent DJN and the rest of the country shows 17 percent DJN. The DJN percentage varies from a low of 11 percent in western medium-size Jewish communities to a high of 23 percent in the small Jewish communities of the Midwest and West. Los Angeles registers 18 percent, which is very close to Massarik's 15 percent. On the whole, then, DJN do form a Jewish population percentage that varies within a reasonably

TABLE 5.3
Distinctive Jewish Name Percentages for Various NJPS Geographic Categories

Sample Category	Percent of NJPS Sample with DJN's
All Sample	16%
New York Metropolitan Area	14%
New Jersey	18%
Philadelphia Metropolitan Area	16%
Boston Metropolitan Area	14%
Baltimore, Washington, D.C., and Providence Metropolitan Areas	14%
Other Eastern Jewish Communities	19%
Midwestern Medium and Large Jewish Communities	19%
Los Angeles Metropolitan Area	18%
Western Medium Size Jewish Communities	11%
Southern Jewish Communities	12%
Small Jewish Communities of the Midwest and West	23%

delimited range. As Massarik cautions, it is best to develop a locality-based DJN percentage before falling back upon the national 16 percent.

Conclusions and Recommendations

It is abundantly clear, based on the NJPS data given here, that the DJN technique must still be used within the clear limits formulated earlier by Massarik. The current tendency to believe that a probability sample of DJN American Jews is an adequate probability sample of all Jews must be avoided.

There does seem to be little difference between DJN and non-DJN

Jews when both subgroups are "known" to the local Jewish community. Here, being known is operationalized by the appearance on a Jewish federation's list of known Jewish households. However, area probability samples of Jewish populations not "known" to federations indicate that the DJN subgroup for this sample division tends to be more traditionally inclined than the non-DJN Jews. Hence, any survey substitution of DJN Jews for non-DJN Jews produces a clear bias away from Jewish marginality. It also produces a bias toward second-generation Jews, better-educated Jews, and those less active in Jewish organizations.

On the basis of these findings, the following recommendations are given to fellow researchers studying American Jewish communities:

1. Try to restrict use of the DJN concept to that for which it has always been meant, namely, for sample designing and, as a less than optimal device, for estimating local Jewish populations.
2. Given the availability of local Jewish federation lists covering a sizable percentage of a locality's Jewish population, there is no obvious survey research reason to work just with DJN Jews on such lists.
3. Do use random digit dialing as the basic sampling and interviewing techniques for locality surveys. This approach will contact all sectors of a local Jewish population—identified or not identified Jews, Jews with or without DJN. Furthermore, it will do it at a reasonable cost.
4. Do integrate a random-digit-dialing survey system with the available list of Jewish households known to the local Jewish federation. Such an integrated system will further reduce survey costs by providing a basic sample stratum containing households, and their telephone numbers, that has high probabilities of yielding survey-eligible Jewish households with a minimum number of telephone calls.[7]
5. Use an expanded random-digit-dialing approach to find and interview Jews not known to local federations. (Nationally, the NJPS found that outside the New York City metropolitan area, 50 percent of its sample did not appear on available local Jewish federation lists.)
6. If, by research chance, one needs to survey Jews in geographic areas not at all or only lightly covered by the nearest Jewish federation, it would be a good idea to use available resources, such as telephone directories, to build a sample stratum of households with an increased probability of yielding Jews. In other words, use a list of DJN for the same sampling tasks as used for federation lists. Then, try to use a "snowball" technique by asking such DJN Jews contacted via telephone to identify locality Jews known to them. This would augment the DJN stratum. Finally, resort to some random digit dialing to try to represent other locality Jews missed by the above efforts.

To this researcher, it makes no sense to restrict use of any decent federation list to just those Jews with DJN. Rather, the obviously proper thing to do is to sample from the entire federation list—DJN and non-DJN alike. Furthermore, in areas with a fairly sizable percentage of the local Jewish population probably not on a federation list, it is not a wise use of available resources to restrict contact efforts to DJN found in sources like telephone directories. First, a researcher would have to make sure that telephone DJN did not appear in the federation list. Then, it is likely that efforts restricted to DJN unknown to local federations hit a mere 10 percent to 20 percent of the "unknown" Jews. It would be better to switch such clerical efforts to more random digit dialing.

These recommendations just sketch out survey design techniques. The actual necessary design details would be more complex and would have to reflect specific local conditions.

Notes

The complex computer programming work for this work was well done by Mr. Matti Ronen of Bar-Ilan University.

1. The full list of 106 distinctive Jewish names, including the original 35, is available from the author.
2. Due to the efforts of Massarik, respondents to NJPS had their names coded into a scheme that gave one code to all those not having DJN and 106 different code entries to those with distinctive Jewish names.
3. As of the date of the NJPS, the very number of Jews in the New York metropolitan area prevented the New York Jewish Federation from having a list of Jewish households that covered a sizable percentage of its local Jewish population. Hence, the necessary resort there to area probability sampling. For a detailed description of the sample design for the NJPS, see Lazerwitz (1973).
4. This caution of work with the full 106 DJN does not apply to lists compiled from sources such as telephone directories and the like. Again, this survey research caution is in line with the DJN usages presented by Massarik. He used DJN to design sample surveys rather than using them for survey data analysis. For use of 35 DJN, see Himmelfarb, Loar, and Mott (1983).
5. For a detailed presentation of the rank-order pattern analysis technique, see Siegel and Lazerwitz (1971).
6. The MNA technique also requires no interaction among its independent variables. The set of independent variables used here have previously been well tested for interaction, and none that needs to be considered were found. For previous use of this Survey Research Center analysis system with NJPS data, see Lazerwitz (1982). For a presentation of MNA, see Andrews and Messinger (1973).
7. The specific sample design procedures for such a combined use of federation lists with random digit dialing are complex and cannot be discussed here.

References

Andrews, Frank, and Messinger, Robert. 1973. *Multivariate Nominal Scale Analysis*. Ann Arbor: University of Michigan, Institute for Social Research.

Himmelfarb, Harold, Loar, Michael, and Mott, Susan. 1983. "Sampling by Ethnic Surnames: The Case of American Jews." *Public Opinion Quarterly* 47 (Summer):247-60.

Lazerwitz, Bernard. 1973. "The Sample Design of the National Jewish Population Survey." New York: Council of Jewish Federations.

———. 1977. "The Community Variable in Jewish Identification." *Journal for the Scientific Study of Religion* 16 (December):361-69.

———. 1982. "Do Denominations Matter?" *American Journal of Sociology* 88 (September): 356-77.

Massarik, Fred. 1966. "New Approaches to the study of the American Jew." *Jewish Journal of Sociology* 8 (December): 175-91.

Siegel, Morris, and Lazerwitz, Bernard. 1971. "Sex, Generation, and Class as Structural Variables in a Large Jewish Community." *Journal of Jewish Communal Service* 47 (Fall): 91-101.

6

The Unreliability of DJN Techniques

Mark Abrahamson

For both research and planning purposes, many organizations and agencies would like to be able to estimate the size of local (e.g. metropolitan area) Jewish populations. Sample survey designs, entailing random digit dialing, are probably the most dependable method. However, they are time consuming and expensive to employ, and they ordinarily require the assistance of professional consultants. For communities that desire a quick and low-cost estimate, the counting of Distinctive Jewish Names (DJN) is a tempting alternative. The potential risks involved in DJN estimates have been noted by Lazerwitz, in this volume, and by several other writers as well. This paper adds to that literature by comparing the results of a 1982 sample survey with several DJN estimates for the Greater Hartford area, Connecticut.

The Sample Survey

The survey was conducted, in the fall of 1982, in two phases (Greater Hartford Jewish Federation 1982). Phase one entailed over 15,000 randomly dialed calls to the twenty-six towns that constitute the Hartford Federation's service area. These calls were utilized to identify households in which one or more persons were Jewish (by background). All such households were retelephoned in phase two, and a fifteen-minute interview was conducted with a Jewish (by background) respondent.

To assess the accuracy of the sample survey, its projections were compared with a number of known "criteria," such as local synagogue memberships, parents in the local Hebrew Home, and contributions to the local federation. The sample projections and known criteria were, on average, only about 5 percent different. Therefore, the sample estimate of the total Jewish population of the Hartford area—25,111—was regarded as likely to be very close to the true figure. In addition, the study provided estimates of the Jewish population of each of the twenty-six towns that constituted the Greater Hartford area. The towns' Jewish populations varied markedly from one another, ranging from over 7,000 to practically none.

DJN Estimates

The most widely used DJN lists appear to be the 35-name list (associated with Kohs) and a slightly modified list of 38 names. The latter list, which is distributed by Chenkin, is an attempt to include fewer German names (e.g. Schwartz) whose bearers may not be Jewish. However, the two lists are very similar; about three-quarters of the names are shared. Population estimates derived from either list are not likely to be very different.

As alternatives, both much smaller and much larger DJN lists have been developed. Specifically, there is a 21-name list designed more completely to eliminate German names, and a 106-name list designed to include more of the more "Americanized" Jewish names.

Past research utilizing DJN has identified as a serious problem the tendency to overestimate the Jewish population by incorrectly including some persons of German background whose names are frequently shared by German Jews. In Cincinnati, for example, where the German population is relatively large, DJN counts appear to result in a 25 to 35 percent overestimation of the Jewish population (Varady and Mantel 1981). Therefore, we will examine two different DJN estimates: the 38-name (modified Kohs) list, and the abbreviated 21-name list; and the results of each will be compared to the sample survey estimates.

The Estimates Compared

Table 6.1 presents a summary of Jewish population estimates for the twenty-six-town Greater Hartford area, comparing the sample survey and the 38-DJN and 21-DJN lists. The footnotes are the assumptions employed in estimating the Jewish population from the DJN lists.

Almost all of the difference between the two DJN estimates is due to different assumptions concerning the percentage of all telephones that are listed. The 38-name list follows the procedure recommended by the *UJA Survey Kit* (Cohen 1981), namely, that 80 percent of all telephones are listed. The 21-name list assumes a lower rate of listed numbers. If the same listing assumption is made, the DJN estimates for the Greater Hartford area differ from each other by fewer than a thousand persons.

TABLE 6.1
Comparison of DJN and Sample Survey Results

Data Source	Total Jewish Population of Hartford Area	Jewish Population of the town with the:	
		Largest Jewish Population	Smallest Jewish Population
38 DJN List[1]	65,022	22,033	28
21 DJN List[2]	68,703	22,003	52
Sample Survey	25,111	7,353	23

1. Assumes multiplying by 9.4 to convert DJNs to total Jewish population; by 1.25 to convert listed phones to all phones; and by 2.5 persons per household, or telephone.
2. Assumes mutliplying by 15.6 to convert DJNs to total population; by 1.30 to convert listed phones to all phones; and by 2.5 persons per household, or telephone.

Because of the procedures by which the sample survey was conducted, and its demonstrated accuracy in predicting known criteria, its estimate of the Jewish population is almost certainly more likely to be accurate than either DJN technique. One must conclude, therefore, that the DJN projections—over two and one-half times larger than the sample survey figures—contain a substantial overestimation bias. It may be very constructive, therefore, to consider why DJN counts may produce highly distorted estimates.

Sources of DJN Error

There are three assumptions that must be made whenever DJN are used to provide population estimates. The assumptions involve (1) the known representativeness of the DJN list, (2) the percentage of all telephones that are listed in directories, and (3) the number of people per household, or telephone. The likely consequences of each assumption will be discussed in turn.

Representativeness

The first assumption that must be made in conjunction with the use of any DJN list is that a local community is typical with respect to the distribution of names of its Jewish population. If too few or too many Jewish residents possess names on the list, the projection will be seriously distorted. Lazerwitz notes that communities vary in this regard from 11 to 23 percent; that is, names on one DJN list correspond with between 11 to 23 percent of all Jews in local communities. This array is viewed by Lazerwitz as falling within a "reasonably delimited range," around an average of 16 to 17 percent.

My conclusion is that this is too variable, given the consequences of the assumption. To illustrate, using the 38-name list, the conventional assumption is that such names represent a little under 11 percent of the population. In the Hartford area, this assumption led to the estimate of about 65,000 Jewish persons. Every 1 percent difference in this assumption, in the Hartford area, corresponds with a difference of approximately 5,000 people. Thus, if the 38-DJN list was assumed to represent 12.5 percent of the Jewish population, then that population would have been estimated at about 55,000 (rather than 65,000).

One uses an average, or conventional, figure in the absence of any information to the contrary. When DJN techniques are employed it is ordinarily because there is no other information. One cannot, therefore, know the representativeness of DJN, and even very small differences between the true and assumed percentages can result in dramatically distorted estimates.

Listed Numbers

The use of any DJN list, by comparison to random dialing, requires the use of published directories. The question that logically arises is, what percentage of all Jewish telephones have listed numbers? The *UJA Survey Kit* (Cohen 1981) recommends the assumption that 80 percent are listed. This is a reasonable figure for some communities, but it is far too high for others. About 70 percent in New York and about 50 percent in Los Angeles appear to be more likely estimates of listed numbers for those metropolitan areas.

Different assumptions about the percentage of listed numbers are less consequential than assumptions about the representativeness of DJN, but they are still consequential. For example, the 80 percent listed assumption produced an estimate of 65,000 Jews for the Hartford area. A 50 percent listed assumption would raise the estimate to over 100,000.

The exact percentage of Jewish telephones that are listed in any community cannot, of course, be known without a systematic investigation. (The percentage listed will be higher if there are relatively few single women, recent movers, doctors and dentists, and so on. Who knows how many of the preceding there are, however, without a study?)

Household Size

The final step in estimating the size of a local Jewish population is to multiply the estimated total number of households (or telephones) by an average household size. The conventional assumption is 2.5 persons. Average household size in many communities is very close to 2.5. Further, variations tend to be relatively small in magnitude. Only in very atypical communities will average household size be less than 2.2 or more than 2.8. Either of these extremes would have added or subtracted only about 6,000 persons to the 65,000 projection in the Hartford area. Thus, by contrast to estimates of either DJN representativeness or proportion of listed telephones, incorrect estimates of household size are not likely to be very consequential.

Conclusion

Without a systematic study of a local community, it is not possible to estimate, with sufficient precision, the percentage of the Jewish community that has either a DJN or a listed telephone number. The consequences of incorrect assumptions concerning either are literally multiplied. DJN techniques all require that the counted directory listing of DJN be multiplied to estimate Jewish persons with non-DJN and to estimate Jewish persons with nonlisted numbers. If the estimates of these values are incorrect, then the counted DJN are multiplied by incorrect numbers, producing wildly unreliable estimates.

To use DJN, therefore, requires that a systematic study be conducted first, but it is to avoid such studies that DJN techniques are even considered. Does this mean that DJN are worthless as a technique for estimating local Jewish populations? Yes, with one possible exception, to judge from the Hartford experience: While both DJN techniques greatly overestimated the Jewish population of every one of the twenty-six towns that constitute the Hartford area, their *rankings* of towns were highly congruent with the sample survey's ranking (Rho = .91). Thus, within metropolitan areas, DJN counts may provide a reasonable basis for ordering subareas relative to one another. More evidence concerning the consistency of DJN rankings of subareas will be most welcome. However, the absolute size of subareas, as indicated by DJN estimates, should be regarded with suspicion.

References

Cohen, Steven Martin. 1981. *UJA Demographic/Attitudinal Survey Kit.* New York: United Jewish Appeal

Greater Hartford Jewish Federation. 1982. *A Study of the Greater Hartford Jewish Population.* Hartford, Conn.: Greater Hartford Jewish Federation.

Varady, David, and Mandel, Samuel J., Jr. 1981. "Estimating the Size of Jewish Communities Using Random Telephone Surveys." *Journal of Jewish Communal Service* 57, no. 3:225-34.

7

Further Comments on the Use of DJN

Harold S. Himmelfarb

The use of Distinctive Jewish Names (DJN) in Jewish population surveys is becoming more popular. It is therefore necessary to inquire to what extent the method biases results.

Our work on DJN has concentrated on the usefulness of a DJN sample versus an organization–list sample (Himmelfarb, Loar, and Mott 1983). Based on the assumption that area housing or phone exchange samples (e.g. random digit dialing) is beyond the means of most social scientific studies on American Jews, we asked whether the use of DJN would not provide a more representative low-cost sample of Jews than the use of Jewish organization lists (i.e. federation lists). The answer, in short, was yes. Using the National Jewish Population Study (NJPS) data, we found that persons with thirty-five distinctive Jewish names were not very different from the other Jews in the sample with regard to demographic characteristics and Jewish identification. The differences that existed were *not* consistently in one direction, e.g. greater identification for the DJN. Moreover, regardless of direction, the magnitude of differences was low. On the other hand, a comparison of the NJPS respondents chosen from Jewish federation lists and the NJPS respondents chosen via area housing probability methods showed more substantial and more consistent differences. The list sample was more Jewishly identified and had many of the demographic characteristics typically associated with greater Jewish identification. Thus, with certain caveats regarding the use of DJN to tap intermarried Jewish women and Russian and Israeli immigrants, we conclude that if researchers must rely on nonprobability sampling methods, the use of DJN should produce a reasonably representative sample with considerably less bias than the use of Jewish organization lists.

Bernard Lazerwitz's article in this volume complements our previous analysis and findings. He also uses the NJPS data, but we worked with different tapes. Lazerwitz uses the entire list of 106 DJN, but we used only the 35 DJN, which constituted 11 percent of the sample. We judged this to be a sufficient number for analysis and a more stringent test of representativeness. We stand by that decision. The two studies also used different modes of statistical analysis. Nevertheless, it is important to note that the differences he finds between the DJN and non-DJN sub-samples with regard to generation, education, denomination, synagogue membership, and participation in voluntary organizations are all consistent with our findings.

What is new in his findings is that DJN persons chosen from federation lists are not statistically different from other Jews on those lists, but nonfederation-affiliated DJN persons (i.e. those chosen by area probability sampling) tend to be more traditional than other non-affiliated Jews. It seems to me that the main implications of this is that a sample of only DJN Jews is less likely than a random sample of Jews to yield those persons who are most marginally involved with Jewish life. Researchers might decide that this small fringe group is not important enough to include, given the economics of using a DJN sample. However, I am not even sure the interpretation of the finding is correct. On Lazerwitz's measures, the area-sample DJN are more traditional with regard to denominational identification and synagogue membership, but they are less traditional with regard to voluntary organizational participation. So, is the group really less traditional overall? Moreover, the same differences are found in our analysis where the area-sample and list-sample DJN are combined (which is the way a DJN sample is likely to be constituted), but in our estimation, the magnitude of the differences are not great enough to cause much concern.

There are two other uses to which DJN are likely to be applied. One, is as a basis for making a population-size estimate. Here, Lazerwitz has shown very graphically that there is a fairly substantial range between geographic regions in the proportion of Jews with DJN. Thus, researchers should be quite cautious about using only DJN persons to establish population-size estimates, unless they have prior knowledge about the actual size of the proportion of the population that DJN persons constitute and the stability of that proportion over time. The other use of DJN is for establishing proportions for stratified sampling. This was elaborate in Massarik (1966) and still seems to be a valid and appropriate procedure.

New uses of DJN are developing. The availability of computerized lists of contributors to Jewish philanthropies and subscribers to Jewish periodicals will allow for research to expand the number of names considered "distinctively Jewish" and to include names from other

Jewish immigrant groups. By expanding the number of names used, assuming that a high level of name efficiency is maintained (i.e. about 90 percent of persons with such names are Jewish), researchers will be able to sample from a larger proportion of the population, and this ought to minimize biases even further.

Initial work in this regard has been undertaken by A.B. Data in Milwaukee. It would be very helpful if research were funded toward the end of making publicly available an updated, expanded, and efficient list of DJN.

There has been some concern expressed (Cohn 1984) about the representativeness of recent national samples of the Jewish community sponsored by the American Jewish Committee (Cohen 1983a, 1983b) that were based on some version of DJN. The first study was based on a sample of 1,700 persons having "about a dozen Distinctive Jewish Names . . . who were listed in the telephone directories of over 40 communities of all sizes throughout the continental United States" (Cohen 1983a,89). The data was collected in the fall of 1981. The second study, conducted in June 1983, used a sample of 1,600 households chosen with the aid of A.B. Data's master list of 80,000 DJN. Both studies had a significant proportion of ineligible or unreachable households (about 18 and 25 percent, respectively), and both studies had about a 50 percent response rate.

Cohen compared both surveys to the 1981 New York Jewish Population Study. Surprisingly, on most demographic characteristics, the smaller list of names produced greater similarities to the New York population than did the larger list, but that result might not be desirable. Indeed, we might expect that New York Jews are older, less educated, and less wealthy than the nation's Jews in general, which is what Cohen found in the later study. We might also expect that nationally the Jews are less Orthodox and less observant than the Jews of New York. Both studies found that they are less observant, but the later study found that more of them considered themselves Orthodox. In fact, the denominational question produced some curious flux. The early study found that 6 percent considered themselves Orthodox—a significant decline from about 11 percent in the 1971 National Jewish Population Study data (Himmelfarb and Loar 1984). However, the later study found that 15 percent considered themselves Orthodox—a dramatic increase from two years earlier! Cohen suggests that slight problems in representativeness in the later national sample might be due to the high nonresponse rate. I think this is only part of the problem. Essentially, we might expect a sample of only 600 to 700 Jews to have a rate of precision of ± 4 percent, even if there was no self-selection bias in the responses. If one survey erred in the minus direction and the other in the plus direction, we could get quite dramatic fluctuations on small segments of the population, like the Orthodox. Thus, before judging the accuracy of using the DJN method (or a particular DJN method) on the results of those data, I would suggest that the sample size should be doubled to yield more stable results.

There is no doubt that the DJN method of sampling needs further refinement. However, I find current research with the method both encouraging and promising.

References

Cohen, Steven, M. 1983a. "The 1981-83 National Survey of American Jews." In *American Jewish Yearbook, 1983*, pp. 89-111.

———. 1983b. *Attitudes of American Jews Toward Israel and Israelis: The 1983 National Survey of American Jews and Jewish Communal Leaders.* New York: Institute on American Jewish-Israeli Relations, American Jewish Committee.

Cohn, Werner. 1984. "What's in a Name: A Comment on Himmelfarb, Loar and Mott." *Public Opinion Quarterly* 48 (Fall): 660-664.

Himmelfarb, Harold S., and Loar, R. Michael. 1984. "National Trends in Jewish Ethnicity: A Test of the Polarization Hypothesis." *Journal for the Scientific Study of Religion* 23 (June): 140-54.

Himmelfarb, Harold S., Loar, R. Michael, and Mott, Susan H. 1983. "Sampling by Ethnic Surnames: The Case of American Jews." *Public Opinion Quarterly* 47 (Summer): 247-60.

Massarik, Fred. 1966. "New Approaches to the Study of the American Jews." *Jewish Journal of Sociology* 8 (December): 175-91.

8

DJN and List Samples in the Southwest: Addendum to Lazerwitz

Bruce A. Phillips

The three sampling techniques most used in Jewish communal research are random digit dialing (RDD), Distinctive Jewish Names (DJN), and lists of known Jews in the community. Only in random digit dialing to the sampled households have a known probability of selection (the inverse of the number of phone numbers sampled for the prefix of the household). The probabilities of household selection are not known because the number of households that do not have DJN or who are not affiliated with a Jewish organization is not known. Thus, only RDD samples are true probability samples in and of themselves.

The problem, then, of DJN and list samples is that the bias introduced by excluding households that are not known or do not have DJN remains unknown, unless discovered from some source outside the sample itself. Goldstein and Goldscheider (1968), for example, checked a random sample of Jewish households located in a general area sample in Providence against the federation list to be sure that their list sample adequately represented the population. In most cases, however, the rationale for using DJN and list samples is generally based on the assumption that people who appear on federation lists or people who have a distinctive Jewish name are basically the same as those who do not.

In this volume, Lazerwitz has challenged the DJN assumption, arguing that "The voluntary retention of a basic label, one's name, which indicates one is Jewish ought to be a sign of a greater Jewish commitment than that of the group of Jews without DJN." Using twenty measures of Jewish identification in the National Jewish Population Survey, Lazerwitz demonstrated that Jews with traditional Jewish names are more likely to be Jewishly involved. Himmelfarb, Loar, and Mott (1983,256) working with the same data, however, reach a different conclusion: "We believe that a random sample of persons with DJN is likely to produce a fairly representative sample of American Jews."

When I worked with the Demographic Study Committee of the Denver Jewish Federation to select a methodology, both DJN and list samples were rejected in favor of RDD. Because new movers to Denver and the Unaffiliated were groups in which the federation was interested, and were not expected to appear in a list sample, the methodology was ruled out categorically. A DJN sample was rejected because there were no data available about the prevalence of DJN in the rapid-growth Jewish communities of the Southwest. The federation wanted the demographic study to develop a long-range plan for a community about which little was known, and the study committee thus chose to adopt the sample design in which the most confidence could be placed. At the conclusion of the data collection, the validity of this decision was checked by creating subsamples of DJN and listed households and comparing them with the full RDD sample to see if the same picture of the Denver Jewish community would have resulted from these two nonprobability samples as from the RDD sample. The results of this comparison show that for Denver a DJN sample would have been superior to a list sample but still would not provide a representative sample of the community.

Methodology

Both DJN and list subsamples were created from the total RDD sample. Two kinds of list samples were created. The first consists of all households found on the federation list; this is called the federation ("Fed.") sample. The second adds to this group all members of synagogues and Jewish organizations; this is called the combination ("Combin.") sample. The combination sample is included primarily for heuristic purposes. There would actually be little compelling reason for using such a comprehensive list sample because the St. Louis experience (where such a sample was employed) suggests that the cost of putting together an unduplicated sample of such comprehensive proportions is the same as conducting a random-digit-dialing study (Tobin 1982).

The DJN subsample was created by looking up every phone number in the sample in a "criss-cross" reverse directory. If the person listed for that phone number had one of the 106 distinctive Jewish names discussed by Lazerwitz, it was included in the DJN subsample. Persons with unlisted phone numbers who might have DJN would not be so identified with this technique. On the other hand, it more closely conforms to the realities of DJN sampling than the method used by Lazerwitz from the NJPS because unlisted DJN would never appear in an actual sample. In other words, a DJN sample combines two sources of bias: the DJN bias and the listing bias. Because the NJPS asked people for their names rather than looking them up in the phone directory, it does not take into account the latter source of bias. Out of the 825 Denver interviews conducted using RDD, only 6 percent (50 cases) were found to be listed with DJN. This figure is consistent with the 11 percent figure for "Western medium-size Jewish communities" reported by Lazerwitz (table 5.3) for the NJPS once the 56.7 percent unlisted rate in Denver is taken into account. This means that the comparison tables were very much lopsided, pairing a sample of 50 DJN with a sample of 725 non-DJN. All the findings reported, however, are significant at the .05 level or better (chi-square distribution).

The approach to data presentation used here differs slightly from that used by Himmelfarb and Lazerwitz. They compare the DJN group with the non-DJN group (and the listed group with the nonlist group) to test for differences in Jewish practice, and identity. In the presentation of the Denver findings, however, the DJN subsample and the two list sub-samples are compared with the RDD sample as a whole by using a number of different variables so as to emphasize the implications of these methodological differences for federation planning.

Findings

Both the DJN and the two list samples tend to overrepresent the affiliated. Both the two list samples and the DJN sample suggest that synagogue members are at least twice as numerous as they really are, as represented by RDD (see table 8.1). Synagogue membership is also over-represented by both the two lists and the DJN sample (see table 8.2). In this case, however, the DJN sample would have been a little closer to the RDD sample, which makes sense, given that the list samples are made up of affiliated households. These findings are consistent with Lazerwitz's analysis of the NJPS. Because it was so heavily planning oriented, the Denver study did not include items on observance or attitudinal questions about Jewish identity, which limits the extent to which Lazerwitz's NJPS analysis can be replicated for this sunbelt community. The planning implications of these sample differences are equally important, however, because they are funded as a planning tool. The two list samples and the DJN sample would not have been adequate in Denver, for each would have missed a significant proportion of a target group.

TABLE 8.1
Number of Jewish Organizational Memberships in Household

	Fed.	Combin.	RDD	DJN
None	26.2	28.4	61.5	40.5
1-3	54.5	57.9	31.1	37.3
4 or more	19.3	13.8	7.4	22.2
TOTAL	100.0	100.0	100.0	100.0

TABLE 8.2
Synagogue Membership

	Fed.	Combin.	RDD	DJN
Household has membership	67.9	71.0	38.6	51.9
Household not a member	32.1	29.0	61.3	48.1
TOTAL	100.0	100.0	100.0	100.0

All three of the nonprobability samples present a picture of the Denver Jewish family than is different from that found in the RDD sample. Never-married household heads and single parents, both of which are considered "target" populations for whom special services are planned, are underrepresented (see table 8.3). The federation sample (typical of most list samples) was particularly far off the mark, excluding close to 80 percent of the never marrieds. The combination and DJN samples come closer to the RDD sample but miss enough of the never-marrieds to be of serious concern. The non-RDD samples also vastly underestimate the extent of intermarriage in Denver (see table 8.4), showing only 14 percent of all married couples to be made up of a born-Jew married to a non-Jew, compared with the 35.6 percent in the RDD sample. Because the intermarriage finding was one of the most dramatic to come out of the study, and because the community began almost immediately to implement programs in this area, the nonprobability samples would have missed a particularly important target population. Data about geographic mobility in Denver would also have been compromised. The effect of new movers (within the five years prior to the study) to Denver would have been missed entirely by the federation sample, and would have been seriously underestimated by the DJN and combination list samples (see table 8.5). Similarly, the number of recent movers to the current residence would also have been underrepresented (see table 8.6).

The age and income distributions of the DJN sample were not significantly different from the RDD distribution (see tables 8.7 and 8.8, respectively). The two list samples, however, undercount household

TABLE 8.3
Household Composition

	Fed.	Combin.	RDD	DJN
Never Married, no children	5.9	16.9	24.7	16.3
Divorced, no children	3.6	4.7	6.6	3.8
Widowed, no children	9.8	7.8	6.1	2.9
Married Couple no children	54.1	41.8	34.0	43.0
Single Parent Family	2.0	3.3	4.1	2.7
Married Couple with children	24.7	25.4	24.5	31.5
TOTAL	100.0	100.0	100.0	100.0

TABLE 8.4
Marriage Pattern

Composition of Couple	Fed.	Combin.	RDD	DJN
Born Jew and born Jew	81.9	79.8	58.3	86.0
Born Jew and convert	4.8	6.3	6.4	0.0
Born Jew and non-Jew	13.3	13.9	35.9	14.0
TOTAL	100.0	100.0	100.0	100.0

TABLE 8.5
Years Lived in Denver

	Fed.	Combin.	RDD	DJN1
5 Years or less	8.0	18.4	35.5	22.6
6 to 10 years	13.0	12.2	15.6	10.3
11 to 15 years	9.9	10.2	9.8	8.1
16 or more years	69.2	59.2	41.0	59.0
TOTAL	100.0	100.0	100.0	100.0

TABLE 8.6
Years at Current Residence

	Fed.	Combin.	RDD	DJN
Less than 1 year	3.1	6.9	11.9	0.9
2-5 years	27.4	39.2	50.6	43.5
6-10 years	15.4	15.7	13.1	16.9
11 or more years	54.0	38.3	24.4	38.7
TOTAL	100.0	100.0	100.0	100.0

TABLE 8.7
Age of Respondent

	Fed.	Combin.	RDD	DJN1
18-29	7.2	16.5	27.4	21.3
30-39	22.2	25.1	29.4	26.5
40-49	14.3	14.6	12.0	13.0
50+	56.3	43.8	31.2	39.2
TOTAL	100.0	100.0	100.0	100.0

TABLE 8.8
Combined Household Income

	Fed.	Combin.	RDD	DJN1
Under $20,000	27.7	31.2	36.8	36.9
$20,000 - $39,999	32.4	32.4	35.0	27.9
$40,000 - $59,999	19.4	17.1	14.5	18.8
$60,000 - $99,999	13.7	14.3	9.9	13.4
$100,000+	6.8	5.0	3.7	3.1
TOTAL	100.0	100.0	100.0	100.0

heads who are under thirty years of age and households with incomes of $40,000 or more.

Conclusion

The DJN sample comes consistently closest to the RDD sample, and the federation sample is consistently the furthest off. The combination list sample falls in the middle but is more similar to the federation sample. The limitations of list samples (even expensive comprehensive ones) are so great as to rule them out of serious consideration in communities such as Denver. The DJN sample, while accurately depicting the community in two areas (age and income), was seriously off in enough of the others to approach it only with great caution. Lazerwitz's cautions about the representativeness of DJN sample on a national scale are even more true in Denver and other new Jewish communities in the Southwest.

References

Goldstein, Sidney, and Goldscheider, Calvin. 1968. *Jewish Americans: Three Generations in a Jewish Community.* Englewood Cliffs, N.J.: Prentice-Hall.

Himmelfarb, Harold S., Loar, R. Michael, and Mott, Susan H. 1983. "Sampling by Ethnic Surnames: The Case of American Jews." *Public Opinion Quarterly* 47 (Summer): 247-60.

Tobin, Gary. 1982. *A Demographic and Attitudinal Study of the Jewish Community of St. Louis.* St. Louis: Jewish Federation of St. Louis.

SPECIAL SUPPLEMENTAL SECTION
Conference Reports on Israelis Abroad

Introduction

Paul Ritterband and *Yael Zerubavel*

Walking through the Diamond district on 47th Street in Manhattan, one hears Hebrew; looking at the name tags of New York taxi drivers, one reads Hebrew; shopping in some neighborhoods in Brooklyn and Queens, one sees Israeli-named stores and Israeli products on the shelves; strolling across college and university campuses in New York, one sees and hears Israelis.

Who are the Israelis in New York? Are they simply sojourners spending a limited time abroad, or do they constitute a new wave of Jewish immigration to the United States? What are their occupations and how do they spend their free time? How do Israelis at home relate to those who have left the country, and how do American Jews receive the newcomers? What are the policies of the Jewish communal organizations for dealing with Israelis in New York?

In the five articles that follow we have attempted to answer these and other questions about the New York Israeli community. Earlier versions of these papers were presented in November 1983 at a conference on Israelis in New York, jointly sponsored by the Center for Jewish Studies of the City University of New York Graduate Center and the Institute for the Study of Modern Jewish Life of the City College. In the articles, analytic methods vary from surveys to literary interpretation to participant observation, and each paper represents the individual author's point of view on the subject of Israelis in New York. But the articles share the recognition of the need to examine this little-studied but highly controversial community from a scholarly, nonpolitical perspective.

By presenting a multifaceted description of the Israeli community in New York, we have tried to illuminate some of the existential, ideological, and organizational dilemmas of New York Israelis and American Jews without passing moral judgment on these issues. We hope that this collection will stimulate further research in this area and will contribute to the sociological study of contemporary Jewry.

9

Israelis in New York

Paul Ritterband

Israelis residing abroad are perceived as a problem both by Israelis at home and by Diaspora Jews. Because they have lived in Israel (and increasingly have been born in Israel) and having decided to leave Israel, their very existence abroad is construed as a rejection of the ideals upon which Israeli society was built. In 1976, then Prime Minister Yitzhak Rabin referred to Israelis abroad as *"nefolet shel nemushot,"* the fallen among the weaklings (cited in Waxman 1983,198). As has been pointed out frequently, rejection of the emigrant from Israel is built into the structure of the Hebrew language. An immigrant to or from anywhere but the Land of Israel is known simply as a *m'hager*, a morally neutral term simply meaning immigrant. An immigrant in the Land of Israel is an *oleh*, one who goes up, a term borrowed from its religious usage referring to *oleh regel*, a pilgrim. One who emigrates from the Land of Israel is a *yored*, one who descends from the holiness of the Land of Israel to the profane world of the exile.

Though most Israelis do not consciously carry the religious vocabulary with all of its overtones into their day-to-day lives, they do grow up with a sense of the centrality of the Land of Israel in the experience of the Jewish people. With that sense comes the moral obligation to live in the Land of Israel. The Israeli folksinger and composer Naomi Shemer recently wrote and recorded a song embodying these sentiments. Parodying Psalm 132 and the Hatikvah, she writes of Hayim "a golden boy," born in Jerusalem and now living in exile (i.e. out of the Land of Israel). Hayim and Tsvikah and the other young men sing the words of the Psalm of the Jews who wept in exile on the banks of the rivers of Babylon as they remembered Zion. The Land of Israel, which has waited for the Jewish people for two thousand years, continues to wait for their return (Shemer 1982).

One Israeli expatriate journalist writing in an American Zionist journal of his own experience and that of his compatriots in the United States entitled his article "Israelis in the America—Moral Lepers" (Nahshon 1976). It is difficult to conjure harsher language in describing or labeling the Israeli who has migrated abroad. Yet, the reality is that during the entire period of Zionist settlement on the land, many Jews migrated to Israel from Europe, then reemigrated out of the Land of Israel to a second exile. There were years in which Jewish out-migration from Israel was greater than Jewish in-migration.

In addition to being a moral problem for the Israeli at home, expatriate Israelis, particularly the well-educated expatriates, are accused of having taken the investment that Israeli society has made in them and used it for their own profit abroad without recompense to the Israeli taxpayer. This perspective on the problem became termed the "brain drain" during the 1960s. Expatriate Israelis are viewed as having taken the investment made in them by Israeli society to a richer society, e.g. the United States.

Given the enormous concern about the Israeli abroad expressed in Israel and the Diaspora communities, one would have expected to find a substantial scholarly and scientific literature on this population. In fact the corpus of scientific literature is quite small.[1] In searching the literature, I could find but one book on the subject (my own) and less than a dozen articles (Ritterband 1978). To paraphrase Steven M. Cohen's insightful essay in this collection, the Israeli abroad is handled in part by denial and in part by outrage; neither of these modes of thought leads to understanding. The purpose of this collection of papers is to advance understanding, not to stand in judgment. While the authors may well have moral positions on the issues, they have set them aside so as to clarify the issues without preachment.

In this paper I will first present some estimate of the size of the Israeli expatriate population in the New York area. That area consists of New York City and the suburban counties of Nassau, Suffolk, and Westchester. Second, I will compare the Israelis with non-Israeli Jews in New York with respect to basic "secular" characteristics. Third, I will deal with the Jewishness of the Israelis in New York.

Estimating the Number of Israelis in the Eight-County New York Area

One might think that counting Israelis is a straightforward simple proposition. In fact, it is not. There are problems of population definition, sample frames, sampling error, and all of the other complications that lurk in wait for the social scientist. There is a wide array of estimates of the number of Israelis (1) living abroad, (2) living in the United States, (3) living in the New York area. The major published estimates as well as some of my own estimates are presented in table 9.1.

At various times Israel's Central Bureau of Statistics (CBS) has published estimates of the number of Israelis residing abroad worldwide. These numbers are necessarily problematic because the CBS has no way of properly enumerating Israeli expatriates. What it can and does do is develop estimates using information collected through passport control

TABLE 9.1
Estimates of the Number of Israelis Abroad

Source	Number
Worldwide	
Israel CBS, 1971 (cited in Guttman and Elizur, 1972)	over 200,000
Israel CBS, 1978 (cited in Elizur, 1980)	over 300,000
United States	
Kass and Lipset, 1979	300,000 (70,000-100,000 in Los Angeles area)
Lass and Lipset, 1982	over 350,000 (70,000-100,000 in Los Angeles area)
Goran, 1980	"as many as 300,000"
Lahis, 1980 (cited in Herman and LaFontaine, 1982)	300,000-500,000 (120,000 in Los Angeles area, 220,000 in New York)
Herman and LaFontaine, 1982	100,000-130,000 in the United States (55,000 in New York area, 13,000 in Los Angeles area)
NYJPS, 1981 (New York area only)	
Jewish householders born in Israel	17,200
Households headed by a Jewish person born in Israel	15,300
Persons in households headed by a Jewish person born in Israel	51,500
Jewish persons in households headed by a Jewish person born in Israel	48,400

TABLE 9.1 (continued)

Source	Number
PUMS (U.S. Census) 1980 (New York area only)	
Householders born in Israel	12,200
All persons born in Israel	18,320
Jewish householders born in Israel	11,400
Households headed by a Jewish person born in Israel	10,020
Persons in households headed by a Jewish person born in Israel	31,060
All persons born in Israel adjusted for under-reported illegals (18,320 x 1.27)	23,270
Jewish householders born in Israel adjusted for under-reported illegals (11,400 x 1.27)	14,480
Households headed by a Jewish person born in Israel adjusted for under-reported illegals (10,020 x 1.27)	12,730
Persons in households headed by a Jewish person born in Israel adjusted for under-reported illegals (31,060 x 1.27)	39,450

at the borders to count Israelis entering and leaving the country. This method obviously has many problems, and we would not expect the estimates to have a high degree of validity.

For present purposes for the United States and the New York area population, I have presented five published estimates in addition to my own estimates. Four of the published estimates present a figure of approximately 300,000 in the United States. One of these estimates proposes that there are at minimum 300,000 and at maximum 500,000 Israelis in the United States. These figures would make the Israelis somewhere between 5 percent and 10 percent of the U.S. Jewish population. That is, on a random basis, one out of twenty to one out of ten American Jews a person would encounter would be an Israeli. That does not jibe with the experience that most observers of the U.S. Jewish community seem to have. To complicate matters, the published estimates cited, more often than not, do not report the method used in arriving at their numbers nor do they tell us their definition of an Israeli. The estimate of 100,000 to 130,000 Israelis in the United States reported by Herman and LaFontaine is the only one to give us precise information on method and definition of the population.

Herman and LaFontaine (1982, 50) take as an Israeli a person who reported Israeli birth or nationality to the Immigration and Naturalization Service (INS) upon entering the United States. They do not include the American-born children of Israelis resident in the United States. For evidence they used records of the INS. Their method is too complex to report in detail here but they give every appearance of being rigorous and thorough. Their estimates are far below those of other sources presented in table 9.1 for the United States and for the New York and Los Angeles areas, the two regions in the country that all agree have the largest concentration of Israelis.

My own estimates are based upon two sources, the New York Jewish Population Study (NYJPS) and the Public Use Microdata Sample (PUMS) of the 1980 decennial census. Using the NYJPS, I estimate that there were 17,200 householders born in Israel in the New York area in 1980.[2] Consistent with census usage, the term *householder* applies equally to husbands and wives. The total number of households in which there is either a male or female Israeli-born householder is 15,300. The total number of persons in a household headed by an Israeli-born house-holder is 51,500, and the total number of Jewish persons in these households is 48,400. There is a second and broader but less precise definition of *Israeli households* that includes both those in which at least one householder was born in Israel and those in which at least one house-holder was not born in either Israel or the United States but who lived in Israel for a year or more. Using that definition, the area has 24,500 Israeli households containing 84,300 persons, of whom 81,900 are Jewish.

It should be kept in mind that both these definitions require that we count as Israeli not only the householder who was born or lived in Israel for a year or more but the American-born spouse and/or children of the Israeli householder. The American-born could be holding dual nationality and thus could be counted both as Americans in New York and Israelis abroad. The complexities of identification and enumeration are evident and confounding.

The last data set comes from the PUMS file of the 1980 United States census.[3] Enumerating within the same eight-county area we find just slightly over 12,000 *householders* born in Israel, and just over 18,000 *persons* born in Israel. Emigration from Israel as a Jewish social problem is concerned with the migration of Jews, but not all of the emigrants from Israel are Jews. Cross tabulating Israeli birth of householders with the new ancestry question posed by the census, we find that 8 percent of the *yordim* report their ancestry as "Arabian," "Jordanian," "Palestinian," or "Armenian." Cross tabulating ancestry with language use, we find that most of the members of these ancestry groups report the use of Arabic or Armenian at home. One "Palestinian" householder reports using Yiddish as his language at home; perhaps he is a member of one of the ultra-orthodox Jewish communities that still withhold recognition from the State of Israel. Removing the probably non-Jewish Israelis from the population leaves 11,400 Israeli Jewish householders and 10,020 Israeli households holding 31,060 persons. These numbers are substantially smaller than those generated by the NYJPS, and much smaller than the previously published estimates presented in table 9.1.

It is of course possible that the Israeli emigrants disproportionately refused to respond to the NYJPS telephone interview, and it is equally possible that there were Israeli illegal immigrants who feared responding to the U.S. census and thus do not appear on the census tapes. As to a possible undercount in the NYJPS, we can only point to corroborating evidence for the NYJPS as a whole and for specific subpopulations that testifies to the accuracy of the population numbers generated by the survey (Ritterband and Cohen 1984,71-79). The Bureau of the Census estimates that there were approximately 23,000 illegal Israelis in the entire United States in 1980 (Warren and Passel 1983; Passel 1983). With New York holding about half of the legal Israelis, we can infer that New York probably holds about the same proportion of Israeli illegals, giving us between 11,000 and 12,000 Israeli illegals in the New York area. The Bureau of the Census believes that well over a third of the illegals were enumerated; thus we can conclude that in the New York area there were about 6,900 Israeli-born persons (= .6 x 11,500) not enumerated in the 1980 U.S. census. Adding 6,900 to the reported census count of Israelis gives us an estiamte of 23,270 Israeli-born persons, or 27 percent more than the officially reported estimate. We still cannot state with absolute certitude precisely how many Israelis there are in the New York area but we now have a good sense of the order of magnitude. We now increase all of our official estimates by 27 percent. Using the NYJPS and PUMS files, we conclude that Israeli-born Jews and their household members (irrespective of country of birth) number between 40,000 and 50,000 persons. All Israeli-born persons, including estimated unenumerated illegals, number almost 25,000 individuals. Using data from Herman and LaFontaine, we estimate that for every two immigrants born in Israel there is another Israeli national not born in Israel, and not born in the United States. We therefore estimate that there are approximately 35,000 to 40,000 Israeli nationals in the New York area including those born in Israel and those born in a country other than the United States or Israel, but not including the U.S.-born children of Israeli nationals. This number is somewhat lower than the Herman-LaFontaine estimate.

Counting Israelis requires that we first define *Israelis*. Given the problems of establishing a "correct" definition, we have here estimates using various definitions. Readers are free to choose which definition they wish to work with, and for that definition estimates are given. It should be noted that the estimates presented here are inconsistent with those of Kass and Lipset (1979), and Goren (1980), but are of the same order of magnitude of Herman and LaFontaine.

The Social Characteristics of New York's Israeli Households

In this section we will briefly review some of the major socioeconomic characteristics of the Israeli households and householders in the New York area. Where available, data will be presented both from the 1980 PUMS and the NYJPS. Where appropriate, comparisons will be made with the non-Israeli Jewish population of the area as reported in the NYJPS. It should be remembered that both the census and the NYJPS findings are based upon small samples. The sample size for the PUMS census file is 570, and the unweighted sample for Israelis in the NYJPS is 94 cases. Given small sample size, we would expect some discrepancies between the two data sets, but with the exception of education and income, the two samples are remarkably close to each other. The data for this discussion are presented in table 9.2.

County of Residence

Israelis are much less likely to live in the three suburban counties than are other New York area Jews. Generally, relatively few first-generation Jews live in the suburbs, and Brooklyn houses a disproportionate fraction of first-generation Jews, including Israelis. The spatial distribution of Israelis is consistent with their immigrant status, and as we shall note further along, with their religious traditionalism as well.

Age of Head of Household

Because the young tend to have the most to gain and the least to lose from immigration, immigrant populations tend to be quite young. The young have a long time over which they can amortize the costs of their migration. About seven of ten Sabra householders are between twenty-five and forty-four years of age, compared with only four in ten of other New York Jewish householders.

TABLE 9.2
Basic Socioeconomic Characteristics of Sabras and
Other Jews in the New York Area

	Israelis		Other
	Census	NYJPS	New York Jews
A. County of Residence (%)			
Bronx	3	3	6
Brooklyn	41	35	24
Manhattan	19	21	23
Queens	24	23	19
Richmond	1	2	1
Westchester	2)	*)	6)
Nassau	7)11	10)16	15)27
Suffolk	2)	6)	6)
B. Age of Head(s) of Household (%)			
24 or less	10	3	4
25-44	67	73	38
45-64	16	20	41
65 or more	8	3	17
C. Period entered United States (%)			
Born to U.S. parents	2		
1975-80	20	14	
1970-74	20	22	
1965-69	13	8	
1960-64	13	28	
1950-59	22	19	
Before 1950	12	10	
D. Current Marital Status (%)			
Married	76	86	63
Widowed	5	2	10
Divorced	7	4	7
Separated	2	*	2
Never married	10	9	17
E. Mean Household Size	3.16	3.51	2.45
F. Country of Birth of Spouse (%)			
Israel	18	11	
United States	46	44	
Other	35	46	

TABLE 9.2 (continued)

G. Education of Head(s) of Household (%)			
No higher education	45	33	28
Some college	17	12	17
College graduate	18	36	34
Graduate training	20	20	21
H. Household Income (%)			
Less than 20,000	52	29	32
20-29,999	23	36	23
30-39,999	10	8	17
40-59,999	9	15	13
60,000 and up	6	16	15
I. Ancestry (% Mid-East or North African)	16	7	
J. Citizenship Status (%)			
Naturalized	65		
Not citizen	34		
Born to U.S. Citizen	2		

Period of Migration

About two out of five of the Sabra householders came to the United States during the 1970s. The apparent bunching up of the immigrant population during the most recent decade could lead one to believe that migration from Israel is on the increase. However, the pool of the Israeli-born has been growing rapidly. It is more likely that the large number of migrants in the 1970s reflects the change in the source pool of adult native-born Israelis than it does a change in ideology, opportunity structure, or other immigration-generating factors. It has also been suggested that migration from Israel tends to increase right after wars. Though the small size of our samples precludes making a definitive statement, analysis of the data on a year-by-year basis does not show increases following wars.

Current Marital Status

Israeli householders are more likely than are other New York Jews to report that they are married. They also report a somewhat lower rate of divorce (as a fraction of the ever married).

Mean Household Size

The Israeli age distribution and marital status would lead one to expect a relatively large average household size. Though there is a discrepancy between the estimates for the two Israeli samples, both samples report average household size much larger than that for other area Jews.

Country of Birth of Spouse

In both samples almost half of the spouses of the Israeli-born householders were born in the United States. It is likely to be the case that a very large fraction of the Israeli migration consists of the movement of single persons rather than whole families. This finding has important implications for our estimate of the number of Israelis in the area. By counting all members of the Israeli-headed household as Israelis, we are including a large number of native-born Americans, thus inflating the count of Israelis inappropriately.

Education and Income

Education and income are the two areas in which the two samples give seriously discrepant estimates. The estimates are internally consistent, i.e. the NYJPS estimates for both education and income are higher than those based upon the federal census. The NYJPS estimate of both variables for Israelis are quite close to those reported for all area Jews; the census estimates are considerably lower. I have no way of knowing which is closer to the truth.

Ancestry

The ancestry issue is handled quite differently in the two sources. The census presented an open-ended question to which the respondent was expected to declare "self-origin, descent, lineage, nationality, group or country in which the person or person's parents or ancestors were born before their arrival in the United States." This question replaced the question that had been asked in 1970 and prior decennial censuses in which the respondent was asked to report the country of birth of his or her parents. For the NYJPS, we report the country of birth of parents. For both samples, we exclude from the analysis those who gave either no response or reported Israel (i) as country of birth/ancestry. In both samples it is clear that Oriental Jews are a small fraction of the migrants.

Citizenship

A small fraction (2%) of Israelis held U.S. citizenship through their parents. In all, two-third of the Israelis were U.S. citizens. The holding of U.S. citizenship usually means that the Israeli will not be returning home (see Ritterband 1978:32).

The Jewishness of New York's Israelis

The popular image of Israeli expatriates is that they are decidedly secular and quite distant from the local Jewish community. The NYJPS data suggest that the image is a distorted one. The data for this discussion are presented in table 9.3. Part A of the table presents information on the household as a unit. In that section we have information on all households in which at least one of the householders is Israeli-born, whether or not the reporting head is him/herself Israeli. In Part B, where we ask about religious observances in the family of origin as well as in the respondent's own home, we restrict our sample to the Israeli-born householders. That is done to be able to distinguish between Israeli and other (usually U.S.) socialization and intergenerational shifts in religious observance.

The data in part A report on three dimensions of Jewishness: social,

TABLE 9.3
Measures of Jewishness

A. Social Indicators (%)	Israelis	Other New York Jews		
3 closest friends Jews	89	68		
Very important to live among Jews	76	49		
Belong to Jewish organization outside of synagogue	31	32		
Orthodox	42	11		

B. Ritual Observance (% observing)	Respondent		Parents	
	Israelis	Other N.Y. Jews	Israelis	Other N.Y. Jews
Passover Seder	93	87	98	90
Chanukah candles	93	73	98	83
Yom Kippur fast	86	65	84	82
Mezuzah on door	91	65	98	77
Sabbath candles	78	35	76	63
Kosher meat only	52	31	63	59
2 Sets of dishes	49	25	57	52
No money on Sabbath	30	10	51	25
Fast of Esther	24	6	39	18

C. Mean Ritual Score (maximum = 9)	5.95	3.97	6.77	5.71

religious, and organizational. Making distinctions among dimensions of Jewishness is admittedly problematic; however, a substantial body of literature and face validity suggest that the distinctions lead to useful results.

On the social dimension, Israelis are significantly more likely to report that all three of their closest friends are Jewish. They are also more likely to report that living among a sizeable number of Jews is very important to them. On the religious dimension, Israelis are more likely to identify with one of the "denominational" groupings, particularly the most traditionalist Orthodox group. When it comes to nonsynagogal organizational memberships and affiliations, Israelis are about as likely to be joiners as are other New York Jews. For the population as a whole, the three dimensions of Jewishness are related, i.e. the more the more. Other things being equal, then, one would expect the Israelis' level of organizational affiliation to be higher, given their higher scores on ethnicity and religious traditionalism. This is not the case. American and Israeli Jews are equally likely to be members of nonsynagogal Jewish organizations. As has been frequently noted, organizational affiliation and voluntarism are peculiarly American habits. Americans are joiners. The affiliational behavior of American Jews is as much American as it is Jewish.

In part B of table 9.3 we present the current ritual observances of Israelis and Americans and the ritual observances in their parental homes while they were growing up. We will want to compare across generations within nationality groups and across nationality groups within generations. Given the fact that a higher fraction of Israelis report themselves to be Orthodox, it is no surprise that Israeli respondents report higher levels of ritual observances when rituals are considered individually and when a summary score of rituals is computed. Even within the Orthodox group, Israelis are more rigorous in their observances. For example, 64 percent of the Orthodox Israelis observe the Fast of Esther, compared with only 42 percent of the other Orthodox.

In comparing respondent observance with respondents' parental observance, we expect to find some level of intergenerational decline as families move from traditional to modern (= secular) societies. This in fact is what we do find; however, the Israelis and the other Jewish New Yorkers report very different experiences in degree. Among non-Israelis there is a serious intergenerational decline in observance beginning with the Yom Kippur fast; for Israelis there is no point at which there is a sharp intergenerational decline. Indeed, there are some instances of statistically insignificant intergenerational increase.

The intergenerational picture is made clearer still by examining the summary scores for the two samples presented in part C. The American respondent score is 67 percent of the Israeli respondent score, while the American parent score is 85 percent of the Israeli parent score. American parents are closer to their Israeli counterparts than are American respondents to their counterparts. Examining scores within nationality groups, we find that Israeli respondents' ritual score is 84 percent of their parents' score; the American respondents', only 68 percent. The Americans start with a lower level of parental traditionalism, but, more significantly, American parents are less successful in reproducing traditional Jewish observance intergenerationally than are the Israelis. There appears to be something about Israeli socialization that makes it possible to maintain traditionalism in the face of the powerful forces of secularization.

Conclusion

This paper deals with three issues: numbers of Israelis, secular social characteristics of Israelis, and Jewishness of Israelis. With respect to the first and third of these issues, the findings presented here are greatly at variance with popular perceptions. There are many fewer Israelis than is usually estimated, and they are far more traditionally religious than is usually thought. Why the discrepancies between popular judgment and data-based estimates is itself an interesting question.

American Jewish estimators no doubt remember meeting Israelis more than they remember encountering local Jews. The purportedly ubiquitous Israeli taxi driver in New York turns out to be a myth (see Korazim and Freedman in this section). Those who exist are simply more likely to be remembered by their New York Jewish passengers. Israeli estimators make a moral point when they present their numbers. Those who do not succumb to the lure of the golden exile are morally superior. Their superiority grows with the growth in the number of *yordim*.

On the question of Jewishness, here, too, I propose selective misperception. The Orthodox Israelis settle in Orthodox communities in New York. In many ways, Boro Park and B'nai Brak have more to do with one another than either has with its secular conationals. The Orthodox Israelis do not become part of the community of "uprooted" Israelis who seek ways of remaining Israelis while yet abroad. The Orthodox Israelis, by virtue of their integration into the local Orthodox network, do not seek services and other resources from the larger Jewish community. Thus they remain invisible to the "secular" Jewish agencies and "secular" observers. The visible Israelis are the secular Israelis, but their number and proportion are both exaggerated.

Notes

1. This has been the experience of other investigators as well. See Kass and Lipset 1982, 289.
2. The NYJPS collected information using both random digit dialing (RDD) and a distinctive Jewish name (DJN) list. Because Israeli and U.S. Jews do not have the same pattern of family names, the analysis in this paper is based upon the RDD sample only.
3. I am grateful to Tony Bernard of the CUNY Data Service for helping me work through the PUMS files.

References

Elizur, Dov. 1980. "Israelis in the United States." In *American Jewish Year-book* 80:53-67.

Goren, Arthur. 1980. "Jews." In *Harvard Encyclopedia of American Ethnic Groups*, ed. Stephan Thernstrom et al., 571-98. Cambridge: Harvard University Press.

Guttman, Louis, and Elizur, Dov. 1972. "Factors Influencing the Reimmigration of Israelis Living Abroad." In *The Israel Yearbook*, pp. 141-43. Jerusalem.

Herman, Pini, and LaFontaine, David. 1982. "In Our Footsteps: Israeli Migration to the United States and Los Angeles." Master's thesis, Hebrew Union College-Jewish Institute of Religion and the University of Southern California.

Kass, Drora, and Lipset, Seymour Martin. 1982. "Jewish Immigration to the United States from 1967 to the Present: Israelis and Others." In *Understanding American Jewry*, ed. Marshall Sklare, 272-94. New Brunswick, N.J.: Transaction Books.

Nahshon, Gad. 1976. "Israelis in American." *Midstream 22*, no. 8 (October).

Passel, Jeffrey S. 1983. Personal communication to Pini Herman, May 19.

Ritterband, Paul. 1978. *Education, Employment and Migration.* New York: Cambridge University Press.

Ritterband, Paul, and Cohen, Steven M. 1984. *The Jewish Population of Greater New York: A Profile*. New York: Federation of Jewish Philanthropies.

Shemer, Naomi. 1982. "New Babylon," recorded in collection, El Borot Ha'Mayim. Tel Aviv: CBS Records.

Warren, Robert, and Passel, Jeffrey S. 1983. "Estimates of Illegal Aliens from Mexico Counted in the 1980 United States Census." Paper presented at the annual meeting of the Population Association of America.

Waxman, Chaim. 1983. *American's Jews in Transition*. Philadelphia: Temple University Press.

10

The "Wandering Israeli" in Contemporary Israeli Literature

Yael Zerubavel

Among recurring themes in contemporary Israeli fiction one can easily identify the theme of the "wandering Israeli." Israeli literature deals with Israelis who left the country and found a temporary or permanent home abroad, and those who live in Israel but constantly dream about life in a faraway country. It describes wandering Israelis' relationships with family and friends in Israel and abroad, and explores their inner world and social environment, motives, and views. Obviously, fiction does not claim to offer a sociological analysis of social facts. Nonetheless, these works portray an interesting and intricate picture and provide us with access to a level of meaning that is often missing from statistical and journalistic treatments of the subject.

This article focuses on several works of fiction written by Israelis in Hebrew and published in Israel during the last few years: Aharon Megged's *Journey in the Month of Av* (1980), Yotam Reuveni's "Mixed Tendency" (1982), Amos Oz's *A Perfect Peace* (1982), Yizhak Ben-Ner's *A Distant Land* (1982), Amnon Jackont's *Borrowed Time* (1982), A.B. Yehoshua's *Late Divorce* (1982), and Arie Semo's *Masquerade* (1983). Although the centrality of the issue of wandering to these works varies, they allow us to make some initial observations about the treatment of the wandering Israeli in contemporary Hebrew literature.

Even though the problem of emigration from Israel is by no means limited to Israeli-born Jews, it is quite revealing that Israeli literature deals primarily with Sabras who become wandering Israelis. Obviously, this focus reflects the Israeli preoccupation with the most painful aspect of *yerida*, namely, the emigration of Israeli-born. Indeed, within the framework of the Zionist ideology, the very combination of these two—"Sabra" and "wandering"—seems like a contradiction in terms. For the generation of the pioneers, the Sabra symbolized the hope to

create a new type of Jew in the land of Israel: young, energetic, resource-
ful, assertive, and self-reliant. Above all, the new Jew was to be rooted in
his or her land, the Land of Israel, in contrast to the wandering Jew of
the Diaspora. It was generally assumed that by reaching the "promised
land," the old wandering Jew would finally arrive at the end of his
historical journey, never to wander again in far and foreign lands.[1]

The fundamental problem of the "wandering Israeli" is further
accentuated by the writers' choice of Sabras who are usually considered
as the "Sabra elite": they are Ashkenazi whose parents, who came to
Palestine as pioneers, are prominent politicians or educators; the sons
received a good Israeli education, volunteered to serve in combat units in
the army, or excelled in their studies. In short, these Israelis appear as
rooted in Israeli life as one could possibly be. Because they seem so
accomplished in Israeli terms, their wish to get away and try a new life
elsewhere reflects even more sharply the personal and ideological crisis
that ignited their urge to leave.

The emergence of wandering Israelis becomes a painful evidence of the
discrepancy between Israeli reality and the vision of the founding
fathers. From this perspective, not only those who have actually left the
country threaten to destroy early dreams about the Sabra and the Jewish
society in Israel but those who obsessively fantasize about life in another
place—even if they may never actually leave—are symbolically a part of
the syndrome of the wandering Isareli and, likewise, challenge the basic
premises of the Zionist dream. Whereas the early Zionists believed that
the return to Zion would solve the problem of the wandering Jew, the
wandering Israelis dream of their own salvation in faraway countries.

Within the context of the Israeli ideology and culture, it is *the wish* to
leave rather than the actual departure or the specific destination that
provides the basic dramatic and emotional tension in this literature. In *A
Distant Land*, Shuvali is obsessed with the dream of taking his large
extended family to New Zealand. Only there will he be able to see his
family peacefully united and prosperous. In his fantasy, his family will
live a utopian life on his farm, working the land together.[2] There is an
obvious historical irony in his attempt to describe his vision in conventional Zionist terminology:

> This is like old time *halutzuit* [pioneering], isn't it? he said passionately—
> like my father and mother who came from Russia. . . .What I have in mind
> is more *aliah* [immigration to Israel] than *yerida*. Just that. That's really
> *aliah*. That's what carries on what we all believed in once.[3]

Yonathan Lifshitz of Amos Oz's *Perfect Peace* spends most of his time thinking over his plan to leave his wife, his parents, and the kibbutz, yet has only a vague idea of where he will go: "His plan was to go as far as possible," for he felt that "it is necessary to go to a totally different environment."[4] For Yonathan, it is the need for dramatic change in his life that motivates him to leave rather than the precise nature of the place where he will go. Although he toys with the idea of traveling to the United States, he ends up in the Israeli desert. Similarly, Giddi of *Journey in the Month of Av* escapes to the desert in his attempt to avoid his family and evade the draft. Although both Yonathan and Giddi hide within Israeli territory, they choose to go to the wilderness, a symbolic no-man's land. It is the provocative act of hiding that is most significant in this context. In both cases, this could eventually lead into leaving Israeli territory, as Yonathan briefly attempts to do and Giddi may later try.

In his novel *Masquerade*, Arie Semo marks the failure of Daniel's attempt to settle back in Israel by the acquisition of a one-way ticket abroad with unmarked destination. The search for his past roots that began with his farewell to New York ends with his departure from Tel-Aviv. Accepting his fate as a "modern wandering Jew," Daniel does not care where he will go.[5] Symbolically, the destination of his last flight from Israel remains unknown.

Along the same lines, Yotam Reuveni's short story "Mixed Tendency" deals with Omer Shlakhin's self-examination before leaving Israel for the United States. After saying farewell to his family and friends, Omer moves into a Tel-Aviv hotel to think over his decision to leave. Hiding among tourists in his own country, Omer examines his reasons for going to the United States for an unlimited period. The reader assumes that Omer will eventually leave the country, but the story ends without a confirmation of this assumption. Within the framework of Israeli literature, the desire to leave and the reasons for leaving are more important than the actual experience abroad.

Whereas the early Zionists yearned for the warmth of the Mediterranean sun, the wandering Israelis often look to the northern countries to cure them from the heat and pressure of life in Israel. It is in the heat of summer that Daniel's apparent reintegration into Israeli society begins to fall apart, and he yearns for the outside world:

> It is still very hot. I listen to the weather forecast. It depresses me when they announce a heat-wave. I detest streams of sweat. They mark—so it seems to me—the disintegration of the body. I walk along the street and decompose within the fetid crowd in the process of decay.[6]

As the situation deteriorates further, Daniel feels increasingly alienated from his friends, family, and work, and experiences a severe anxiety attack in the midst of a summer night. In describing this haunting nightmare, Arie Semo uses imagery often associated with hell: darkness, fog, fire, the smell of burning pitch, and the odor of death and decay. In this context, Daniel's dreams of "far districts of northern legends" or life in a small village built upon snow-covered slopes reinforce his final resolution to leave: "Far and cold countries await me and I cannot linger anymore."[7]

A similar contrast between the tormenting heat in Israel and the inviting coolness of other countries also appears in *A Distant Land, Journey in the Month of Av*, and *Late Divorce*. The heat and the sweat inflame Shuvali's anger and the motionless air seems to reflect his own feeling of being hopelessly stuck.[8] His fantasy of green forests and blue lakes in New Zealand temporarily relieves him from the intense blinding light of the sun that turns his taxi into a "prison of heated steel."[9] Aharon Megged uses similar imagery in describing the abrupt transition from life in the United States to the heat of midsummer in Israel. As Daniel Levine leaves the green lawns, the trees, and flowers of a quiet university town, he feels totally invaded by the heat and the light of Israeli summer. Pain and fury, altars, and death become a part of his vision in the journey through the desert and into his own past.[10] For Kaminka of *Late Divorce*, life in Israel is marked by aging, madness, and confinement. In contrast, the "quiet and cool Diaspora" is associated with rejuvenation and an unexpected surge of creativity and fertility in his old age.[11]

While the Sabra was often described in early Israeli literature as "the son," the literature about wandering Israelis often relates to them as "the lost sons." In fact, in four of the literary works discussed here, sons intentionally get lost by hiding: Omer Shlakhin and Yonathan Lifshitz leave without informing their families and friends where they stay. Giddi Levine and Arik Ben-Dor hide not only from friends and relatives but also from the authorities: Giddi escapes from the Israeli army, and Arik hides from the Israeli secret service.

The theme of the "lost son" is most striking in *Borrowed Time* and *Journey in the Month of Av*. In the former, Arik Ben-Dor, who serves in Teheran, cuts himself off from the secret service and disappears without leaving any trace. The book revolves around the search for Arik and the secret service's attempt to bring him back to Israel. Because Arik is the son of a famous Israeli politician, the service relates to him as a collective symbol and acts as if it has a claim on his life. Although Arik himself is a middle-aged person and his father is long dead, he continues to serve the

sociological role of a "son," and Kugel, who conducts the search for
him, represents the "father." Even when Arik becomes very ill and
transforms into an aging man, Kugel still regards him as the child who
needs to be disciplined for his own good as well as for others' benefit.

The search for a lost son is the focus of the novel *Journey in the Month
of Av*. Here, Daniel Levine presents an interesting case, because he
functions as both a father and a son. As the son of a prominent figure in
the Labor party, he shares the "symptoms" of the "lost son" who
wanders away in search of his individual needs. Daniel, the scientist, first
uses outer space as a way to wander away from Israeli reality and the
pressures at home. Later, his scientific pursuit leads him to the United
States, where he wishes to extend his one-year stay for at least another
year or two. However, if Daniel has the potential of remaining a
wandering Israeli as a son, as a father he feels bound to the Land of
Israel by the blood of his elder son, Nonni, who was killed during the
war. Even as he thinks of staying abroad, he says to himself:

> Forever—no. We have a family grave. And he said to himself: To die, only
> there![12]

> To die—it should be there. Near Nonni. At his side. Not in the snow, in a
> foreign land. On the sun-heated ground.[13]

But Daniel is forced to return to Israel because of his younger son,
Giddi, who disappeared so as to evade the draft. As he travels through
the desert in search of Giddi, Daniel also begins an inner journey by
examining his relationship with his father, wife, and two sons. (The
Hebrew title of the novel, *Massa Be'Av*, has, in fact, a double meaning.
It implies both "a journey in the month of Av," as the official English
translation suggests, but it also means "a journey within a father.")
During this journey we learn that in rejecting his pregnant lover, Daniel
also lost a third son through abortion a few years earlier. Although at the
outset of his journey, Daniel still has a chance of regaining his only living
son, Giddi, he eventually neglects the search for him and wanders away,
following the route to the place where he lost his elder son, Nonni.
Obviously, for Daniel, the trauma of Nonni's loss in the war is more
intense than the problem he faces with the younger son who ran away.
But by choosing to go after Nonni, whom he loved more but could not
bring back to life, the father ultimately misses his last opportunity to
bring back the other son and loses him forever.

In a country like Israel, where parents often lose sons in wars, the
theme of the lost son in reference to wandering Israelis is particularly
significant. Whereas the loss of a son in war conforms to Israeli patriotic

sentiments and the value of sacrificing for the country, the loss through wandering clearly violates basic Israeli norms and values. Although in both cases parents lose their sons, there is a fundamental difference in the social meaning attributed to this loss. In the context of Israeli national ideology, the wandering Israeli betrays the very cause for which the sons who are lost in war gave up their lives. Nonetheless, the two kinds of losses have become part of Israeli reality and, as the literature suggests, are interrelated. As we shall see later, the stale political situation and the constant threat of death intensify the wandering Israelis' desire to break away from a reality that offers no real hope for the future.

Whereas all the other wandering Israelis we deal with are Israeli-born, Yehuda Kaminka of *Late Divorce* was born in Eastern Europe and came to Palestine as a young man. Kaminka, who belongs to the generation of the pioneers, leaves his mentally ill wife and his grown-up children and goes to the United States. In his desire to begin a new life there, Kaminka resembles other wandering Israelis. But as a father and a founder, he disrupts the sociological pattern of wandering Israelis. By raising the theme of the "lost father" instead of the "lost son," A.B. Yehoshua deliberately creates a role reversal consistent with the history of distorted relationships within the Kaminka family. The father who expected his sons to act as judges and protectors toward him and his wife continues to play the role of the son when he leaves. While his impotent young son cannot have children, the sixty-five-year-old father expects a new baby abroad. Under the stress of the late divorce, it is the grandson, and not Yehuda, who suffers chest pains and is hurried to the hospital. It is only when Yehuda Kaminka dies that the "lost father" is recovered by his sons and the Kaminka family's role relations might become less confused.

In accounting for their wish to leave, wandering Israelis emphasize the need for a change of environment that will allow them the personal space they lack at home. In referring to their life in Israel, they often use metaphors of imprisonment and suffocation. Shuvali feels that he is trapped in a situation that offers him only increasing pain and embarrassment. Burdened by mounting economic pressures, his sons' moral deterioration, and the disintegration of his large family, Shuvali sees no way out of this inevitable process of decline. His dream of life in New Zealand allows him to experience the freedom and the open space that he misses so greatly in Israel and provides a new, if unreal, frontier for striving for a better future.

Feeling oppressed in a small, tightly knit society, wandering Israelis often express their need to find their own way in life without the constant direction and interference of parents, relatives, and the society at large. At the age of twenty-six, Yonathan Lifshitz feels an intense urge to leave his wife, parents, and the kibbutz and start a new life. He is haunted by the feeling that if he does not make this move soon, it might be too late:

> In his childhood, as he was growing up, during his military service, he was always being surrounded by a close circle of men and women who never ceased interfering with his life. He began to feel that these people constricted him and there was no point in continuing to yield.[14]

Omer Shlakhin experiences a similar feeling of being constantly directed without having the capacity or right to choose:

> I am thirty one years old. And I don't know who Omer is. Everything I've done so far—and you can argue what that's worth—doesn't belong to me. I was steered and pushed and programmed. At least, in the beginning. Then I just acted out of inertia.[15]

Omer, who divorced his wife and left the kibbutz, presents his decision to go abroad as only one further step away from conformity. For him, the trip to the United States becomes an opportunity to assert his individuality and satisfy his need to define the future on his own terms.

The conflict between social control and individual needs is often manifested in the relationship between the parents and their sons. In *Masquerade*, much of Daniel's desire to break the law and do the unexpected stems from his anger at his father's rigid universe of rules. Similar is Giddi's reaction to his father's withdrawal into the world of science while rejecting Giddi and ignoring his needs. The frustration and anger toward parents is even more salient in those cases where the fathers belong to the generation of the pioneers. Typically, the fathers are portrayed in this literature as leading figures in the kibbutz or at the national level. Being used to leadership roles, they expect their sons to fully conform to their worldview and follow in their steps. Indeed, one often has the impression that these fathers feel more comfortable in their public roles than their roles as parents.

Inhibited by their fathers' overpowering presence and resentful of their verbosity and pathos, the sons often express their hostility by withdrawing into silence. This is the case with Yonathan Lifshitz, Daniel Levine, and Arik Ben-Dor, who choose to escape into silence and eventually to wander away than confront their parents with their own opinions and needs. The sons' desire to leave the country becomes another manifestation of their need to get away from their parents and establish their identity as independent, mature men. The fathers, who tend to celebrate themselves and the achievements of their generation, are often condescending toward, and overly critical of, their sons. Whereas the sons express the individual's right and need to determine the individual's own way, the fathers dismiss their sons' doubts as weaknesses, or answer them in the name of collective good:

> It doesn't suit me—said Yolek—I feel, I don't feel, it suits me, it doesn't suit me; what is it here. . . .Maybe you can explain to me once and for all what's the matter with you here; it suits me, it doesn't suit, self-realization, pampering, whims. . . .What does it mean 'it doesn't suit me' when someone talks to you about a job, eh?[16]

Kugel, the representative of the fathers' generation in *Borrowed Time*, says to Arik's friend:

> Your whole generation, ex-Palmachnicks, soldiers, kibbutzniks, politicians —you're all transparent. . . . When my generation was in charge, everything went much better. You have to admit it.[17]

The fathers of both Arik Ben-Dor and Omer Shlakhin tend to blame the next generation for the inevitable disparity between their old dreams and the present Israeli reality. Arik describes his father's attitude:

> My father had a dream. A magic, vague dream. Something that was born in Russia. His Land of Israel was kind of a heavenly Land of Israel: no Arabs, no melting pot, no heat waves, no inflation. . . .Then, when the country began to look like those who built it, he cried that they ruined his vision. . . .[18]

Omer portrays a similar picture:

> Now, after his wars and his sons' wars, he is still longing for this peace of the beginning. You can scream at him till you're blue in the face that it will never come back. . .we talked of this more than once. Like right after the Yom Kippur War. I asked him, 'what did you think?' And he blamed me and my commanders and my whole generation. 'In our time'. . .he said—'this wouldn't have happened.' I remarked that Golda was his peer, but he only smiled.[19]

In Amos Oz's novel, Yolek, the father, repeatedly expresses his contempt for the young generation:

> A kind of genetic collapse must have occurred here. . . .Where have we made mistakes, Srulik? Why did such pitiful guys like them grow here?[20]

In his long and silent inner monologue before he leaves, his son, Yonathan, expresses his own exasperation with his father's moral superiority:

> O.K. I'm contemptible, O.K. I'm a deserter whatever you say you're right you've taken hold of righteousness and it will always be yours. . . .[21]

Although the sons' urge to wander is largely motivated by personal needs, it is also, in part, a response to the social and political reality of Israel. The wandering Israelis who were raised on their parents' idealized image of Israel often express the feeling of being cheated and trapped in a hopeless situation. In *Journey in the Month of Av*, Daniel Levine experiences a sudden wave of terror when he realizes that he returned to a small besieged country whose fate is doomed "and sooner or later the end will come."[22] In *Masquerade*, Daniel remarks that the country's funeral has already started and he cannot stay there and join the funeral march.[23] Omer Shlakhin and Arik Ben-Dor, who used to be kibbutzniks and combat pilots, feel that they have gone through a deep change in their attitude toward the country. They who internalized the values of their parents and conformed to the social expectations of the Sabra have reached the point in their lives when they begin to question the political reality and ideological premises of Israeli society. Omer believes that his decision to leave the country is directly linked to the political change in Israel:

> It was that night we learned that Menahem Begin will be Prime-Minister. . . .Watching this strange old man march toward the central platform, I experienced the first shock.[24]

Omer maintains that the apathy and materialism of the silent majority in Israel leave the country at the hands of a few hundred extremists, and as a result, threaten any prospects of a real peace. He vehemently dismisses the assumption that the large wave of emigration from Israel is an "economic exodus" and argues: How can anyone believe that former kibbutzniks and paratroopers who were ready to sacrifice their lives for the country would leave it to become taxi drivers and mechanics?

Arik began to express his doubts following the Yom Kippur War. For the first time he confronted his father with his growing doubts about the future. He tells his friend about this last conversation he had with his father:

'They found the forgery,' I told him; 'Dad'—I told him—'they found the catch. . .' and he asked: 'What is the catch, Arik? What's wrong? What's wrong?' 'The future is wrong,' I told him. . . . 'The future is wrong. Anyone who stays here has to choose between a war that will eventually end up in disaster or a peace that will lead to assimilation and make all these wars that we've fought and will fight totally meaningless.'[25]

It is the menacing violence of the masses during the Islamic revolution in Iran that finally convinces Arik that Israel has no future. Life in Israel, he believes, is like a trap in which a time bomb will explode and shatter the Zionist dream to pieces:

We live at the mercy of borrowed time, a borrowed time that history has granted us absentmindedly. And now, time is running out. . . .And what do we do?. . . .I'm scared. Maybe I'm neurotic, disturbed. . .but history repeats itself! A few borrowed decades of war from within and without and at the end, what is the end? Destruction! You win one battle, two, a dozen, a hundred and twelve—and the war is still lost![26]

As if to indicate the process of "de-Sabraization" that takes place during this period, Arik Ben-Dor changes his name to Albert Bodinger, his father's old name. This name change is essentially the reversal of the Hebraization of names in Israel, which is one of the rites of passage into Israeli society. As his Hebrew name implies (Ben-Dor literally means "one generation old") Arik's Sabra image did not survive beyond one generation. The old Jewish identify surfaced from underneath the Israeli cover.

Arik deliberately wishes to peel off his Sabra image. However, in returning to the image of the wandering Jew, he also accepts his fate of wandering and persecution. Arik's friend, who remembers his youthful Sabra image before this change, comments:

Little has remained of you since you cut yourself off from the country. I almost didn't recognize you. . . .A body without a soul, a wandering Jew, faceless and hollow.[27]

Ironically, as a part of the historical reversal in this novel, it is the Israeli secret service that acts as the persecutor of the wandering Israeli. It forces Arik to wander from one country to another, to separate from his Palestinian lover and the child she adopted, and, finally, to give in.

Although Arik eventually dies, *Borrowed Time* shows that the ideological crisis does not end with him. While his friend is exploring Arik's motives for staying abroad, the friend undergoes a similar process of "de-Sabraization," including the name change, a relationship with a non-Jewish woman, and the plan to stay abroad. More dramatic is the transformation of Kugel, the man in charge of the search for Arik, from the persecuting Israeli to the sympathetic Jew. Although this change takes place too late for Arik to enjoy it, Kugel finally acknowledges the individual's right to have dreams of the individual's own, even if they merely provide an illusion of change and improvement.

Indeed, the literature about wandering Israelis shows us time and again that the wandering is ultimately a form of escape that cannot offer a long-lasting solution of fundamental problems. Whether the wandering Israelis dream about leaving or actually wander away from Israel, they can enjoy only a temporary relief from the immediate pressures of every-day life in Israel. Even when they seem to experience a new sense of freedom and creativity, these are inevitably short-lived. In this respect, there is no fundamental difference between those who leave Israel in fantasy or reality. In both cases, the wandering leads into the world of dream and illusion that, sooner or later, is bound to crumble.

The theme of escape and illusion is central to *Journey in the Month of Av*. Both father and son, Daniel and Giddi, attempt to find a new freedom (in the university in the United States and the desert resort, res-pectively). But the reader is well aware of the precarious nature of their escape and the limits of their freedom. In the idyllic atmosphere of his new home, Daniel suffers a heart attack. When he is finally forced out of his retreat by Giddi's decision to evade the draft, he is overwhelmed by the intense pain of his thoughts and memories. Although during his double journey Daniel acknowledges the extent to which he has used his work to escape from other realities, he is incapable of using these insights constructively. Replacing one form of escape by another, he lets the past take over the present and, once again, chooses Nonni over Giddi. His inability to confront the present is symbolized by his own collapse near Nonni's burned tank, marking his final escape from life to death. His son, Giddi, wishes to believe that he can now enjoy his newly gained free-dom in the hiding place. But whereas the sun, the beach, and his free-spirited friend are real, his liberation from his family and the Israeli army is only an illusion. Giddi continues to carry his parents' presence in his own mind as he mentally argues with them about the past and the future. It is also clear that eventually the military police will invade this natural paradise and his ultimate fall is inevitable.

Along similar lines, Arik Ben-Dor and Yehuda Kaminka only deluded themselves that they could find a better future outside Israel. Arik, who criticizes Israeli society for living on borrowed time, finally realizes that his time too is running out. If the State of Israel, according to Arik, has an unrealistic dream, his attempt to create a world of his own with a

Palestinian lover appears to be equally unrealistic. Likewise, Yehuda Kaminka returns to Israel to get a divorce from his institutionalized wife in order to protect his new American family. Although the purpose of the one-week visit is to seal off his past, as time progresses he becomes increasingly entangled in his past relationship with his Israeli family. By the time he obtains his legal freedom, he is totally imprisoned by his past. The divorce he desired for the sake of his American future acquires a new meaning for him in the context of his past relationship with his former wife:

> At the end, she expelled me from here. She managed to tear me away from here. She is punishing me for not losing my sanity, for refusing to fall into the pit with her.[28]

Underlying *Late Divorce* is a strong sense of historical determinism. Yehuda Kaminka cannot escape his fate. From this perspective, his stay in the United States is like "time out" during which he could briefly enjoy his rejuvenation. But faced again with his Israeli past, his American life gradually fades out until it becomes unreal as a dream. At the end, Yehuda incites his own murder, which he had managed to escape a few years earlier. His death is so much a direct continuation of his Israeli past that when his American lover finally arrives with his child, the Israeli family is shocked to remember that the American episode was indeed real. This visit also confirms the impression that, by escaping to the United States, Yehuda Kaminka only created an illusion of change. As his son-in-law remarks to Yehuda's daughter:

> It's amazing that your father went so far as America to find the very same thing he'd run away from.[29]

In contrast to these wandering Israelis, Omer Shlakhin of "Mixed Tendency" is aware of the limited freedom he is likely to enjoy abroad. Although the cold countries appeal to him, he knows that he will never be able to relinquish his bond to Israel. Like Isaac, he feels bound to the altar, but unlike him, he believes that he will remain bound forever, carrying the altar within him wherever he goes.[30]

If the literature suggests that wandering is a form of escape that eventually fails, one would suspect that it will attempt to present the return to Israel as the appropriate solution for wandering Israelis. And yet, in the works discussed here, one does not perceive a sense of relief with the return to Israel. In *Masquerade, Late Divorce,* and *Journey in the Month of Av*, the protagonists are overwhelmed by the renewed

contact with their families and the Israeli society. The failure of Daniel's
attempt to settle down in Israel after ten years of wandering abroad is the
essence of the novel *Masquerade*. In *Late Divorce* and *Journey in the
Month of Av*, Yehuda Kaminka and Daniel Levine unconsciously lead
themselves to their own deaths shortly after they return to Israel.
Similarly, the search for Arik Ben-Dor in *Borrowed Time* eventually
leads to his death: Although Arik's fragile world abroad collapsed, he
has no more a place in Israeli reality either.

It is interesting to note the recurrent theme of death in this literature.
As we have seen, three of the novels discussed here end with the
protagonist's death. In other works, wandering Israelis court death, or
think of it, although they stop short of suicide. Yonathan Lifshitz of *A
Perfect Peace* risks his life when he sneaks across the Jordanian border
and exposes himself in an outburst of rage and despair;[31] Daniel of
Masquerade challenges death as he recklessly drives across the country in
an aimless search, until he decides to finally leave.[32] And in his last day
before leaving Israel, Omer Shlakhin plays with the idea of suicide.[33] The
prominence of the theme of death in these works suggests the depth of
despair of the wandering Israelis, who cannot find their own place either
in Israel or abroad.

Ultimately, the literature about the wandering Israelis reflects the
current social and ideological crisis in Israeli society. In contrast to the
more prevailing economic explanations for *yerida*, it focuses on the
conflict between generations, the disillusionment with the myths of the
past, and mostly on the oppressive feeling of confinement that is
associated with a continuous state of siege and magnified by the strong
demand for conformity in a small, tightly knit society. Contemporary
Israeli fiction reveals the growing unrest of a generation that was brought
up on the pioneers' romantic vision of the Sabra and the Sabra's future
in the Land of Israel but faces that vision's discrepancy with the present
Israeli sociopolitical reality. By exploring the impact of a situation that
offers no valid solutions for the future, this literature illustrates the
fragile line that separates the Sabra from the wandering Jew as the Sabra
searches for an answer to his existential dilemma.

Notes

I would like to thank Eviatar Zerubavel for his most valuable comments on an
earlier version of this paper. I am also grateful to Ammiel Alcalay for his helpful
suggestions on the English translations of the Hebrew texts.
  1. For a more extensive discussion of the images of the Sabra and Diaspora Jew
     in Israeli culture, see Yael Zerubavel, "The Last Stand: On the Trans-

formation of Symbols in Modern Israeli Culture" (Ph.D. dissertation, University of Pennsylvania, 1980), pp. 313-18; Samuel Klausner, "The New Hebrew Man," *Zemanim,* 1-3 October, 1954 (in Hebrew); Ferdinand Zweig, *Israel: The Sword and the Harp* (Rutherford, N.J.: Fairleigh Dickinson University Press, 1969), p. 4; Ammon Rubenstein, *To Be a Free People* (Schocken, 1977; in Hebrew), pp. 101-6; G. Shaked and J. Yaron, eds., *Life on the Razor's Edge; An Anthology of Israeli Fiction* (Hakibbutz Hameuchad, 1982; in Hebrew), pp. 11-14, 33-40.

2. Yizhak Ben-Ner, *A Distant Land*(Keter, 1981; in Hebrew), pp. 150-51.
3. Ibid., p. 183.
4. Amos Oz, *A Perfect Peace* (Am Oved, 1982; in Hebrew), p. 9.
5. Arie Semo, *Masquerade* (Sifrait Poalim, 1983; in Hebrew), pp. 194, 201.
6. Ibid., p. 170.
7. Ibid., pp. 179, 195, 213.
8. Ben-Ner, *A Distant Land*, p. 158.
9. Ibid., pp. 150-51, 173.
10. Aharon Megged, *Journey in the Month of Av* (Am Oved, 1980; in Hebrew), pp. 9, 14-15.
11. Abraham B. Yehoshua, *Late Divorce* (Hakibbutz Hameuchad, 1982; in Hebrew), p. 289.
12. Megged, *Journey in the Month of Av*, p. 165.
13. Ibid., p. 51.
14. Oz, *A Perfect Peace*, p. 7.
15. Yotam Reuveni, "Mixed Tendency," in his short stories collection, *Mixed Tendency* (Am Oved, 1982; in Hebrew), p. 67.
16. Oz, *A Perfect Peace*, p. 11.
17. Amnon Jackont, *Borrowed Time* (Am Oved, 1982; in Hebrew), p. 184.
18. Ibid., pp. 282-83.
19. Reuveni, "Mixed Tendency," pp. 65-66.
20. Oz, *A Perfect Peace*, p. 252.
21. Ibid., pp. 221-22.
22. Megged, *Journey in the Month of Av*, p. 88.
23. Semo, *Masquerade*, p. 195.
24. Reuveni, "Mixed Tendency," p. 60.
25. Jackont, *Borrowed Time*, p. 272.
26. Ibid., p. 270.
27. Ibid., p. 274.
28. Yehoshua, *Late Divorce*, p. 251.
29. Ibid., p. 241.
30. Reuveni, "Mixed Tendency," p. 85.
31. Oz, *A Perfect Peace*, pp. 343-50.
32. Semo, *Masquerade*, pp. 172-73.
33. Reuveni, "Mixed Tendency," p. 88.

11

Israelis in the New York Area Labor Market

Marcia Freedman and *Josef Korazim*

Among the new waves of immigrants to New York, the Israelis are among the least understood. Casual observation makes it clear that in New York they are engaged in car and taxi services, in diamond trading, and in retail enterprises dealing in photo and electronic goods. These are not, however, the Israelis who were traditionally sampled in social science studies. Influenced by the 1970s focus on the "brain drain" as an important phenomenon in immigration, these studies were mostly limited to students and well-educated population segments, and their results served to reinforce the conclusion that Israeli immigrants were highly educated, cosmopolitan types (see, for example, Ritterband 1969, 1978; Fein 1978).

Kass and Lipset (1982) provide an example of how this conclusion has influenced discussions of reasons for leaving Israel. They see the basic problem in Israel's large population of educated people, more of whom aspire to professional status than the country can employ, with the implication that there is a group of secular intellectuals who do not have enough scope for their talents and who thus become prime candidates for emigration. The authors, however, did notice that Sephardic Jews, whose origins are on the Mediterranean littoral and the Near East and who have lagged behind the primarily European and/or Western Jews (Ashkenazim) in educational achievement and social status, were also emigrating to the United States. So wedded are they to the "brain drain" thesis that they have to turn the evidence around through a paradox: the success of the dominant Ashkenazi population "in transmitting its achievement values . . . is manifest in the growing number of Israeli-born Sephardim among immigrants to the United States" (Kass and Lipset 1982, 284).

Of course, the conventional wisdom is never wholly incorrect; an unknown proportion of the Israeli population of New York City is made up of highly educated professionals, some of whom came as students and others who left Israel after they were established there, but, as we shall see, the group is more heterogeneous than that, and the economically related reasons for emigration are by no means limited to professional underemployment in Israel. The purpose of this paper is to expand our knowledge of the nonprofessional segment and its opportunities in the New York labor market. In particular, we shall explore the role of self-employment in making the transition and how family and friends create an ethnic dimension in the labor market that smoothes the way into small business.

Family Ties and the Ethnic Network of Employment

The circumstances of Jewish history in the twentieth century increased the probability that a family might extend across national borders. As time went on, these extensions became particularly common between Israel and the United States. One important contribution was the 1965 U.S. immigration law that gave family reunification priority in the criteria for accepting newcomers. What is apparent, however, is that the same networks that account for who may become a resident alien with a green card permitting employment also account for the particular kind of work the newcomer will find. The importance of this ethnic dimension for immigration and for employment emerges clearly from a sample of Israeli families in New York City (Korazim 1983). Table 11.1 arrays the respondents on a continuum according to the strength of the relationship that ties each one to the labor market. Here, the data relate to both men and women; for men taken alone, the proportion with no ethnic dimension is lower.

Almost three-quarters of the individuals in the sample were working in some relationship in the Jewish, and more specifically, the Israeli community; of these, half were in small businesses. The case examples presented later in the paper illustrate the details of the relationships that create this pattern.

A Taste for Self-Employment

Studies that have examined differential self-employment among religious groups in the United States have had conflicting results, but there is little doubt that Jews, whether viewed as a religious group and compared to Catholics and Protestants, or as an ethnic group compared to national-origin groups, show an unusual affinity for self-employment. National data for the late 1950s show significantly greater self-employ-

TABLE 11.1
Ethnic Dimensions in the Employment of Israelis in New York

Ethnic Dimension	N	%
Family Business	21	24.4
Israeli Partnership	10	11.6
Israeli Government	4	4.7
Israeli Employer	10	11.6
Many Israeli Colleagues or Clients	9	10.5
American-Jewish Partner or Employer	8	9.3
No Ethnic Dimension	24	27.9
Total	86	100.0

ment for Jews among both professionals and managers, a finding supported by later studies. (For the relevant literature, see Goldscheider and Kobrin 1980.)

A Rhode Island study at the end of the 1960s for example, turned up large differences in self-employment between Jews and non-Jews (Goldscheider and Kobrin 1980, 275, 277):

> Not only are more than half the Jewish males currently self-employed but this high level is not solely dependent on the self-employment patterns of their fathers. . . .The evidence points to the need for the greater appreciation of the salience of ethnic community networks in facilitating the process of ethnic variation and change in self-employment.

When we compare self-employment among Jews in the United States with Jews in Israel (table 11.2), it is apparent that in a nation (contrasted with an ethnic group), the occupational distribution must cover the entire spectrum, and therefore it is not surprising that the level of self-employment in Israel is more like that in other developed countries and less like the proportions for Jews in the Diaspora.

From 1955 to 1979, the self-employed in Israel (including those categorized as "employers") declined from 23 to 15 percent of the work force according to the Central Bureau of Statistics. This group probably includes those who would be omitted from the U.S. figure (8.7 percent in

TABLE 11.2
Jewish Self-Employment

Date	Study	Percent Self-Employed	Jewish Sample
1957	U.S. Current Population Survey	37	Professionals
	U.S. Current Population Survey	69	Managers
1967–69	Goldscheider & Kobrin	52	Rhode Island men
1979	Statistics of Israel	11	Men in labor force
1981	Greater NY Jewish Population Study	41	Men in Greater NYC
	Greater NY Jewish Population Study	53	Israeli men in NYC
1982	Korazim	63	Israeli men in NYC

1981) because the organizational form of their businesses was either a partnership or a corporation. Even so, the real figure in Israel is probably slightly higher than the figure in the United States. The underlying reasons for the decline in both countries are related to economies of scale, real or imagined, but in Israel the decline seems also to have involved a certain degree of social unacceptability and been reinforced by national policy on job security.

The majority of wage and salary workers in Israel are granted a form of lifetime tenure after six months of probation, a practice that reflects, among other things, the suspect nature of entrepreneurship from a Zionist perspective. The tax authorities also tend to enforce this ideology with particular vigor when they are prodded by the complaints of salaried workers that the self-employed are tax evaders who do not contribute their fair share to the building of the nation. The self-employed therefore have had a double burden of "parasitism," deviant both ideologically and practically.

The official Israeli attitude contrasts sharply with the situation in France and Italy, where small business is protected and encouraged through subsidies as a way of obviating unemployment and political pressure from the traditional petite bourgeoisie (Berger and Piore 1980). The United States, typically, has no official policy on this question. In the nation as a whole, there is some admiration for risk takers, balanced by a distaste for tax evaders, but overall people are free to try out truly private enterprise within wide limits of tolerance. Given the high level of risk, many who yearn for independence are self-employed only as moonlighters or as secondary earners in the family. From time to time, these ventures turn into full-scale activities, but more often they never reach the takeoff stage. The federal agency that is mandated to support this kind of activity, the Small Business Administration, is itself small and ineffective, a fact that demonstrates the difficulties both of risk reduction and of creating entrepreneurs where none existed before.

In spite of the risk, the prospect of self-employment seems to play a part in the emigration decision of many Israelis, just as it does among other immigrants. The "brain-drain" hypothesis, as we have seen, was based on competition among the well-educated, but it may well be that unfulfilled tastes for self-employment constitute a more powerful spur to seeking opportunity elsewhere. In Israel, those who opt for an independent role lack security in a state where they also have diminished chances to flourish outside the ranks of salaried workers. In the event, well-educated emigres require courage to leave home, but the less-educated emigres, who are the more obvious risk takers, may also be rational maximizers who see in self-employment a profitable way to use their energies.

Two Israeli Samples

The discussion in this paper is largely based on a sample of eighty-six New York City families surveyed by Josef Korazim (1983), a sample described in greater detail below. This study was conducted in face-to-face interviews and is therefore rich in detail. In contrast, the much larger New York Jewish Population Study of 1981 (NYJPS) (Ritterband and Cohen 1982), conducted on behalf of the Federation of Jewish Philanthropies, was a telephone survey providing minimal labor-market information and only the place of birth and date of immigration for the foreign born.

In the NYJPS sample there were in the end only seventy-two men who could with confidence be counted as Israelis. About half had college graduate or professional degrees. Their occupational distribution is summarized in table 11.3 With its high proportion of professional and technical workers, this group seems to resemble the Jewish population of the city as a whole. Certainly it conforms more closely to the conventional picture. On the other hand, compared to 41 percent of all men in the study, 52.8 percent of the Israelis were self-employed. Of these thirty-eight men, only eight were professionals—a rabbi, a writer, a teacher, a lawyer, an economist, an engineer, and two systems analysts; the rest were storeowners and craftsmen. The remainder of the professionals, like most Americans, were wage and salary workers.

The Korazim sample, which provides our main focus, was purposively selected to produce a data set with characteristics suitable for investigating the social-service needs and service-utilization patterns of Israeli immigrants. In the sample, half of the families resided in Queens and the other half in Brooklyn; half were Ashkenazi and half Sephardi; half were "newcomers" who had lived in the United States one to three years, and half were "old-timers" who had lived in the United States four to ten years. All of the families were composed of husband, wife, and at least one child living at home, and all were Israelis by virtue either of having been born in Israel (two-thirds) or having lived there at least ten years before emigrating (one-third). It is noteworthy that although none of the criteria for inclusion in the study had any bearing on employment, the sample produced a distinctively Israeli spectrum of occupations.

Table 11.3 shows the difference between Israel and the United States in the broad occupational categories of the men in the sample. After immigration, the shift was away from the professions and toward management, with a decline in craft jobs and an increase in operatives. These changes are paralleled by a significant difference in the level of self-employment. These men already had an unusually high level of self-employment, 34 percent, perhaps indicating a tendency to self-selection for immigration, but in New York, the proportion almost doubled, to reach 63 percent, even higher than among the Israelis in the NYJPS sample.

When the men were asked directly, "What brought you and your family to the U.S.?" the three most frequent of their multiple responses were family reunification (54 percent), job opportunities (35 percent), and curiosity and adventurousness (26 percent). These suggest that Israelis as a group are positively selected migrants who respond primarily to "pull" factors in the country of destination. Rather than being pushed out, they are attracted by perceived opportunities. Such migrants have been characterized as highly educated persons who are comfortably situated in their country of origin but who respond to perceived opportunities elsewhere (Lee 1969). Although this picture seemed to characterize about half of the Greater New York sample, it represents only about a quarter of the Korazim sample. All but two of the men with college or postgraduate degrees were Ashkenazi, and about two-thirds lived in Queens. The Brooklyn group, not so well educated and somewhat less prosperous, tells a different story. Among these respondents,

TABLE 11.3
Occupations of Israeli Immigrant Men

| | Korazim Sample | | | | NYJPS Sample | |
| | In Israel | | In New York | | In New York | |
Occupation	N	%	N	%	N	%
Professionals and kindred	14	16.3	10	11.6	20	30.8
Managers/ Administrators	21	24.4	32	37.3	12	18.5
Sales and Clerical Workers	10	11.6	11	12.8	13	20.0
Craft workers	24	28.0	18	20.9	10	15.4
Operatives	7	8.1	12	13.9	7	10.8
Service Workers	3	3.5	3	3.5	3	4.6
Not in Labor Force	7	8.1	0	---	0	---
Total	86	100.0	86	100.0	65	100.0
Self-Employed	29	33.7	54	62.8	38	52.8[a]

the leading reason for emigration, "family reunification," was followed by adverse economic experiences in Israel—harassment by income-tax authorities, small-business failure, and a generalized economic pessimism.

One such case involved a Sephardi family with three children:

> The husband had tried for two years to operate a business of his own as an elevator constructor. He attributed his lack of success to harassment by the income tax authorities. Furthermore, the business suffered from the interruptions occasioned by his military service obligations. His brother, who had been in the States since 1966, provided him with a job in his shoe factory and later helped him to become self-employed in New York as a small contractor in the home-improvement sector of the construction industry.

This case, like others, illustrates not only the importance of self-employment but also the critical role played by relatives. Among real people, motives interact. U.S. immigration law stresses family reunification, but as we have already pointed out, the networks that serve to bring relatives to the U.S. also account for their labor-market activities once they arrive. In describing their decision to emigrate, many respondents spoke of family members in the United States who encouraged them with specific promises of help in finding employment or going into business. As we have noted, fifty-four of eighty-six men were self-employed; table 11.4 shows the activities in which they were engaged.

The person closest to being an independent professional in the group of self-employed men is a computer consultant. For the most part, however, Israeli immigrants display two patterns of labor-market behavior that result in small-scale entrepreneurship: one is characterized by the diamond industry; the other, by the taxi business. In the first case, self-employed Israelis move to New York while keeping their attachment to an industry; in the other, they find a way to make a living in small business by taking advantage of the particular conditions they find upon arrival. In both situations establishment occurs by virtue of preexisting networks of family and friends.

Diamonds

Both the findings of this study and other sources (Mackay-Smith 1982) agree that Jews control about 80 percent of the diamond business in New York City. Many of these are immigrants from Israel, including some who profess a form of religious orthodoxy that rejects belief in a Jewish homeland until the coming of the Messiah. At the very least, this group

TABLE 11.4
Activities of Israeli Self-Employed Men in New York City

Type of Business	Number
Manufacturing	4
Diamonds (inc. retail establishments)	11
Retail Stores, exc. Diamonds	14
Wholesale Suppliers	2
Construction and Building Trades	4
White Collar Services	6
Taxis and Car Service	13
Total	54

feels as at home (or as alien) in one place as in another. Survivors of the Holocaust who emigrated to Israel from the Netherlands and Belgium carried with them skills involved in the cutting, setting, and trading of precious stones, making Israel into the primary marketplace after World War II.

The diamond business, which flourished under the conditions of steadily rising diamond prices, gradually became centered in New York, but it retained an international flavor, with family members likely to reside both in Israel and in the United States, and for the larger firms, also in European cities. A case in the sample illustrates these connections:

> The respondent has an uncle who moved to New York from Israel many years ago. When the uncle fell ill, he summoned the nephew, who also was in the diamond business in Israel, to take over for him until his children would be old enough to do so. The respondent's loyalty to the family was evidently stronger than any reluctance he may have had to leave Israel. At the time of the interview, he had been in New York less than two years out of a total five-year commitment.

After 1980, diamond prices plunged precipitously, and it is now doubtful whether the business community centered on West 47th Street in Manhattan will continue to grow larger. In fact, a follow-up about a year after the initial interview found several of the most recent Israeli arrivals in new activities. One who had traded in diamonds had become a furniture salesman; a cutter was selling used cars; and a broker had turned to importing watches. The ties that had encouraged them to emigrate to New York were also useful in helping them find other jobs that involved such entrepreneurial skills as selling, and so they were maintaining a somewhat precarious foothold in New York.

Taxis

The place that Israelis have found in the taxi and car-service business in New York illustrates how rapidly a network to absorb newcomers grows in an activity where skill requirements are nil and capital requirements small. As late as 1970, only 5 percent of New York City residents employed in the taxi industry were foreign-born. Subsequently, changes in the structure of the industry made it especially attractive to new immigrants. First, a *de facto* relaxation of standards occurred when drivers were hard to recruit, thus making it possible to incorporate new-comers whose spoken English and knowledge of the city was marginal. The second development was related to the nature of industry regulation. Because the right to operate and accept street hails from riders is restricted to those who own a taxicab medallion, a decline in the profit-abililty of large fleets in the 1970s freed up medallions for newcomers (Gilbert 1981). The 1981 medallion price was $60,000, but a network of brokers and banks made it fairly simple to finance a purchase over a five- to seven-year period at an average annual cost of about $15,000. Over half of individual medallion owners and two-thirds of fleet owners in 1981 had bought their medallions in 1976 or later.

New owners pay for medallions from three sources (Roistacher and White, 1982):

- by revenues provided through the established fare;
- by taxpayers in general if there is unreported income more easily "sheltered" by an owner than by a hired driver; and
- by "self-exploitation" of the owner-operator who is willing to work for less than he would as a hired driver because a medallion guarantees him a job.

Medallion taxis are only part of the business. A parallel car-service system that responds to telephone calls has created a full-fledged second tier that is particularly dominant outside Manhattan. In effect, it also provides camouflage for a third tier, nonmedallion gypsy cabs that operate illegally.

The attractiveness of the business, therefore, lies in ease of entry and the possibility of moving from employment to ownership. (As time has gone on, the fleets have become even less of a factor. The most recent development is a flat-rate leasing arrangement that has loosened the last ties between workers and employers.) Again, a case from the study illustrates the nexus between family ties and finding a labor-market niche:

> This case involves a couple, born in Rumania and brought to Israel as children. The wife's father, however, had long harbored a wish to emigrate to New York, and he did so in 1968 after the Six-Day War. Having become a citizen, his children were eligible for visas as resident aliens. In 1975, the young couple in Israel became restless even though the husband was settled in a job as foreman in a heavy-duty equipment enterprise, with the usual "tenure." They agreed to take advantage of their chance to enter the U.S. by taking one year's leave as an experiment. The parents supported them initially, and helped them buy a taxi. Now the wife drives during the day and the husband, at night. Unlike most families, they are clearly determined to stay and to expand their business.

In the sample study reported here, thirteen men own one or more taxis, and another four are drivers for owners. In addition, five are in businesses related to automobile maintenance. The ethnic network is strengthened by factors on both the demand and the supply sides. In Brooklyn, for example, there is a symbiosis of the local American-Jewish community and the Israeli immigrants, especially among those who prefer a segregated life-style and so tend to prefer Jewish taxis and car service. This interdependence is said to create a "communal harmony" with the Israelis that is considered a stabilizing force, implicitly supported by the police even though they often have knowledge of illegal drivers (Karp 1983). It is an example of the importance of social and institutional integration that Carmenza Gallo (1983) found to be a factor in small-scale construction activities.

On the supply side, the labor force is fed by four streams:

1. Transient newcomers who need money upon their arrival to finance their travels. They stay for a short time and move on, but their presence provides a flexible work force at the margins.
2. Temporaries who either cannot find a job in their own occupation or who need supplementary income from part-time work. Here there is complementarity with the entertainment and diamond industries.
3. Permanent drivers who are seeking to establish their own businesses.
4. A downwardly mobile residual who have no other choice. They are often ashamed or bitter and hide their actual occupation from family and friends in Israel.

The boundaries among these groups are permeable. From the interviews with the sample in this study, it is clear that although no one may come to New York precisely to own a taxi, certain immigrants do find such an outcome satisfactory, given their educational level, their lack of other skills, and their taste for self-employment.

Conclusion

Any conclusions drawn from two small and imperfectly drawn samples such as those presented here can only be tentative. What these data do suggest, however, is that the Israeli immigrant population in New York City is not homogeneous. Different types can be found in varying proportions depending on where one dips into the immigrant pool. There is certainly a well-educated cohort made up of those who came as students and married in the United States, as well as those who came after being professionally established in Israel. About this group, the two samples are in agreement: the highly educated are predominantly wage and salary workers.

In both samples, the large number of self-employed seem to have a different occupational orientation. They are traders and craftsmen who encounter less disapproval and more scope in New York and an atmosphere conducive to the risk-taking aspects of small business. Their families and kinship networks afford some protection from the vagaries of the marketplace, but just as important is an increasingly less formal style of doing business.

In the United States generally, the ties between workers and employers have grown weaker, thus creating more space in the interstices and at the margins. Among the growing numbers who face a more uncertain labor market with fewer long-term protections, immigrants have some advantages. Foremost among these is the extended family and kinship structure that facilitates their coming to the United States in the first place. Newcomers can count on at least a modicum of support and assistance in becoming established from those relatives who sponsor and encourage them. For Israelis, this situation arises naturally from the historic movements of the Diaspora. In occupational terms, it is most clearly expressed in the international network of the diamond business, which encompasses all facets of manufacture and trading.

Somewhat less obvious is the contribution of self-employment to the settlement process of immigrant groups in general. Different classes of immigrants have found in small business a way of gaining a foothold in a relatively unstructured labor market. Thus, well-educated Koreans who might have worked as engineers or technicians in their home country become shopkeepers in New York (Kim 1981). Among Israelis, it seems to be the less-educated who find it attractive to go into business for themselves. It is an interesting question for further research how much of this attraction stems from a lingering taste for self-employment, and how much is the lack of an alternative route to success. In any case, emigration to a place where risk taking offers the possibility of economic rewards becomes an obvious step.

Not everyone who takes this route succeeds, but for those with little education and great energy, business in New York seems worth a try. Israelis are cosmopolitan by nature and by nurture; what draws them to the United States is not only the rejection of provincialism by the educated but the search for profit by those who feel undervalued at home.

Note

The authors are listed in alphabetical order.

References

Berger, S., and Piore, M. 1980. *Dualism and Discontinuity in Industrial Societies.* New York: Cambridge University Press.

Fein, A. 1978. "The Process of Migration: Israeli Emigration to the United States." Ph.D. dissertation, Case Western Reserve University.

Gallo, C. 1983. "The Construction Industry in New York City: Immigrants and Black Entrepreneurs." New York: Columbia University, Conservation of Human Resources.

Gilbert, G. 1981. "Operating Costs for Medallion Taxicabs in New York City." New York: Mayor's Committee on Taxicab Regulatory Issues.

Goldscheider, C., and Kobrin, F.E. 1980. "Ethnic Continuity and the Process of Self-Employment." *Ethnicity* 7:256-78.

Karp, D. 1983. "Israeli Car Service in New York City." *Israel Shelanu*, 18 February.

Kass, D., and Lipset, S.M. 1982. "Jewish Immigration to the United States from 1967 to the Present: Israelis and Others." In *Understanding American Jewry*, ed. M. Sklare. New Brunswick, N.J.: Transaction Books.

Kim, I. 1981. *New Urban Immigrants: The Korean Community in New York.* Princeton: Princeton University Press.

Korazim, J. 1983. "Israeli Families in New York City: Utilization of Social Services, Unmet Needs and Policy Implications." Ph.D. dissertation, Columbia University.

Lee, E.S. 1969. "A Theory of Migration." In *Migration*, ed. J.A. Jackson. New York: Cambridge University Press.

Mackay-Smith, A. 1982. "Faded Luster." *Wall Street Journal*, 20 August.

Reeves, R. 1982. "Democracy in America, Reconsidered." *Washington Monthly* (July/August):52.

Ritterband, P. 1969. "The Determinants of Motives of Israeli Students Staying in the U.S." *Sociology of Education* 42 (Fall).

———. 1978. *Education, Employment and Migration.* New York: Cambridge University Press.

Ritterband, P., and Cohen, S.M. 1982. "The Greater New York Jewish Population Study." Report 1. New York: Federation of Jewish Philanthropies/United Jewish Appeal.

Roistacher, E.A., and White, J.J. 1982. "The Pricing of Taxicab Medallions in New York City." New York: Mayor's Committee on Taxicab Regulatory Issues.

12

Israeli Emigres and the New York Federation: A Case Study in Ambivalent Policymaking for "Jewish Communal Deviants"

Steven M. Cohen

In the Spring of 1983, concluding a year of intensive deliberation, the Federation of Jewish Philanthropies of New York adopted a comprehensive policy to provide a limited array of services to Israeli emigres living in New York. The considerable controversy that preceded that decision reflected deep value conflicts within the federation about the propriety of serving a very special group of Jews in need. It aroused passionate feelings of ambivalence, embarrassment, and anger. But the case of policymaking for Israeli emigres should not be seen in isolation. In fact, it can be placed within a larger context of communal decision making about several subpopulations in U.S. Jewry, all of whom may be referred to as "Jewish communal deviants."

Communal Deviants: Problematic Groups for U.S. Jewry

"Communal deviants" are those whose behavior (even if "through no fault of their own") departs—or deviates—from the expectations of the organized community. They include such unconventional family types as never-married adults, childless couples, the intermarried, and the divorced. They also include young adults who move to areas of sparse Jewish settlement in order, according to some, to escape from their Jewishness. Many communal leaders have, in effect, also termed deviant (or worse) those Soviet emigres who settle in the United States, allegedly for mere material reasons, instead of heading for Israel, as many of their more praiseworthy Zionist predecessors did (some call the former *noshrim* or dropouts). Communal deviants also include emigrating Israelis (some call them *yordim*, or descenders, in contrast with the more admirable *olim*, ascenders, those who migrate from the Diaspora to Israel).

In the ideal world of organized Jewry, Jews should marry Jewish spouses of the opposite sex, stay married, and have children quickly (and plentifully). The American-born also should live in areas of high Jewish density with established networks of community services that they ought to use and support. The international refugee, though, ought to settle in Israel. When significant numbers of Jews fails to conform to these expectations, lay and professional communal leaders typically manifest a variety of now-classic reactions. Many of these reactions, in fact, emerged among communal leaders in New York and elsewhere when the migration of Israelis to the United States became noteworthy.

We may identify at least seven broad types of reactions to Jewish communal deviants generally. Some are cognitive, having to do with the image of the group in question. Others are action oriented, having more to do with communal policy toward the group. The three cognitive reactions are (1) denial, (2) cover-up, and (3) exaggeration. The four policy-oriented reactions are (4) malign neglect, (5) benign neglect, (6) containment, and (7) accommodation. Each reaction bears elaboration, both in general terms and in the specific case of providing services to Israelis in New York.

Seven Reactions to Communal Deviants

Denial

One of the first reactions many communal leaders have to the initial presentation of a problem of growing numbers of communal deviants is to deny the problem exists, to try to refute the notion that large numbers of Jews might be contravening conventional notions of how Jews should behave. If Jews are family oriented, then it is hard to believe they are staying single longer, or divorcing, or emerging as homosexuals. If the Jewish State is so wonderful and Israelis are so heroic and committed to its survival, then the very presence of Israelis in the United States runs contrary to the idealistic and idealized images of the Zionist endeavor. In the early 1970s in particular, several communal leaders reacted to the reports of a slow but mounting Israeli migration to the United States by denying the veracity of the claim, or by denying that Israeli emigres constituted a social problem worthy of communal attention.

Cover-up

A second typical response entails conceding that the communally deviant group may indeed exist in some notable number, but that attention to the group can serve only to impugn the character of the Jewish community. Of course, this reaction does not characterize all groups, only those whose existence might in some way serve to diminish Jewish communal influence or its putatively positive image in the eyes of impressionable Jews or Gentiles. Particularly embarrassing groups that have been the object of such a reaction include drug and alcohol abusers, child abusers and violent spouses, nonelderly Jews needing public assistance, and, in an earlier era, criminals.

To this fairly standard list of genuine social deviants we can add a special, admittedly less serious case, that of Israeli emigres. As noted, for some, the appearance of many Israelis in the United States constituted an embarrassment, a threat, an indictment of the quality of life in Israel and a rejection of Zionist values. Many communal leaders believed emigrating Israelis represented to elected officials and other U.S. influentials a sign of weakening resolve in the beleaguered country. To their fellow Jews—especially those whose commitment to Israel may be subject to wavering—leaders thought Israeli emigres might provide a rationale for diminished financial and political support for Israel. After all, if *Sabras,* who are closest to Israel and its problems can reject the Jewish State, then why should American Jews invest considerable time, money, and energy in its support?

Despite determined and insistent efforts at cover-up, if the communally deviant group is large and enduring enough, the tactic is doomed to failure. Members of the group—especially if they feel stig-matized—need to demonstrate that their individual decisions have been replicated by many others. Journalists, social workers, and communal leaders whose area of interest and involvement focuses on the group have compelling interests not only in placing the group on the agenda of organized Jewry and in resisting efforts at cover-up but even in magnifying the dimensions of the group and the problems it allegedly presents.

Exaggeration

When organized Jewry officially discovers a new group of communal deviants and admits to its presence, one typical reaction is to exaggerate its size. Lay and professional leaders, eager to call attention either to the problem group or to themselves, are quick to focus on the most shocking and startling piece of evidence. For example, many people have the im-pression that half of all Jews marrying today are intermarrying. One source for this figure derives from the National Jewish Population Study, which found that 48 percent of new couples involving Jews in the late 1960s were indeed mixed *couples*, but this meant that less than a third (32 percent) of Jewish *individuals* were marrying born non-Jews. (Some Israeli demographers, in reanalyzing the data, suggest that less than a quarter may be a more accurate fraction for the individual rate.) Similarly, evidence of decline in Jewish fertility prompted one author to predict in a *Midstream* magazine article that the United States Jewish population will dwindle to about ten thousand in the next century. Following this piece of "yellow demography" came a more reasoned and better-documented article by two reputable demographers in the same journal. They projected a slight increase, in fact, in the Jewish population because of the bulge in new parents owing to the post-World War II "baby boom," followed by a decline—assuming quite low birthrates—to a little over four million in the next century. The doomsday article received far more attention than did the subsequent less-spectacular presentation. Still another self-serving and distortionist example is provided by a prominent Orthodox rabbi's comments upon making aliyah. After years of unusually successful work in building a vibrant Orthodox community around several institutions, he declared U.S. Jewry doomed. In remarks published in the *Jerusalem Post*, the new *oleh* cited as proof text the high interreligious cohabitation rate among a small sample of young adults in a study of an isolated and very recently settled mountain-states Jewish community.

The phenomenon of exaggeration also emerged in the case of Israeli emigration. An Israeli official in the late 1970s, anxious to draw attention and money to his portfolio—the cause of dissuading emigration or promoting reimmigration of Israeli abroad—trumpeted the figure of 500,000 to 600,000 Israelis in the United States. At the same time, demographers at Israel's Central Bureau of Statistics were saying that no more than 300,000 Israelis were living abroad throughout the world. Where some in Los Angeles suggested that its Israeli population numbered about 100,000—which would mean that one Los Angeles Jew in five was Israeli—a detailed and careful academic study of diverse governmental records as well as the recent Los Angeles Jewish population study suggested a figure closer to 15,000. Where some had estimated the New York Israeli population in excess of 200,000, the federation's population study found somewhere between 50,000 and 80,000, depending upon the definition of *Israeli*.

Interestingly, the phenomenon of exaggeration also extended to the images of the Jewish identity of Israelis. Most communal leaders assumed that Israeli emigres' identity is quite weak (otherwise, if they were good Jews and good Zionists, why did they not stay in Israel). Research has demonstrated that, in many respects, most Israeli emigres'

Jewish identity is far stronger than that of the typical American Jew. Moreover, it shows that the emigres' overall Jewish commitment profile—at least in New York, where many Hassidic and other Orthodox Israelis settle—is greater than that found in Israeli society generally (in other words, observant Israelis are at least as likely to emigrate as are the nonobservant) (see Ritterband in this section). The one exception to these generalizations is that recently arrived Israelis are far less likely to join U.S. Jewish organizations and they are far, far less likely to support the UJA/federation campaign. Campaign leaders encountering stiff Israeli emigre resistance to their entreaties for support reasoned that there must be something woefully amiss with the Israelis' Jewish identity. This assumption underlies one policy-oriented reaction to Israelis and other communal deviants, a reaction we can call, "malign neglect."

Malign Neglect

As noted, malign neglect arises from the assumption that communal deviants are bad Jews. Thus, intermarriers are rebelling against their parents and their Jewish upbringing. Childless couples must be unaware of their demographic responsibilities to the Jewish people. Migrants to outlying communities with few Jews are trying to escape their Jewish roots. Soviet emigres coming to the United States are rejecting Israel, which has done so much for them and needs additional human energy desperately. And Israeli emigres are, objectively if not subjectively, anti-Zionists.

The malign neglect argument maintains that organized Jewry should have nothing to do with the deviant groups because they are such terrible Jews. The Israeli government has, for years, pressured HIAS not to assist Soviet emigres heading for the United States. When one high cabinet official was informed that they may turn to those Christian charitable agencies that also administered per capita United States government relief funds, he was said to have responded, "Any Jew who turns to Christian agencies we don't need anyway."

Some Israeli officials and U.S. Jewish communal leaders reacted in a similar way to Israeli emigres. One top Israeli government official referred to the emigres as *zevel* (garbage) and urged consulates world-wide to have little if anything to do with them. Since the early 1970s, the New York consulate repeatedly urged the federation to provide no special services to Israelis. Consular officials and their UJA/federation supporters took the view that Israelis in New York were the province and responsibility of the Israeli government and not of the local organized Jewish community. When the federation ultimately resisted this approach, the consulate shifted to a second argument—one that found considerably more support among lay leaders—that of "benign neglect."

Benign Neglect

Opponents of special services for communal deviants argue that the provision of special services will have at least two adverse effects. First, it will call attention to the emergence of the deviant group, causing embarrassment to the Jewish community. Second, the very provision of services will be taken as a symbol of legitimacy.

Some Orthodox communities, until recently, resisted the institution of special services for young singles on the grounds that such programs would detract from the image of strong and secure Orthodox familialism. Many synagogues, congregational movements, and others have been struggling with the issue of intermarriers and how to cope with them, their Gentile spouses, and their children. Certainly one impediment to involving them in Jewish communal life is the fear that such action will further lower normative inhibitions to intermarriage. Homosexual Jews, even those organized affirmatively as Jews in their own synagogues and the like, have also encountered fear, aversion, and exclusion. Opponents of gay synagogues have argued that homosexuals should participate as individuals in Jewish communal life, but that the establishment of formal gay Jewish institutions is an unwarranted and unsupportable claim to legitimacy.

Those against extending any special services to New York Israelis likewise argued that the emigres are as free to avail themselves of community services as any other Jewish New Yorkers. The very act of extending specially tailored services to them—as had been provided to recent Soviet and Iranian immigrants—might be taken as a sign of approval of their decision to migrate and might actually stimulate more emigration. Rather than promoting Israeli migration to New York, they argued, federation policy ought to stanch the flow of immigrants and even reverse it. That is, rather than serving the Israeli immigrants, some preferred to "contain" the phenomenon.

Containment

One frequent reaction to the emergence of a Jewish communal deviant group is the urge to combat the social trends that gave rise to the group in the first place. The policy of containment, as I call it, has many illustrations in Jewish communal life. Numerous conferences have sought to devise incentives for Jews to have more babies. Several cities have started new programs to introduce marriageable Jewish singles to one another so as to curb singlehood and intermarriage. Several neighborhood groups have tried to entice young Jews to move into declining Jewish residential areas. These efforts remind one of the Jewish Agency's efforts to persuade Soviet emigres to choose Israel rather than the United States as their ultimate destination.

Consular and other Israeli officials have taken some tentative steps to encourage the reimmigration of Israelis to their homeland. Federation officials believed that such activities, though admirable, were both beyond the federation's competence and philanthropic philosophy. Moreover, research on international migration in general and on Israeli emigration in particular supports the view that kinship and friendship networks along with push and pull market factors are the dominant influences on the decision to migrate. The notion that the provision of federation services to emigres will stimulate further emigration, or that its denial will retard emigration, is ludicrous in light of this research.

My own view is that communal efforts to alter Jewish demographic trends in a significant way are doomed to failure. Entire governments have struggled to alter birthrates with marginal effect at best (and that effect is the subject of dispute among reputable demographers). Parents do all they can to persuade their children to marry Jews quickly and have children. If persuasion and motivation are the missing ingredients in understanding allegedly disappointing Jewish marriage and childbearing behavior, then certainly parents have more opportunity to influence their offspring than does the voluntary formal Jewish community, especially in light of the low affiliation rates among singles and childless couples. (All of this is not to argue against social programs for singles, counseling for troubled marriages, or day school tuition. These are admirable programs that should be enacted for their own sake, but not with the expectation that they will alter rates of marriage, divorce, or births.)

Accommodation

Although "demographic jawboning" (trying to persuade Jews to change their familial, professional, or migratory decisions) may well be effective only in affirming communal principles, organized Jewry does frequently come around to accommodating a newly or recently emergent group of deviants. Often, it stops viewing them as an embarrassment or a social problem subject to some sort of conversion and adopts an "accommodationist" approach. This type of policy seeks to bridge the gulfs that often separate communal deviants from Jewish institutional life.

The typical profile of communally active Jews embraces the following characteristics. They are married, have schoolchildren home, have lived for many years in the same town or neighborhood, and are American-born, college educated, and reasonably affluent. Those who depart from this paradigm in any way are less likely to be active in Jewish communal life. Those who deviate in several ways, such as single mothers with modest incomes, are even less likely to participate in Jewish institutional life.

As I see it, the central task of organized American Jewry vis-à-vis its potential constituency, is to extend formal Jewish communal life to several communally deviant groups now standing on the periphery of the institutions. Research I conducted demonstrated that singles, childless couples, intermarrieds, and divorced are not only more numerous but more distant from conventional Jewish life than were their counterparts in the mid-1960s.

Accommodation to these and other deviant groups has taken either or both of two directions. One entails the creation of Jewish networks and institutions composed primarily of the communally deviant. Examples include *havurot* geared for the young single or couple and several *landsmanschaft*-like structures among Israelis in New York. The other course involves fully integrating the communal deviants into conventional structures such as Y's and synagogues.

My own sense is that we need both separationist and integrationist options and that the former are, in fact, a prelude to the latter. My experience with federation leaders, however, uncovered a strong bias against fostering new networks or organizations outside the established communal infrastructure. Federation leaders were hard put to understand why Israeli Jews would prefer their "own" institutions. Many were honestly concerned about the proliferation of institutions in a heavily institutionalized community. Others viewed Israeli-only organizations (which, significantly, the federation could not control) as an implicit rejection of the New York Jewish community and as a precursor of permanent alienation of Israeli emigres from the rest of New York Jewry. Paradoxically, then, some federation leaders reject the institutional expression of pluralism within local Jewry, even as they insist that American Jews can and should maintain their own voluntary network within a multiethnic and multireligious pluralistic society.

A Policy Emerges: Cultural Services for Israelis

Despite the New York federation's sentiments, its lay Committee on Services to Israelis agreed on a general policy statement, one that successfully bridged conflicting ideological differences and obtained consensual support, albeit at times hesitant, tentative, and wary. In the spring of

1982, as a prelude to the establishment of the committee, several federation lay and professional leaders collaborated on a "Mandate Statement" that would serve as a charge to that committee. The statement had to elicit the support of a wide circle of federation leaders. In so doing, it had to maneuver between two basic orientations—the "proto-Zionist" and "liberal philanthropic" positions—at least one, if not both of which, could be interpreted so as to preclude any special services to Israeli emigres. The policy options these two orientations generated were as follows.

Proto-Zionist Option

The proto-Zionist option combined elements of several reactions outlined above, particularly malign neglect. Several UJA/federation leaders, particularly those heavily involved in the campaign, were highly sensitive to the objections of Israeli consular officials to any sort of special services to Israeli emigres. In their view, the provisions of such services would have several adverse effects, including encouraging additional emigration, legitimating such emigration, and, not least, causing unnecessary friction between campaign leaders and the consulate. Thus, initially, the proto-Zionists forcefully opposed the provision of any special service to Israeli emigres.

Liberal Philanthropic Option

A fundamental element of the federation's philosophy prescribes service to all Jews in need regardless of their Jewish orientation. In recent years, the federation had provided special services to Iranian and Soviet immigrants. By logical extension, the liberal philanthropic philosophy meant that Israeli emigres should receive the same high level of attention commensurate in nature and extent with their special needs. Liberal philanthropists could argue—although few ever did—that this might mean federation advocacy in obtaining "green cards," the Immigration and Naturalization Service document that permits resident aliens to work in the United States. Or, they might argue, as some did, that Israelis in need can and should avail themselves to preexisting services, using established mechanisms available to all Jews (i.e. benign neglect).

The "Option 3" Option

Columnist William Safire wrote, "In bureaucratic. . .manipulation, Option 3 is always set up as the choice between extremes" (*New York Times*, 16, October 1983, sec. 4).

The federation's "Mandate Statement" and the subsequent directions of the Committee on Services to Israelis maneuvered between, and in fact drew upon elements of, the proto-Zionist and liberal philanthropic options. The committee advanced the view that Israelis should indeed receive special services (in accord with the liberal philanthropic philosophy), but those services should focus on their children's Jewish education and the parents' Jewish cultural and communal involvement. Few proto-Zionists could argue against Jewishness. Even the consulate genuinely had no objections to Jewish education for Israeli youngsters, although it did quietly voice reservations about special communal outreach efforts to Israeli adults.

Most federation leaders favorably received the proposed policy orientation, although the proto-Zionists still wanted to be reassured that the consulate was not forcefully objecting to the approach. The liberal philanthropists, with less of a stake in the outcome, merely wanted something to be done for Israeli emigres in New York.

Following adoption of the "Mandate Statement," the Committee on Services to Israelis, meeting over several months, recommended establishing, expanding, and replicating several educational and cultural programs for Israeli emigres. Some examples include a Hebrew-language day school with relatively little emphasis on traditional observance as well as an afternoon school teaching the Israeli school curriculum to prepare youngsters for Israel's precollege matriculation (*bagrut*) examination. Others entailed a Hebrew community library, Hebrew worship services in synagogues, and Israeli/American social events in certain Y's. At this writing, these and other projects seem to be advancing within the federation organizational infrastructure.

Thus, while Israelis may not need Jewish cultural or educational services much more than the typical Jewish New Yorker, their very presence prompted the federation to expand its commitment to fostering Jewish identity in New York. For those interested in moving the federation away from a predominant commitment to philanthropic social services for the down-and-out and toward what some have called "community building," the case of policy-making for Israelis in New York emerges at least as a step in the right direction.

Lessons and Implications

Both members of and advocates for communally deviant groups have often complained that organized Jewry is slow to respond to their special needs. This paper has tried to give some flavor to the nature of the inhibitions and objections to recognizing and serving the diverse cluster of groups called Jewish communal deviants. Yet, even while cognizant of the community's inhibitions, there is good reason to end on an optimistic note. Like all bureaucracies and formal organizations, organized Jewry initially resists innovation and responding to new external constituencies. But all is not bleak. If, indeed, enough members of a communally deviant group emerge, they are likely to form their own networks and institutions of a Jewish character. These in turn attract not only attention and advocates but some measure of legitimacy as well. Moreover, communal deviants and their allies come to exert influence within established institutions. (For example, it is no accident that Reform Judaism, with the largest percentage of intermarriers of the three major denominations, has adopted the most welcoming official policy to Jewish out-marriers, their spouses, and their children.)

This is not to say that all communally deviant groups will eventually receive substantial recognition, legitimacy, and service. It is to say that a Jewish community vitally concerned with its survival and participation rates will not long want to ignore any potential constituency, even those that at first blush appear objectionable or embarrassing. Thus, although in response to current and emerging groups of Jewish communal deviants we will undoubtedly witness expressions of denial, cover-up, exaggeration, malign neglect, benign neglect, and containment, we will also eventually see sure signs of accommodation as well.

13

Israelis in New York and the Federation of Jewish Philanthropies: A Study of Anomie and Reconnection

Linda G. Levi

Formulating policy and developing programs to serve the needs of the diverse population of Jews in New York is a primary communal planning task of the Federation of Jewish Philanthropies of New York. In the last few years, the federation grappled with and resolved an exceedingly complex and sensitive planning issue: developing a policy and program to serve Israelis in New York. In 1982, the Committee on Services to Israelis in New York took a fresh look at this issue and prepared a service plan. A policy report, approved by the federation's Communal Planning Committee in 1983, was affirmed by the federation's Executive Committee and Board of Trustees.[1] This paper examines the process whereby the federation formulated a policy direction regarding Israelis in New York.

The philosophical questions and dilemmas faced by federation leadership in formulating a rationale for singling out Israelis as a population with special needs have been discussed elsewhere in this section.[2] The tension between what we can call the "pro-Iraelists" and the "philanthropic liberals" was resolved by the determination to concentrate on reaching out to Israelis as an unaffiliated group. It was believed that a major effort was needed to reinforce a sense of Jewish identity among the Israelis while strengthening their ties to the Jewish community.

In May 1982, following more than half a year of intense, emotional, and ideological discussion among federation lay and professional leaders, the Communal Planning Committee issued the following mandate statement setting forth general policy on services to Israelis and establishing a subcommittee on the matter:

The Communal Planning Committee believes that the Israeli population temporarily or permanently living in New York frequently lacks adequate ties to the local Jewish community, and lacks appropriate vehicles for connection to the Jewish community and Israel and for transmission of Jewish identity.

The mandate of the Committee on Services to Israelis is as follows:

1. To assess the needs of the different Israeli communities of New York from the vantage point of Israelis as an unaffiliated group and to identify service gaps.
2. To recommend policies, priorities and programs to the Communal Planning Committee as to how to enhance the Jewish identity of Israelis in New York.
3. To recommend mechanisms (which may include specific programs) to increase the access to and utilization of the local Jewish service network by Israelis.
4. To recommend ways in which Israelis might participate in and contribute to New York Jewish communal, philanthropic and cultural life.
5. To encourage self-help groups among the Israeli population.

Towards these ends, the Sub-Committee on Services to Israelis in New York will prepare a service plan for presentation to the Communal Planning Committee.

UJA-Federation is committed to the security, welfare and continuity of the State of Isarel. Although Federation will continue to provide to Israelis the full range of services in its network, Federation does not intend to create a support situation which would de facto be viewed as an encouragement to immigration to New York nor is its role vis-à-vis Israelis to respond to primary initial immigrant needs.[3]

With this general direction set as the frame of reference for further deliberations, the Committee on Services to Israelis in New York was appointed in June 1982. In a sense, this committee in its development epitomized some of the major issues, tensions, and dynamics inherent in creating bridges and channels of communication between the Israeli communities and the American Jewish community. The committee served as a forum to further learn about American Jewish and Israeli Jewish identities, values, needs, and mutual expectations. This was not always smooth and easy. In selecting members, top federation leadership tried to involve broad segments of federation and UJA-Federation Campaign[4] leadership as well as various segments of the Israeli population. The selection of Israeli members took into account such factors as geographic, socioeconomic, and ethnic representation as well as the ability to participate in a committee process, something familiar to Americans but not as common to Israelis. Also crucial was the ability of the candidate for committee membership to see beyond personal needs to a broader, more generalized perspective. Because the local Israeli community is not organized, it was difficult to comply with some of these desired criteria. With all this, a small committee size was preferred to facilitate fruitful discussion.

Two examples may help to illustrate some of the dynamics of the committee: At the first meeting, during the discussion of the mandate statement, one federation leader suddenly burst out, "I don't belong here." He began a lengthy confession expressing his personal conflict with directing energies toward helping Israelis in New York when support and efforts should be directed toward Israel. He went on to say that he left home that morning with the following parting words from his wife: "Don't make it too easy for them." The heated debate that followed reflected the deep ambivalence of American Jews with regard to Israelis in the United States. It is interesting to note that the initiator of the discussion did not attend any further deliberations of the committee. At a subsequent meeting, Israeli committee members had difficulty explaining to the American members some of the cultural differences between Israelis and American Jews. The Americans had trouble understanding the needs of Israelis, including the importance of Hebrew as a medium of communication in reaching out to Israelis, the attitudes to celebrate holidays in Israeli fashion. They, on the other hand, countered with the attitude that while you are in the United States, you must conform to its culture, i.e. "If you want to be a part of the community, you must be like us." The American committee members did not understand the Israelis' ambivalence about "joining" the community.

One of the first tasks of the committee was to gather all available data on the Israeli population in New York. One source was the Greater New York Jewish Population Study, which provided demographic data as well as information on Israeli utilization of Jewish social services and charitable giving patterns.[5] In addition, the committee canvassed existing programs and resources serving Israelis and collected enrollment statistics of Israeli children in Jewish schools. The following picture emerged:

1. Relatively few Israelis are affiliated with New York Jewish communal agencies or utilize the social service network.
2. Many Israeli children are not involved in any form of formal Jewish education.
3. Very few Jewish organizations and agencies have developed programs to reach out to Israelis, either to integrate them into the local Jewish community, or to benefit from their potential contribution to the New York Jewish community.[6]

Psychology of Israeli-Jewish Identity

To understand the needs of Israelis in New York, develop policy, and plan programs, it was important to understand the Israeli-Jewish identity, particularly the psychology of the Israeli living in New York.[7] For these purposes, it is useful to differentiate among three aspects of the Israeli-Jewish identity:

Attitudes toward being Jewish: Jewishness as Nationalism

For most Israelis, Israeli and Jewish identities are closely intertwined and, for some, almost indistinguishable. Jewish identity, particularly for the non-Orthodox Israeli, is often expressed as Jewish nationalism and is closely tied to living in Israel: Israel is a Jewish state; Jews constitute a majority; national holidays are Jewish holidays; and the public school curriculum includes Jewish history, literature, and Bible. Within Israeli society, the religious and secular communities are in many ways socially, culturally, and physically separated. Since the creation of the state in 1948, ideological differences divided the Orthodox community and the socialist pioneers rebelling against the traditions of their Eastern European past. Today's Israeli public school system, which maintains two parallel structures of religious (Orthodox) and secular (nonreligious) schools, reinforces that separation. The non-Orthodox or nonreligious Israeli identifies Jewishly through Israeliness, and religion per se often does not play a role in his or her Jewish identity. Secular Israelis often see the synagogue as a strictly religious institution, the domain of the Orthodox rather than as a central Jewish communal institution in a broader sense.

Thus, Israelis in New York have moved from a culture in which Jews constitute a majority to one in which they are a minority, and from a culture where Jewish identity is a heavily national, secular expression to one where it is religious and ethnic in character. Orthodox Israelis easily find their way to synagogues and other Jewish communal institutions, easing the adjustment to American Jewish life. They are already accustomed to the synagogue as a central Jewish institution and to a religious orientation to their Jewishness. For non-Orthodox Israelis, though, it is more difficult to adjust to their new minority Jewish status, and they must develop new ways to express their Jewishness in a very different, often alien, environment.

One of the committee's tasks was to clarify these differences in Jewish identity between Israelis and American Jews as well as the problems related to adjusting to American Jewish life. To succeed in maintaining the Jewish identity of the Israeli in the United States, the committee realized it was important to recognize and validate the ways in which

Israelis identify as Jews, as well as to expose Israelis to other options of Jewish identification and affiliation within the framework of the American Jewish community. Accepting the "Jewish authenticity," so to speak, of Israelis is central to fostering ties between Israeli Jews and American Jews.

Attitudes toward Israel: Emigration as an Act of Betrayal

As has been noted elsewhere in this section, in the Israeli ideology, migration to Israel is morally praised while emigration from Israel is morally condemned. Israel's educational system and ideology place great value on settling in Israel as the ultimate expression of Jewish fulfillment. For Israelis, leaving Israel is often accompanied by guilt for betraying the homeland or for appearing to do so as perceived by other Israelis or American Jews.

Israelis make distinctions among reasons or intentions for being abroad. "Legitimate" reasons include official Israeli government or institutional assignments or advanced study with the intent of returning. To comport with this thinking, many if not most Israelis in New York view themselves as "sojourners,"[8] that is, temporary residents planning to return shortly or "some day" to Israel; maintaining such sojourner status is important to their Israeli identity. The sojourner mentality, often misunderstood, is in fact a very real and crucial component of the Israeli's identity. The sojourner mentality, which inhibits creating deep roots in the United States or connections with American Jewish institutions, also at times impedes adjustments to and integration within American Jewish life. Maintaining the psychological and social connection with Israel, no matter how long one actually remains in the Diaspora, and maintaining the sojourner status and mentality are of paramount importance. The stigma assigned the *yored* ("descender," permanent emigrant) by both Israelis and American Jews alike, reinforces the desire not to cross the line between "sojourner" and "immigrant."

The committee accepted the legitimacy of the sojourner identity yet sought to establish vehicles of connection for Israelis in New York with the local Jewish community. There is a delicate balance between not losing Israelis to the Jewish community, yet not encouraging *yerida* or a support system for *yerida*. At issue here is a crucial value conflict for American Jews supporting Israel who recognize Israel's need to diminish *yerida* and encourage *aliyah*. The committee believed, however, that it is in the interest of both Israel and the American Jewish community to connect Israelis who are in New York with the local Jewish community. Ignoring *yordim* as if they do not exist is self-defeating and will not yield ultimate positive results for the Jewish community or for Israel. Parenthetically, proliferation of the derogatory term *yored* evokes a condescension and a value judgment somewhat ironic to hear from Jews in the United States.

Attitudes toward American Jews and Organized Jewry: Ambivalence and Distance

The stereotypes and values prevalent in Israeli society generate ambivalent views of Diaspora Jewry among Israelis. On the one hand, many Israelis hold that *galut* (Diaspora) Jewish life is trivial, inauthentic, and precarious. At the same time, Western culture and material opportunities have become increasingly popular and attractive. Moreover, many Israelis view American society as culturally advanced and socially progressive. Upon moving to New York, Israelis encounter the adjustment problems of any immigrants. They experience the culture shock of moving to a new society, and they must go through the typical stages of absorption and cultural change. The significant cultural differences between how Israelis and American Jews express their Jewish identity have already been stated.

Most Israelis are ignorant about the U.S. Jewish organizational structure and are unfamiliar with many of the central institutions of U.S. Jewish life. Moreover, what they do know is often colored by images formed in Israel. As already mentioned, secular Israelis view the synagogue as a limited institution serving limited (religious) needs for a limited (Orthodox) population. As a result, non-Orthodox Israelis often avoid synagogues and other religiously based institutions. Moreover, since its establishment, Israel has not had a tradition of voluntarism; thus, Israelis are not accustomed to "joining" formal organizations, self-help groups, or other voluntary groups. For them, the UJA, to take an important example, not only is a voluntary charity but also represents the quintessentially "Diaspora way" of affirming one's Jewishness as opposed to the "Sabra way." Thus, giving to the campaign signifies joining the Diaspora and severing one's insider status with respect to Israeli society. The perceived dichotomy between a Sabra identity and a Diaspora identity makes it difficult for the Israeli to adjust to U.S. Jewish life.

Like other migrants, recently arrived Israelis feel most comfortable with their compatriots. Even after several years, many Israelis still feel separate and distant from the larger Jewish community. The vastness of New York and the existence of a large Israeli subculture that tends to be insular, reinforce their remoteness from the U.S. Jewish community. On the other hand, American Jews' lack of familiarity with the characteristics and needs of Israelis is an additional barrier to the affiliation of Israelis with New York Jewish communal institutions. Similarly, American Jews do not recognize the potential contribution of Israelis to the U.S. Jewish community at large in such areas as the proliferation of the Hebrew language.

Central to establishing connections between Israelis in the United States and the U.S. Jewish community is a sense of mutuality and a recognition of the Israelis' potential cultural contribution to New York Jewish life so as to benefit from it and to establish a mutual symmetric rather than a client-patron relationship. The committee recognized the need to understand and interpret these issues and dilemmas. Both the Jewish continuity of the Israelis and their children as well as the vitality of the New York Jewish community are at stake. In relating to "Israelis" it is important to recognize the pluralism of Israeli society and to address a number of Israeli communities, with different ethnic and socioeconomic backgrounds and different motivations and intentions for living in the United States. The subcommittee also sought to address similar needs of different groups (children, families, adults, singles) in different ways.

In keeping with its mandate, the committee focused on two high priority areas: Jewish education of children of Israelis, and Jewish identification and communal affiliation of Israeli adults.

Jewish Education of Children of Israelis

Estimates gathered through the Board of Jewish Education indicate that while 40 percent of New York's Jewish children receive a Jewish education, only 25 percent of the children of Israelis in New York are enrolled in Jewish educational programs. Some schools are not appropriate for the Israeli child for whom Hebrew is a mother tongue; others are not acceptable to many Israeli parents because of their religious orientation and auspices. The result is that large numbers of Israeli children go without any form of Jewish education or the opportunity to learn Hebrew. Much of this is the outcome of the Israeli educational system with its separation of religious and secular schools.

The committee identified several factors inhibiting Israeli enrollment in Jewish schools and other educational programs. Recent Israeli immigrants earn less than native American Jews, and thus the high costs of Jewish education prevent many Israelis from seeking a Jewish education for their children. In Israel, they did not need to pay tuition for Jewish education. Israelis, accustomed to being part of a Jewish majority, are likewise accustomed to sending their children to the Israeli "public school.'' Many Israelis in the United States, like many American Jews, see the public school as a valuable vehicle of integration and advancement. Moreover, religious factors often prevent Israelis from sending their children to Jewish schools. As already stated, non-Orthodox Israelis often avoid religiously based schools, synagogues, and other such institutions. Israelis are also unaccustomed to the concept of institutional belongings. Thus, synagogue membership as a condition to enrollment in some schools poses problems for the Israelis.

Many Jewish day school officials are reluctant to admit too many Israelis for fear of changing the religious and cultural ambience of their schools. Some schools accept only Orthodox children, and others resist adjusting their curriculum to accommodate the special needs of Israeli students, which include English language remediation, advanced studies in Hebrew language, and opportunities for preparation for *bagrut* (the Israeli high school matriculation examination).

After gathering data on enrollment statistics, hearing testimony from educators and Israeli parents, and conducting several site visits, the committee recommended the following general policy directions: It is crucial to conduct outreach to Israelis in New York to examine the reasons that Israeli families do not participate in existing programs, to seek ways to motivate Israelis in determining directions for new programs. Likewise, it is vital to further promotional and informational activities to publicize existing schools and programs among Israelis. The assumption can be made that many do not know about the Jewish educational system in the United States and its different philosophies, curricula, and formats.

The committee proposed that the problem of attracting Israelis to religious schools should be first approached from the perspective of Israeli identity, and then Jewish content can be further enriched and incorporated. Thus, for example, a curriculum stressing Hebrew language and literature and Jewish history might be a useful starting point in developing Jewish educational programs that would appeal to the secular Israeli. Once the initial relationship has been established between the school and the Israeli family, it is possible to deepen gradually the connection with the synagogue and include prayer in the curriculum, for example.

Several other points should be considered in targeting children of Israelis for enrollment in Jewish educational institutions. It is important that programs that meet the specific educational needs of Israeli children not be ghettoized but, rather, incorporated into existing Jewish educational structures. If the ultimate goal is connection with the local Jewish community, segregated Israeli schools would not be effective in achieving this goal. Sometimes separate programs may be desirable, but it is advisable to incorporate such programs within, and parallel to, existing schools. For example, Gachelet, a supplementary school for Israeli children, was established at Temple Israel in Great Neck, New York, parallel to the temple's religious school. A second example is Etgar, a supplementary school based on the Gachelet model, which is sponsored by the Central Queens YM and YWHA. Both schools, while geared to the specific needs of Israeli children and conducted in Hebrew, are within U.S. Jewish communal institutions, and thus encourage interaction with both the institution and other American Jews.

Israelis, like American Jews, demand performance and prestige in the quality of their schools, and this should be recognized in developing educational programs. Opportunities for formal as well as informal Jewish education should be explored. Youth groups, community centers, and camps can reach some who cannot be reached by schools. For example, among more than one hundred Israeli children involved in the Hebrew-speaking Israeli Scouts *(Zofim)* group in Forest Hills, New York, most do not attend Jewish schools; Zofim thus serves as a vehicle for their Jewish education. Attention needs to be directed toward both high school and primary school children.

The committee believed that leadership of existing schools needs to be sensitized to the special needs of Israeli students as well as the potential contribution of Israeli students to Jewish schools in creating an Israeli ambience in song, dance, drama, and celebration of Israeli national holidays, as well as in fostering use of the Hebrew language. Experimentation with innovative, untried programs should be encouraged. Camps, particularly those connected to community centers located in areas of high concentration of Israelis, should be encouraged to focus recruitment efforts on children of Israelis and this should be backed up with scholarship opportunities, where the need exists. Hebrew-language groups within English-speaking camps and possibilities for a Hebrew-speaking camp with strong outreach to Israelis are areas for exploration. Camps could also be excellent settings for family vacationing programs.

Jewish Identification and Communal Affiliation of Israeli Adults

Elsewhere in this paper I have discussed some of the fundamental problems that prevent Israelis from affiliating with the U.S. Jewish community. The communication problem involves both Israelis in New York as well as the New York Jewish community. Lack of contact and little understanding of cultural differences have created stigmas that must be overcome by both communities. To build understanding and trust, there is a need for education and more diversified contact and interaction between Israelis and American Jews. The committee recommended that staffs and boards of Jewish communal institutions should be educated about the characteristics and potential contributions of Israelis; likewise, Israelis should learn about the Jewish communal structure of U.S. Jewry, the federation service network, and how one affiliates as a Jew in the United States. Lectures on Israelis might be directed to agency leadership groups as well as to more general audiences. Dialogues between different types of American Jews and their Israeli counterparts would also facilitate communication.

Several principles were formulated as a pragmatic approach to enhancing Israeli affiliation. An incremental, community-based approach was recommended for outreach to Israelis on a neighborhood basis; Israelis would be involved in the planning and implementation of programs for Israelis. Different sectors within the Israeli population may need different types of programming. By offering programs geared to Israelis, agencies would encourage Israelis to affiliate with Jewish institutions. In outreach activities, a concentrated and consistent, rather than diffuse and sporadic, effort would be more effective. Based on testimony from the directors of existing programs for Israelis and from Israeli groups, as well as a gained understanding of the Israeli mentality and the barriers to Jewish affiliation, the committee focused on religious, cultural, and social needs.

Despite the lack of familiarity of secular Israelis with the synagogue, outreach efforts centered on the Jewish communal and cultural needs of Israelis—in areas such as holiday celebration programs, home hospitality for holidays, or Hebrew libraries—can be a means toward involving Israelis with the synagogue as a central American Jewish institution. Synagogues within areas of concentration of Israelis should be encouraged to develop special High Holy Day Services for Israelis. All the available evidence suggests that this model should be free of charge (because Israelis are not accustomed to and react negatively to the concept of synagogue dues) and conducted and publicized in Hebrew. The importance of language and mother tongue in communication must be stressed. Hebrew is also the bridge between the Israeli and the synagogue. An additional bridge between the "secular" Israeli and the synagogue is the desire and need to celebrate Jewish holidays among Israelis in a manner familiar to Israelis. Holiday celebration represents an excellent vehicle to establish connection with the Israeli community. For example, a self-help group, Israelis in New York, Inc., had its beginnings in planning holiday celebrations and often approached synagogues for space and as the setting for these activities. Synagogues should encourage these contacts. The alternatives, as seen in recent years in New York City, are mass Israeli holiday celebrations in discotheques.

Israelis take great pride in their cultural heritage and are seeking to capture the nostalgic memories and common experiences of Israel. Israeli arts, culture, and entertainment are important vehicles to respond to this need, and they also represent areas in which Israelis can make a significant contribution to New York Jewish cultural life. The B'Tzavta coffee house, until recently a program of the Educational Alliance in New York, was an excellent example of this, serving as a major center of Israeli cultural events.[9]

Israelis place a high value on reading and, in the United States, have limited access to Hebrew books for either adults or children. Establishment of Hebrew libraries and the proliferation of Hebrew literary programs within Jewish institutions such as community centers and synagogues would not only serve Israelis but also represent a significant contribution to the American Hebrew-speaking public, promote the Hebrew language among the New York Jews, and provide a meeting ground for Israelis and Hebrew-speaking New Yorkers. Lectures, forums, and discussions in Hebrew on contemporary Israeli issues in such areas as politics, the economy, and social issues would also help Israelis retain and express their connection with Israel.

Beyond the general need to create opportunities to meet with other Israelis and other Jews, the committee focused on several specific areas. Israeli traditions of family outings and vacations and the Israeli love of nature, camping, and the sea suggest the use of residential camping facilities as settings for family vacations. Such settings might also be an appropriate forum for dialogue between Israeli and American Jewish families.

Because of the nature of their programs and facilities, their neighborhood base, and their relatively neutral ideology, community centers could play a leading role in outreach efforts to the Israeli population. Involvement of Israelis in program planning and use of the Hebrew language are central to the success of these efforts. Community center efforts should focus on informal Jewish education and camping for children of Israelis, and on meeting the cultural and social needs of Israelis.

The committee made some recommendations that related to the New York Jewish Federation and the UJA-Federation Campaign. A Hebrew brochure describing the federation and its network of agencies would be a useful resource to acquaint Israelis with the local Jewish community. The Jewish Information and Referral Service should be encouraged to recruit Hebrew-speaking volunteers and to publicize this service in the

Hebrew media. The federation should initiate an ongoing forum for professionals working with Israelis for the exchange of ideas and experiences. It was suggested that the campaign seek ways by which to connect Israelis with it by tailoring fund-raising efforts to the Israeli communities and developing Hebrew fund-raising materials. The subcommittee suggested that a full-day conference be planned for Jewish institutional leadership on the topic "Israelis in New York."

After developing its policy on service to Israelis, the New York federation approved an incremental, three-year implementation plan. One year later, many positive and concrete developments are already evident, particularly outreach programs in four community centers and the creation of Jewish educational settings for children of Israelis. Most of these programs have become possible through leverage funding offered by the federation. It is doubtful that many of these initiatives would have occurred were it not for this encouragement from the federation. Some resistance still exists on the part of some segments of the federation community to viewing service to Israelis as a communal priority. Continued reinforcement by the federation of its policy direction and active encouragement of the relevant agencies is necessary.

The policy and service plan emphasizes Jewish education and affiliation with the local Jewish community. The community saw fit to differentiate Israeli emigres from Jews who have left countries of persecution, e.g. Jews from the Soviet Union or Iranian Jews, and, thus, to avoid development of special services for Israelis in areas with primary immigrant needs, e.g. jobs, housing, language. The analogy with these other Jewish newcomers was deemed inappropriate, and it was believed that Jewish communal dollars should not be allocated for specific programs to help Israelis settle in New York. The adopted policy views Israelis as an unaffiliated (rather than immigrant) group, and the service plan reflects this.

Many gray areas remain to be addressed, some of which call into question central social values of the Jewish community: Should New York's interagency homeless project accept the growing numbers of Israelis seeking its services, some of whom are in the United States on expired tourist visas? What are the implications of providing temporary food and shelter for Israelis who cannot legally find employment? And what of those Israelis who wish to return "home" but need some financial assistance to do so? Is this a responsibility of the individual? the local Jewish community? the Israeli government? the Jewish agency? What of the many Israelis who come to New York for medical reasons, e.g. special operations, and turn to the local community for financial assistance? Should the organized community have an infrastructure in place to respond to these needs?

In summary, regardless of one's political and philosophical opinions and leanings in regard to the Israeli population in New York, the fact is that there are substantial numbers of Israelis living in New York. The Federation of Jewish Philanthropies of New York has attempted to determine a concrete direction and plan to reach out to Israelis so as to connect them to the New York Jewish community and so that the community can benefit from their contribution to New York Jewish life. The first critical step was the development of a policy. Beginning with a policy conflict that first appeared to be irreconcilable, the New York Jewish community was able to move forward with a resolution of policy and direction. The next critical stage was the development of an incremental implementation plan and the securing of the necessary resources, both financial and organizational commitment, to implement the programmatic recommendations. Some of these recommendations have already been implemented. Some are in the planning stages. Others depend on the response and interest of both Israelis and local Jewish organizations.

Notes

1. Report of the Subcommittee on Service to Israelis in New York to the Communal Planning Committee of Federation of Jewish Philanthropies of New York, March, 1983.
2. Steven Mr. Cohen, see article in this collection.
3. Minutes, Communal Planning Committee, Federation of Jewish Philanthropies of New York, 26 March 1982.
4. Unlike other Jewish communities in the United States, in New York three distinct organizations exist: United Jewish Appeal of Greater New York, Federation of Jewish Philanthropies of New York, and the UJA-Federation Campaign, which conducts a united fund-raising effort.
5. Federation of Jewish Philanthropies of New York, New York, 1984.
6. For further information on demographic data on Israelis in New York, see Paul Ritterband's article in this collection.
7. Drora Kass has conducted research on the identity of Israelis in the United States for a book on this subject.
8. For an analysis of migration, Jewish identity, and Israeli migration to the United States, see Pini Herman and David LaFontaine, 1983.
9. Moshe Shokeid of Tel Aviv University is currently working on a study of the social and cultural significance of Israeli sing-alongs. His work is based on an analysis of the sing-alongs sponsored by the Israeli club at the Central Queens YM-YWHA.

References**References**

Cohen, Steven M. 1985. "Israeli Emigres and the New York Federation: A Case Study in Ambivalent Policy Making for 'Jewish Communal Deviants.' " *Contemporary Jewry*, this volume.

Federation of Jewish Philanthropies of New York. 1984. *The Jewish Population of Greater New York: A Profile.*

Herman, Pini, and LaFontaine, David. 1983. "In Our Footsteps: Isareli Migration to the United States and Los Angeles." (Master's thesis, Hebrew Union College-Jewish Institute of Religion and the University of Southern California.

Ritterband, Paul. 1985. "Israelis in New York." *Contemporary Jewry,* this volume.

BOOK REVIEWS

In this section we include three book reviews that were written for previous publications of Contemporary Jewry *but were not published at that time. In an effort to be faithful to our reviewers and readers, we have made the publication of these book reviews a priority. Future volumes of* Contemporary Jewry *will seek to publish a small number of review essays about the books regarded to be the most central to our field of interest. Reviewers will be asked to write one essay on preferably two or more related books recently published. Suggestions as to books to be reviewed and authors to write the reviews are welcomed by the Editorial Office.*

Values and Violence in Auschwitz
by Anna Pawelczynska
Berkeley: University of California Press, 1979, 169 pages.

Reviewer: *Celia S. Heller*

The Spring/Summer 1980 issue of *Contemporary Jewry* carried a full-page advertisement of this book without realizing its nature. But how can one explain that a serious university press published such a grotesque book, let alone advertised it in a Jewish journal? For this is a book about Auschwitz that omits the Jews who died there. Nowhere in it do we encounter any statement that the Jews, as a people, were marked for total destruction. The author also omits the important fact that more than half of those killed in Auschwitz were Jews. Thus, for example, she begins chapter 5, "Social Differentiation and the Odds for Survival," with the sentence, "The transports that arrived at Auschwitz brought men and women representing all the traditions of Europe," but fails to add that foremost among them were Jews. In the beginning of her book, Pawelczynska presents a short history of Nazism (pp. 6-10) but does not mention the Nazi ideology and programs concerning Jews. Even when she specifically writes about Nazi racism, she avoids mentioning the central role that Jews occupied in that ideology. Jews were considered the lowest, the most dangerous race, devoid of all humanity.

Since the author almost completely omits the unique situation of the Jews, she can generalize about an important factor in the survival of inmates, which applied to Poles but, alas, not to Jews. As she puts it, "Every camp, every prison of Poland was surrounded by a similar atmosphere of fraternal support. . . . No matter how—given the circumstances under Nazi terror—that support might be actualized, the very awareness that it existed had incommensurable moral and emotional consequences both for prisoners and outside supporters." Clearly, the author does not tell us that this kind of support was lacking not only in the case of Jews from other lands, but in the case of Polish Jews outside, as well as in, the death camps. Polish Jews who were passing as Poles or hiding were in constant fear of being handed over by Poles to the Nazis. Frequently, the Nazis could not at first tell some Jews apart from Poles.

But, as the murdered Jewish historian Ringelblum expessed it in his diary found after the war, there were enough Poles to point out to the Nazis who was a Jew. Nevertheless, the painful remembrance of this horrible reality must not overshadow the existence of other Poles. The fact that some, even if few, Jews survived on Polish soil is a testimony not only to their indestructible will to live but also to the supreme humanity of some exceptional Poles who risked their lives to make such survival possible.

For an American sociologist it is unquestionably hard to visualize a book by a fellow sociologist who claims "to consider the concentration camp in objective categories," and yet fails to mention, let alone discuss, the Nazi program and treatment of Jews. The book could have achieved some sociological objectivity had the author explicitly confined herself to the treatment of Poles and other non-Jews in Auschwitz. But no, she sets no limitations. She states at the very beginning that her aim was an "objective" study of "mechanisms which the concentration camp operated" and "the mechanisms which caused some of the prisoners to survive" (p. 1). However, in her last chapter, "People and Values," Pawelczynska inadvertently admits that under the guise of writing a general treatise on Auschwitz, she wrote a book about Poles in Auschwitz. She tells us openly that she limits her discussion of values to Polish values "on the assumption that the majority of conclusions pertain to the prisoners as a whole, regardless of what cultural system shaped them, or what values were instilled by their milieu in the process of their upbringing, or of what authorities uphold the moral standards they recognized" (p. 135). This is quite an assumption, and yet the author does not bother to spell out what its basis is. And so she continues to tell us how the Auschwitz inmates, brought up in Christian values (mind you, not Judeo-Christian), changed their moral dicta under the impact of camp brutality.

Those acquainted with the official ideology in today's Poland would not be surprised that such a book appeared in Poland. And, indeed, the book was written in Polish by a Polish sociologist and first published in Poland. As such, its character of skipping over Jewish martyrdom fits well with the official line of the Polish government. Like the Soviet one, it has decided that Jews must not be cited as *particular* victims of the Nazis. For example, the special nature of the Warsaw Ghetto uprising of 1943 is not to be mentioned; the uprising must be seen as part of the "national Polish struggle against the forces of racism and fascism" (see "Epilogue" in C.S. Heller, *On the Edge of Destruction: Jews of Poland. . .*, 1977, paperback, 1980).

That Pawelczynska's book in English translation appeared in the U.S., not published by one of the anti-Semitic or racist presses but by the prestigious University of California Press, Berkeley, is surprising. Until now—during the entire post-World War II period—it has been inconceivable that a respected American university publishing house would come out with a "scholarly" book, so glaring in its distortion of a not-too-distant historical reality: the reality of the Holocaust.

The Religious Drop-Outs
by David Caplovitz and Fred Sherrow
Beverly Hills: Sage Publications, 1977, 196 pages

Reviewer: *George Kranzler*

Though one may raise some questions about the methodology and approach of *The Religious Drop-Outs* from the perspective of Jewish community research, it is a highly significant study of the loss of faith among college graduates.

The phenomenon of apostasy came into focus in the 1960s, and continues to grow and concern scholars and lay leaders because of its portents for the future of organized religion in this country. Caplovitz and Sherrow's superior analysis of three major sources of data—the National Opinion Research Center (NORC) studies of 35,000 college seniors between 1961 and 1968, the 1969 Carnegie study of undergraduates, graduates, and faculty, and the annual studies of entering college freshmen of the American Council of Higher Education between 1966 and 1976—seems to justify this concern in their conclusion, based on the findings of 15 years of research: "Apostasy increased dramatically in all three religions, a growth that judging from the ACE date on incoming freshmen, is an inexorable process" (p. 188). On these grounds, Caplovitz and Sherrow estimate that "Were this trend to continue unchecked, it may well mean that in fifty years or so, America's religious communities as we know them today, will have disappeared" (ibid.).

It will be difficult to find fault with the sophisticated techniques, the superior structure, and the underlying reasoning of this valuable study. The authors construct a theoretical framework—based on their own and related research—that contains the crucial elements of religiosity and what they call the five major "germs" of apostasy. Since all of their major sources used the same two NORC questions on the religious upbringing and the current religion of the students sampled, *The Religious*

Drop-Outs yields invaluable information on the change of faith and the broader dynamics of apostasy and provides a sound test for some of the hypotheses of previous studies. Thus, for example, the authors are able to debunk the popular notion of apostasy as a "static" phenomenon and to develop a meaningful profile of the types of students susceptible to it, and the processes involved in it. They do confirm the common assumption that the college scene in general, and graduate school in particular, breed religious drop-outs because of the positivist scepticism and the secular humanism endemic to academia.

In their update, particularly of the American Council on Education studies of incoming freshmen, analyzed in the later phase of their research, Caplovitz and Sherrow go beyond the early findings based mainly on the study of college seniors. They conclude that the roots of apostasy are increasingly to be found in the students' precollege life. They also find that denominational colleges, which had been a strong bastion against religious defection in the early 1960s, no longer serve this function. This is particularly true for Catholic students, whose enrollment in denominational colleges dropped from 42 percent to 15 percent. As they flock to secular colleges in ever growing numbers, including the "high apostasy" prestigious universities, apostasy among Catholics has increased by an alarming 172 percent. This raises their rate of defection close to that of Jewish students, who, in spite of greater variations in the trends of apostasy and return to religion, rank highest with 21 percent, at the peak of this research. Caplovitz and Sherrow suggest that Catholics do so "under the pressure of upward mobility," because, as already found by Lazarsfeld and Thielens, Jr. in *The Academic Mind* (New York: 1958), the education at denominational colleges is generally considered inferior. *The Religious Drop-Outs* also confirms that women are generally more deeply religious and that socioeconomic status is not a crucial factor of apostasy for most. It emphasizes that conversion is not, as is generally assumed, the next step in the process of religious defection that starts with apostasy. Conversion constitutes a minor phenomenon: 2 percent for Jews, 4 percent for Catholics, and 6 percent for Protestants. Frequently it serves merely to solve problems created by intermarriage. Of the five crucial germs of apostasy—poor parental relations, maladjustment, religiosity, radical orientation, and commitment to intellectualism and universal values—the authors, not unexpectedly, find the degree of religiosity to be the most important.

In their theoretical framework, Caplovitz and Sherrow place major emphasis on the differences between the two types of religious commitment which they, with Lenski and Herberg, label "religiosity" and "communality" or "ethnicity." They use this distinction to explain the variations in the dynamics of apostasy among Protestants, Catholics, and Jewish students. In their opinion, "In spite of their propensity for the germs of apostasy, the overwhelming majority of Jews have little difficulty retaining their identity as Jews even though they are not religious" (p. 180). Based on this assumption and on the phenomena of recent religious revival and charismatic movements dedicated to communal living, Caplovitz and Sherrow conclude: "The future may yet see the emergence of 'secularized religions that have their wellsprings in the psychic energy that is generated by communal life' " (ibid.).

Since *The Religious Drop-Outs* is an expansion of what started as a study of Jewish identity among college graduates, it may not be improper to raise some questions about it from the vantage point of Jewish social research. Granted that Caplovitz and Sherrow have provided valuable empirical evidence and conceptual research models for the dynamics of religious defection and return, a glance at the foreword of Milton Himmelfarb will indicate what worries the scholar about this otherwise superior study. Himmelfarb questions the authors' attribution of the dramatic increase of religious defection among Catholics to the pressure of upward mobility. He does not question the authors' findings concerning the Jewish studnets' apostasy or return; but he does suggest a serious lack of reference to current events in the period studied, mentioning the effect of such "numerous" occurrences as the Six-Day War in Israel and the Jewish awakening of Soviet Jewry's "dry bones" to explain changes in the attitude of the Jewish students.

Although there is little room here for more intensive exploration of the historical context, it seems mandatory to make a few points concerning the meaning and approach of *The Religious Drop-Outs*. Methodologically, one may question whether the Jewish samples in the three major sources of data—the NORC, the 1969 Carnegie study, and the American Council on Education studies of freshmen—are representative. The peculiarities of the composition and the geographical location of the bulk of the American Jewish community require a distribution different from the standard national sampling of college students. Furthermore, since the primary studies were not concerned with the religious background per se, even though they used the NORC questions about it, their populations may not yield reliable information. More important, on the conceptual level, scholars like Caplovitz and Sherrow (who, before his untimely death, had played a significant role in the religious reorientation and search for Jewish meaning on the Columbia University campus) should have made a clear distinction between Jewishness and Judaism. They should have emphasized that in the context of their research one cannot speak of "Jews" in the same manner as one does of

Catholics and Protestants. First, there is no single Jewish community; there are three distinct Jewish communities: the Reform, the Conservative, and the Orthodox. The terms *ethnicity or communality* are hardly adequate to characterize the differential behavior and values of the students that have grown up in them, have defected from them, or have returned to one of them or to a new, alternate form of Judaism or Jewishness. The crucial differences between the three main communities (the roughly 35 percent of American Jews who identify with the Reform movement, the approximately 40 percent who identify with the Conservative movement, and the close to 15 percent whose whole lifestyle is determined by their membership in the Orthodox community) are not simply more or less religiosity or variations in doctrines and theology. What sets them apart is largely a matter of their perception of the nature of the Jewish identity as a religion, a race, an ethnic minority, a secular nation, or a religio-cultural community. Perhaps, had this study been done prior to World War II, when American Jews were still caught up in their headlong flight from the Old-World taint and the *shtetl* mentality of their immigrant parents' or grandparents' lifestyle, one might have accepted the findings of the Caplovitz and Sherrow research on apostasy of college students without much qualm about oversimplification. Yet even then, at the height of the successful assimilation of American Jews into the mainstream of middle-class suburbia, the authors' approach would have overlooked the fact that the more than a third of American Jews who identify with the Reform movement reject the age-old Jewish identity to peoplehood, of the synthesis of the religious, national, and cultural elements that had enabled the Jewish people to survive in exile under the best, as well as the worst, of conditions, in order to create a "church" of their own, very much like that of their Protestant neighbors. Equally, *The Religious Drop-Outs*, if written a generation ago, would have disregarded the essence of political Zionism that had swept up the Jewish world since the end of the nineteenth century. Its national, international, and cultural elements became as meaningful to the majority of American Jews as these elements had been for the vast masses of East European Jews caught in the throes of severe oppression and persecution, and gradually to those of Central and Western Europe, with the darkening horizon of the approaching Holocaust. Terms like *communality* or *ethnicity* hardly do justice to the impact of Zionism and its "old-new" dream of a new, secular reunion of the land, the people, and its historical mission. Charles Liebman, in a superb article (*Commentary*, August '77) rejects the favored sociological "accommodationist" theory and emphasizes the essential distinctiveness of the American Jewish community that survived even among the most anti-Zionist or nonreligious elements. This distinctiveness defies such simplistic generalizations as the greater "communality" of Jews to explain the variance and inconsistency of the trends of Jewish religious defection among the Jewish students in *The Religious Drop-Outs*.

Still, one might have accepted the book's format a generation ago. But it is incomprehensible how any research into Jewish identity and apostasy among Jewish college youth in the 1960s and 1970s disregards the significant events and changes that shook the Jewish students of the hippie/yippie, Haight-Ashbury, and Woodstock generation. They were jolted out of their complacency by the growing awareness of the real dimensions of inhumanity emerging from the still incomplete records of the Holocaust. They were disillusioned by the attitude of the radical left, who admittedly chose to ignore it in favor of other, less "tainted," causes. They were no less shocked by the inaction of the "free World" than by the crimes committed by Nazi Germany—a traditionally highly cultured nation of superior contributions in most realms of intellectual, aesthetic, and technological endeavor—against Jews and other human beings. The Jewish students of the 1960s and 1970s were alternately elated, as well as shaken, by the triumphs of the Six-Day War and by the events that preceded and followed it—by the losses, handicaps, and agonies of Israel's survival under harrowing circumstances imposed on it by the combined power and influence of the Arab nations, the Soviet Union, and a largely hostile world. No matter how accurate, the astringent statistics of *The Religious Drop-Outs* do not adequately reflect to what degree personal acquaintance with, and the experience of, Israel, and the conduct of the United Nations, orchestrated by the Soviet Union and its satellites, disillusioned or inspired Jewish youth everywhere in their Jewish Middletowns or Lakevilles and turned them back to their roots long before roots became fashionable. A glance at the Jewish student publications indicates that revulsion from the typical Jewish suburban middle-class spirit—from the emphasis on "cardiac" and "culinary" Judaism, as they called it. The intellectually mobile, like Fred Sherrow himself, went in search of their Jewish identity via intensive study, seeking Jewish knowledge other than what they had been fed in their Hebrew or Sunday schools, and achieved a level of active commitment. Thousands who had become disillusioned with the "isms" of their radical past, moved towards greater "Jewishness." Hundreds flocked to the idealism of Kibbutz life, temporarily or permanently. Others formed *Havurot* and similar groups or institutions that developed their own forms and rituals, or they joined traditional communities and schools for intensive study and a total commitment to Judaism on a scale that could hardly have been anticipated in the 1950s.

A study of Jewish identity and drop-out among Jewish college students cannot totally overlook facts such as that hundreds of American colleges and universities, among them some of the most prestigious, established flourishing Jewish studies departments, that 35 instituted Yiddish language and culture courses that unquestionably contributed to the potential renaissance of interest and involvement in Jewish cultural and religious activities among the Jewish students under investigation in the later years of the Caplovitz and Sherrow study. Quite a few Jewish college students have even moved so far as to join the so-called ultra-orthodox Hasidic and similar Jewish subcommunities, as evidenced in a number of recent Jewish community studies.

Finally, apropos Hasidim (or Chassidim) a footnote in the book indicates its stereotypical approach when the authors state: "Within the Jewish community, the one group that has rejected the goal of upward mobility in favor of religious purity and continuity of the religious community is the Chassidim" (p. 190). Anyone familiar with the large Hasidic communities in the United States knows that in spite of their emphasis on religious purity and their "wanted otherness" or outright isolation, they have displayed an amazing ability to engineer their upward mobility with equal, if not greater, success than many of the previous waves of Jewish immigrants who entered and remained part of the American proletariat. Among them are still large segments of the Jewish poor, who constitute about 25 percent of the Jewish community. But among them are also a large number of highly successful business-men, manufacturers, professionals, academicians, and officials in the lower and middle levels of city, state, and federal bureaucracies. While they retain and perpetuate their intensive Jewish religious and communal identity, they have entered the mainstream of the American work force and are as successful and upward bound as other groups with fewer handicaps and self-chosen or self-created problems. Their major sub-communities have thousands of members with large families. One has only to visit such centers as Boro Park and Flatbush, in Brooklyn, or their new exurban communities in upstate New York or New Jersey to find the display of middle and upper-middle class status symbols, as well as the tokens of their intentional distinctiveness.

The mere statistics of historical or sociological research have hardly ever come to grips with the essence of existence and survival. In spite of the significant findings they have yielded in *The Religious Drop-Outs*, Caplovitz and Sherrow miss their very significance because they do not relate them to the historical context of the period they have researched. They fail to realize or adequately emphasize the fact that in their study four or five college students sampled have not defected from their Jewish community, and that only 2 percent admit conversion. Nor do they point to the significance of their findings when related to the dangerously low Jewish birth rate and the growing rate of intermarriage, which in the 1960s affected a third of all Jewish marriages.

Whereas one cannot deny the importance of this superior study of religious apostasy among college students, Jewish community researchers must question some of its approaches and interpretations.

Magic Carpet: Aleppo-in-Flatbush—
The Study of a Unique Ethnic Jewish Community

by Joseph A.D. Sutton. Foreword by S.D. Goitein.
New York: Thayer-Jacoby 1979, 304 pages

Reviewer: *Abraham D. Lavender*

Magic Carpet is a sociological and historical study of the Syrian Jewish community in Flatbush, Brooklyn, New York. The methodology utilized is a mixture of participant observation (the author is a descendant of a Jewish family from Aleppo, and for sixty-five years has been a member of the New York Syrian community) and historical analysis.

Moving from the present to the past, *Magic Carpet* is divided into Book I, "The American Experience," and Book II, "Life in the Orient." In addition, there are fifty pages of appendixes that discusses a variety of topics. In Book I, Sutton begins with a social portrait analyzing the Syrian Jewish migration to the United States in the early twentieth century. He further describes the trials they "underwent in a sea of a million East European Jews with a culture so alien to the accustomed tranquility of their minaret-studded city in the Orient" (p.x). The immigrants brought with them a commercial background, a strong sense of *gemeinschaft* values, and a strong devotion to Judaism. Established more than seventy years ago (1907-1908), and now numbering 20,000 to 25,000, the community is today well-off economically, still religiously observant, and still "insular" in its interaction with other groups. Sutton explores several issues: the ways of experiencing sorrows and joys, occupational change, religious life, youth and education, and class structure. He closes Book I with a social profile of six families, noting such practices as cousin marriages—"a not uncommon marriage among Jews from the Orient." The author suggests several factors underlying the maintenance of tradition by the Syrian Jews: the longevity of Jewish life in the Fertile Crescent, the combining of religious practices with the life and culture of the Arab world, the status of Jews as a self-governing group under Islam, and the drawing together of the immigrants in the United States for comfort and survival.

Book II traces the history of Jewish life in Syria, a history of unequal but tolerant treatment. The author notes in detail the interaction of Jews and Moslems, and concludes that persecution of Jews was not widespread in the Near East. A number of specific topics, illustrating the history of Jews in Syria, are discussed.

Sutton integrates the points from Books I and II, and concludes, regarding the present Syrian Jewish community in New York, that "barring major unheavals in the life of the country, it is reasonable to look to a perpetuation of the Syrian community life for the foreseeable future" (p. 229).

Magic Carpet makes several major contributions to the sociology of Jewry and to the sociology of ethnicity. It is a major factual, descriptive addition to the sociology of world Jewry—to Jewish life in the Near and Middle East in the medival era and to Jewish-Arabic life today. The book's preservation and recording of "Jewish-Arabic memories and customs in the old world before the erosion of time makes this an impossibility" (p. xii) should be a model for other Jewish communities. The book also makes an important contribution to several specific issues in the study of Jewry. For example, in addition to contributing more information to the controversy over the relative treatment of Jews by Christians and Moslems, the book also reaffirms that Sephardic Orthodoxy is different from Ashkenazic Orthodoxy. The analysis of the interaction of Arabic values and customs with Jewish values and customs, and the analysis of "a community where exceptional pressures of assimilation, pressures which have markedly altered the character of other immigrant generations" (p. ix), make important contributions to the sociology of ethnicity. The book does not follow a particular theoretical orientation, but relates a number of findings to theoretical concepts—particularly assimilation and pluralism.

Magic Carpet is interesting and written in an easily read style. It is strongly recommended for students of Jewry and ethnicity, particularly for those who know little about the "Sephardic, Oriental, Arabic" side of the Jewish family.

APPENDIX

Recent Research on Contemporary Jewry: A Compendium of Abstracts

Rena Cheskis and *Arnold Dashefsky*

1981

American Sociological Association

S13271. Hartman, Moshe, Familistic Tendencies and Religiosity.

S13272. Hartman, Moshe & Stinner, William F., International Migration and Labor Force Participation of Married Women.

S12565. York, Alan S. & Lazerwitz, Bernard, Religious Affiliation as the Gateway to General Voluntary Activity and Communal Leadership.

Sociology of the Arts

83N1360. Cohen, David, Remarques historiques et sociolinguistiques sur les parlers arabes des Juifs maghrébins.

83N1411. Sephiha, Haïm Vidal, " 'Christianismes' en judéo-espagnol (calque et vernaculaire).

83N1420. Tannen, Deborah, New York Jewish Conversational Style.

Association for the Sociology of Religion

S12845. Kohn, Rachel L.E., Dual Membership and Sectarian Status: The Case of a Hebrew-Christian Group.

Community Development

83N0279. Rayman, Paula, Co-Operative Movement Confronts Centralization: Israeli Kibbutz Regional Organizations.

83M8666. Waxman, Chaim I., The Fourth Generation Grows Up: The Contemporary American Jewish Community.

Complex Organizations (Management)

83N0924. Bergman, Gerald S., Work Satisfaction and General Adjustment of Migrants.

Culture and Social Structure

83N4203. Fredman, Ruth Gruber, Cosmopolitans at Home: The Sephardic Jews of Washington, D.C.

Delinquency

82M3720. Cromer, Gerald, Repentant Delinquents: A Religious Approach to Rehabilitation.

Demography and Human Biology

82M4905. Berman, Yitzhak, Internal Migration Patterns in Israel.

83N0032. Medoff, Marshall H ., Some Differences between the Jewish and General White Male Population in the United States.

82M2468. Soldinger, Roberto B., Sociologia de la immigración.

Rural Sociology and Agricultural Economics

83M8009. Baker, Wayne & Hertz, Rosanna, Communal Diffusion of Friendship: The Structure of Intimate Relations in an Israeli Kibbutz.

Sociology of Education

82M4757. Rich, Yisrael, Amir, Yehuda & Ben-Ari, Rachel, Social and Emotional Problems Associated with Integration in the Israeli Junior High School.

83M9819. Sigal, John, August, David & Beltempo, Joseph, Impact of Jewish Education on Jewish Identification in a Group of Adolescents.

82M6325. Stahl, Abraham, The Americanization of Educational Research in Israel.

The Family and Socialization

83N0106. Lazerwitz, Bernard, Jewish-Christian Marriages and Conversions.

81L9253. Peres, Yochanan & Katz, Ruth, Stability and Centrality: The Nuclear Family in Modern Israel.

83N0119. Steinmetz, Suzanne K., A Cross-Cultural Comparison of Marital Abuse.

Feminist Studies

83M8732. Izraeli, Dafna N., The Zionist Women's Movement in Palestine, 1911-1927: A Sociological Analysis.

Group Interactions

83M7489. Bernstein, Deborah, Immigrant Transit Camps—The Formation of Dependent Relations in Israeli Society.

82L9872. Bensimon, Doris, Sociologie des jucaïcïtés contemporaines: bilan et perspectives de la recherche française.

82M3165. Bernstein, Judith & Antonovsky, Aaron, The Integration of Ethnic Groups is Israel.

82M5755. Carmon, Naomi, Economic Integration of Immigrants.

82L9875. Driedger, Leo & Mezoff, Richard A., Ethnic Prejudice and Discrimination in Winnipeg High Schools.

82M3186. Rofé, Yacov & Weller, Leonard, Ethnic Group Prejudice and Class in Israel.

83M7522. Rose, Peter I, Blacks and Jews. The Strained Alliance.

S11471. Rosenstein, Carolyn Nancy, Rates of Return, Processes and Assets: Status Attainment of Israeli Jews.

82M4167. Shamir, Roas, Some Differences in Work Attitudes between Arab and Jewish Hotel Workers: An Exploratory Study.

82M5781. Soen, Dan, Cultural Confrontation of an Algerian Family with Israeli Reality and the Effect on Its Social Adjustment.

83N0872. Walker, Ian, The Jews of Cheetham Hill.

83M7528. Weinfield, Morton, Myth and Reality in the Canadian Mosaic: "Affective Ethnicity."

Sociology, History and Theory

82M3170. Gartner, Lloyd P., Urban History and the Pattern of Provincial Jewish Settlement in Victorian England.

82M3174. Lambroza, Shlomo, Jewish Self-Defence during the Russian Pogroms of 1903-1906.

82M5616. Porter, Jack Nusan, The Urban Middleman: A Comparative Analysis.

83N0652. Silberman, Alphons, Zur Problematik einer "Soziologie der Juden."

Sociology of Knowledge

83N0247. Eisenzweig, Uri, An Imaginary Territory: The Problematic of Space in Zionist Discourse.

82M6818. Miller, Justin, Interpretations of Freud's Jewishness, 1924-1974.

Sociology of Leisure

82M1914. Dubin, Robert & Aharoni, Yair, Ideology and Reality: Work and Pay in Israel.

Marxist Sociology

82M6981. Clark, Joseph, Marx and the Jews: Another View.

Mass Phenomena

83M7758. Prokop, Dieter, "Holocaust" and the Effects of Violence on Television: A Report on Interviews Conducted in Frankfurt.

82M3329. Semyonov, Moshe & Yuchtman-Yaar, Ephraim, Professional Sports as an Alternative Channel of Social Mobility.

Political Interactions

82M6024. Coser, Lewis, Afterthoughts on the Israeli Election.

82M3383. York, Alan S., American Jewish Leaders from the Periphery.

Sociology of Relegion

82M3549. Furman, Frida Kerner, Ritual as Social Mirror and Agent of Cultural Change: A Case Study in Synagogue Life.

82M3553. Löwy, Michael, Messianisme juif et utopies libertaires en Europe centrale (1905-1923).

83M9881. Wasserman, Harry, Bubis, Gerald B. & Lert, Alan, a Study of *Havurot* in Five Synagogues in the Los Angeles Area.

Social Anthropology (and Ethnology)

83M7542. Goldberg, Helene S., Funeral and Bereavement Rituals of Kota Indians and Orthodox Jews.

Social Control

82M6453. Saltman, Michael, Legality and Ideology in the Kibbutz Movement.

Social Differentiation

83M9592. Kraus, Vered & Weintraub, Dov, Community Structure and the Status Attainment Process of the Jewish Population in Israel.

Social Psychology

83N2350. Guttman, Joseph, Various Measures of Moral Judgment as a Function of Social Pressure.

83M7405. Huneke, Douglas, A Study of Christians Who Rescued Jews during the Nazi Era.

83N2353. Jaffe, Yoram, Shapir, Nahum, & Yinon, Yoel, Aggression and Its Escalation.

Social Problems and Social Welfare

83M8626. Landau, Simha F., Juveniles and the Police. Who Is Charged Immediately and Who Is Referred to the Juvenile Bureau?

83N0242. Shichor, David & Ellis, Ruth, Begging in Israel: An Exploratory Study.

83N0238. Rahav, Giora, Culture Conflict, Urbanism, and Delinquency.

Society for the Study of Social Problems

S13021. Glassner, Barry & Berg, Bruce, Jews and the Medicalization of Alcoholism.

Studies in Violence

83M8710. ———, Americans Confront the Holocaust.

83N3658. Dietrich, Donald J., Holocaust as Public Policy: The Third Reich.

83M8706. Levinsohn, Hannah, The Television Series "Holocaust" in Israel.

82M3788. Weinfeld, Morton, Sigal, John J. & Eaton, William W., Long Term Effects of the Holocaust on Selected Social Attitudes and Behaviors of Survivors: A Cautionary Note.

1982

American Sociological Association

S15062. Lazerwitz, Bernard, Class, Ethnicity, and Site as Planning Factors in Israeli Residential Integration—A Post-Occupancy Study.

Sociology of the Arts

83N3045. Bunis, David M., Types of Nonregional Variation in Early Modern Eastern Spoken Judezmo.

83N3046. Chumaceiro, Rita Mendes, Language Maintenance and Shift among Jerusalem Sephardim.

83N3054. Harris, Tracy K., Reasons for the Decline of Judeo-Spanish.

83N3062. Malinowski, Arlene, A Report of the Status of Judeo-Spanish in Turkey.

Collective Behavior

83M9452. Kimmerling, Baruch & Backer, Irit, Voluntary Action and Location in the System: The Case of the Israeli Civilians during the 1973 War.

Community Development

83N0272. Kirschenbaum, Alan, The Impact of New Towns in Rural Regions on Population Redistribution in Israel.

83N0280. Semyonov, Moshe & Kraus, Vered, The Social Hierarchies of Communities and Neighborhoods.

Demography and Human Biology

83N1645. Goldstein, Sidney, Population Movement and Redistribution among American Jews.

Sociology of Education

82M6287. Cohen, Elizabeth G., Expectation States and Interracial Interaction in School Settings.

The Family and Socialization

83N0093. Cnaan, Ram A., Notes on Prostitution in Israel.

83N3396. Davids, Leo, Divorce and Remarriage among Canadian Jews.

83N0095. Farber, Bernard & Gordon, Leonard, Accounting for Jewish Intermarriage: An Assessment of National and Community Studies.

83N1731. Glenn, Norval D., Interreligious Marriages in the United States: Patterns and Recent Trends.

83N0104. Hartman, Moshe, Cultural Change and Married Women's Economic Activity.

83M8427. Ichilov, Orit & Chen, Michael, School-Club Activity and Social Integration in Two Educational Frameworks in Israel.

83M8493. Rosen, Sherry, Intermarriage and the "Blending of Exiles" in Israel.

83N3462. Shamgar-Handelman, Lea, The Concept of Remarriage among Israel War Widows.

Group Interactions

82M5764. Hobsbawn, E.J., Are We Entering a New Era of Anti-Semitism?

83M9192. Benkin, Richard L. & DeSantis, Grace, Creating Ethnicity: East European Jews and Lithuanian Immigrants in Chicago.

82M5762. Heilman, Samuel C., The Sociology of American Jewry: The Last Ten Years.

83N4153. Hofman, John E., Social Identity and the Readiness for Social Relations between Jews and Arabs in Israel.

Sociology of Health and Medicine

83N5197. Snyder, Charles R., Palgi, Phyllis, Eldar, Pnina & Elian, Beatrice, Alcoholism among the Jews in Israel: A Pilot Study. I. Research Rationale and a Look at the Ethnic Factor.

Sociology: History and Theory

83N0840. Cohen, Stuart A., Selig Brodetsky and the Ascendancy of Zionism in Anglo-Jewry: Another View of His Role and Achievements.

83N1201. Weill, Georges, The *Alliance Israelite Universelle* and the Emancipation of Jewish Communities in the Mediterranean.

83M7153. Fahey, Tony, Max Weber's Ancient Judaism.

International Sociological Association Supplement No. 116

S13701.   Berthelot, martine & Puig I Moreno, Gentil, La Communauté israélite de Barcelone face au processus de normalisation de la société et de la langue catalanes.

S13711.   Blasi, Joseph R., A Critique of Gender and Culture: Kibbutz Women Revisited.

S13750.   Cais, Judith, Cultural Heritage, Socialization and Verbal Behavior: Formal and Informal Speech of Middle- and Lower-Class Israeli Girls.

S13822.   Demarest, Jan & Gordon, Haim, From Dialogue to Responsibility: Bridging Conflict Resolution and Peace Education.

S13856.   Ehrenfeld, Rachel & Sebba, Leslie, The Social Policy towards Drug Addict Offenders in Israel: Detention in Mental Hospitals.

S13951.   Goldberg, Albert I., Commune Professionals: The Impact of Social Structure on Work Commitments.

S14001.   Hartman, Moshe & Hartman, Harriet, Methodological Problems in the Study of Changes of Social Status Resulting from International Migration.

S14004.   Hassin, Yael, Use of Vehicle without Permission (Joy Riding) by Minors in Israel.

S14150.   Landau, Simha F., Trends in Violence and Aggression: A Cross-Cultural Analysis.

S14418.   Rubin, Nissan, Encounter with Death: A Religious Problem in a Non-Religious Kibbutz.

S14448.   Sebba, Leslie, Attitudes of New Immigrants to White-Collar Crime: A Cross-Cultural Study.

S14458.   Shamgar-Handelman, Lea, The Hidden Costs of Family Intervention Programs.

S14459.   Shamir, Boas, The Relationships between Work and Leisure and the Kibbutz and the Town.

S14466. Shlonsky, Hagith R., Principles Regulating Selection into Poverty: A Re-Examination of the Notion of "Cycle of Poverty."

S14491. Spolsky, Bernard, Avoiding the Tyranny of the Written Word: The Development of Jewish Literacy from the First to the Tenth Centuries.

S14565. Toren, Nina, National Styles of Orientation toward Scientific Work: A Comparison between Soviet and American Scientists Who Have Recently Immigrated to Israel.

Market Structures and Consumer Behavior

83N4363. Avruch, Kevin, New Markets and Good Deeds: On Altruism and Exemplary Entrepreneurship.

Mass Phenomenon

83N1073. Rosenfield, Geraldine, The Polls: Attitudes toward American Jews.

North Central Sociological Association

S13566. Nagi, Mostafa H. & Nigem, Elias, International Migration and Fertility with Special Reference to Kuwait and Israel.

Political Interactions

83M7818. Abu-Lughod, Janet, Israeli Settlements in Occupied Arab Lands: Conquest to Colony.

83N1158. Lehman-Wilzig, Sam N., Public Protests against Central and Local Government in Israel, 1950-1979.

83N1184. Saltman, Michael, The Use of the Mandatory Emergency Laws by the Israeli Government.

83N1203. Yishai, Yael, Israel's Right-Wing Jewish Proletariat.

Public Opinion

83N4381. Kats, Rachel, Concerns of the Israeli: Change and Stability from 1962 to 1975.

Sociology of Religion

83N1483. Cutwirth, Jacques, Jews among Evangelists in Los Angeles.

83M8215. Harrison, Michael I. & Lazerwitz, Bernard, Do Denominations Matter?

83M9850. Heilman, Samuel C., Prayer in the Orthodox Synagogue: An Analysis of Ritual Display.

82M3573. Zerubavel, Eviatar, Easter and Passover: On Calendars and Group Identity.

Social Change and Economic Development

82M3259. Bernstein, Deborah & Swirski, Shlomo, The Rapid Economic Development of Israel and the Emergence of the Ethnic Division of Labour.

Social Control

83N4909. Shamir, Boas & Drory, Amos, A Cross-Cultural Comparison of Prison Guards' Beliefs regarding the Rehabilitation Potential of the Prisoners, the Rehabilitative Potential of the Prison and Their Own Supportive Role.

Social Differentiation

83M7976. Jacobsen, Chanoch & Sadan, Arie, Busdrivers in Israel: An Anomaly of Occupational Status and Its Explanation.

83M8003. Toren, Nina & King, Judith: Scientists' Orientation toward Their Work: The Relative Effect of Socialization versus Situation.

Social Psychology

83N2378. Bizman, Aharaon & Amir, Yehuda, Mutual Perceptions of Arabs and Jews in Israel.

83N2351. Haber, Gilda Moss, Spatial Relations between Dominants and Marginals.

83N2431. Helmreich, William B., Making the *Awful* Meaningful.

Society for the Study of Social Problems

S14772.   Agassi, Judith Buber, Testing Theories of Work Attitudes of Men and Women.

S14835.   Hankin, Janet R. & Goodman, Allen C., Determinants of Depressive Symptoms in Elderly Jews.

S15193.   Weiner, Richard R., Bund Socialism, *Yiddishkeit* and the Challenge of Modernity.

Urban Structures and Ecology

83M9739.   Varady, David P., Neighborhood Stabilization in Jewish Communities: A Comparative Analysis.

83M9743.   Zweigenhaft, Richard L., Recent Patterns of Jewish Representation in the Corporate and Social Elites.

Studies in Violence

83N0331.   Pollak, Michael, Des mots qui tuent

About the Contributors

Mark Abrahamson is a professor in the Department of Sociology at the University of Connecticut. His current research is examining the effects of city size and region upon people's attitudes and values in the United States between 1947 and 1982.

Efraim Ben-Zadok is a lecturer in the Department of Political Science and the Center for Urban and Regional Studies at Tel-Aviv University. He received his Ph.D. (urban planning program) and M.P.A. from New York University, Graduate School of Public Administration. His research interests are in the areas of urban policy and politics and social planning.

Rena Cheskis works as a demographer for Yale University's Office of Institutional Research. Her current research is diverse, ranging from a study of intermarriage and conversion among Catholics to an economic model of student loan default.

Steven M. Cohen is an associate professor of sociology, Queens College.

Arnold Dashefsky is an associate professor of sociology and director of the Center for Judaic Studies and Contemporary Jewish Life at the University of Connecticut. His current research interests focus on a comparative investigation of sources and consequences of American emigration (to Australia and Israel, with J. DeAmicis and B. Lazerwitz) and a study of successful supplemental schools in the Jewish community.

Marcia Freedman is a senior research scholar, Conservation of Human Resources, Columbia University.

Eva Etzioni-Halevy is a political sociologist currently a senior lecturer at the Australian National University. She is the author of *Bureaucracy and Democracy: A Political Dilemma* (1983); *Social Change: The Advent and Maturation of Modern Society* (1981); *Political Manipulation and Administrative Power* (1979); and (with Rena Shapira) *Political Culture in Israel* (1977). Her forthcoming book is *When Prophecy Fails: On the Socio-Political Role of Intellectuals in Modern Society*.

Celia S. Heller is a professor of sociology at Hunter College and Graduate Center, CUNY.

Harold S. Himmelfarb is an associate professor in the Department of Sociology at the Ohio State University, and immediate past president of ASSJ. Currently he is completing a cross-cultural analysis of Jewish educational systems and a detailed review of the empirical literature on Jewish education in the United States.

Joseph Korazim is a lecturer, Paul Baerwald school of Social Work, Hebrew University of Jerusalem.

George Gershon Kranzler is a professor of sociology at Towson State University, Baltimore.

Abraham D. Lavender is a clinical sociologist in the Miama area.

Bernard Lazerwitz is a professor in the Department of Sociology of Bar-Ilan University (Israel). Currently he is engaged in a survey of the Tel-Aviv metropolitan area, studying the operations of the Israeli condominium system, neighborhood involvement, and changing religious characteristics.

Linda G. Levi is director of the Management Assistance Program, Federation of Jewish Philanthropies.

Bruce A. Phillips is an associate professor of Jewish communal studies at Hebrew Union College-Jewish Institute of Religion, Western Campus. He has conducted Jewish population studies in Los Angeles, Denver, Las Vegas, Phoenix, and Milwaukee (the latter conducted with Policy Research Corporation in Chicago), and is currently working on a book comparing the Jewish population in western communities with the non-Jewish populations as well as with the Jewish populations in midwestern communities.

Paul Ritterband is a professor of sociology and Jewish studies, City College and the Graduate Center of the City University of New York.

Ronald Tadao Tsukashima is a professor in the Department of Sociology at California State University, Los Angeles. His interests are in the areas of Black anti-Semitism and patterns of adjustment of Japanese immigrants. In addition, he is coordinator of the Japanese Studies Center at his campus and editor of the *California Sociologist*. Currently he is serving as a Fulbright lecturer in Japan.

J. Alan Winter, associate editor of this volume, is a professor of sociology at Connecticut College, where he has served as department chair. He is the author of various articles and books in the areas of social problems and the sociology of religion, including *Continuities in the*

Sociology of Religion. Recently he served as research consultant to the Council of Jewish Federations and as visiting professor at the Center of Judaic Studies and Contemporary Jewish Life at the University of Connecticut.

Yael Zerubavel is associate director of the Center for Jewish Studies of the City University of New York, the Graduate Center.